DISORIENTATION AND MORAL LIFE

Studies in Feminist Philosophy is designed to showcase cutting-edge monographs and collections that display the full range of feminist approaches to philosophy, that push feminist thought in important new directions, and that display the outstanding quality of feminist philosophical thought.

STUDIES IN FEMINIST PHILOSOPHY
Cheshire Calhoun, Series Editor

Advisory Board

Harry Brod, University of Northern Iowa
Claudia Card, University of Wisconsin
Lorraine Code, York University, Toronto
Kimberle Crenshaw, Columbia Law School/UCLA School of Law
Jane Flax, Howard University
Ann Garry, California State University, Los Angeles
Sally Haslanger, Massachusetts Institute of Technology
Alison Jaggar, University of Colorado, Boulder
Helen Longino, Stanford University
Maria Lugones, SUNY Binghamton
Uma Narayan, Vassar College
James Sterba, University of Notre Dame
Rosemarie Tong, University of North Carolina, Charlotte
Nancy Tuana, Penn State University
Karen Warren, Macalester College

Recently published in the series:

Visible Identities: Race, Gender, and the Self
Linda Martín Alcoff

Women and Citizenship
Edited by Marilyn Friedman

Women's Liberation and the Sublime: Feminism, Postmodernism, Environment
Bonnie Mann

Analyzing Oppression
Ann E. Cudd

Ecological Thinking: The Politics of Epistemic Location
Lorraine Code

Self Transformations: Foucault, Ethics, and Normalized Bodies
Cressida J. Heyes

Family Bonds: Genealogies of Race and Gender
Ellen K. Feder

Moral Understandings: A Feminist Study in Ethics, Second Edition
Margaret Urban Walker

The Moral Skeptic
Anita M. Superson

"You've Changed": Sex Reassignment and Personal Identity
Edited by Laurie J. Shrage

Dancing with Iris: The Philosophy of Iris Marion Young
Edited by Ann Ferguson and Mechthild Nagel

Philosophy of Science after Feminism
Janet A. Kourany

Shifting Ground: Knowledge and Reality, Transgression and Trustworthiness
Naomi Scheman

The Metaphysics of Gender
Charlotte Witt

Unpopular Privacy: What Must We Hide?
Anita L. Allen

Adaptive Preferences and Women's Empowerment
Serene Khader

Minimizing Marriage: Marriage, Morality, and the Law
Elizabeth Brake

Out from the Shadows: Analytic Feminist Contributions to Traditional Philosophy
Edited by Sharon L. Crasnow and Anita M. Superson

The Epistemology of Resistance: Gender and Racial Oppression, Epistemic Injustice, and Resistant Imaginations
José Medina

Simone de Beauvoir and the Politics of Ambiguity
Sonia Kruks

Identities and Freedom: Feminist Theory between Power and Connection
Allison Weir

Vulnerability: New Essays in Ethics and Feminist Philosophy
Edited by Catriona Mackenzie, Wendy Rogers, and Susan Dodds

Sovereign Masculinity: Gender Lessons from the War on Terror
Bonnie Mann

Autonomy, Oppression, and Gender
Edited by Andrea Veltman and Mark Piper

Our Faithfulness to the Past: Essays on the Ethics and Politics of Memory
Sue Campbell
Edited by Christine M. Koggel and Rockney Jacobsen

The Physiology of Sexist and Racist Oppression
Shannon Sullivan

Disorientation and Moral Life
Ami Harbin

DISORIENTATION AND MORAL LIFE

Ami Harbin

OXFORD
UNIVERSITY PRESS

OXFORD
UNIVERSITY PRESS

Oxford University Press is a department of the University of Oxford. It furthers the University's objective of excellence in research, scholarship, and education by publishing worldwide. Oxford is a registered trade mark of Oxford University Press in the UK and certain other countries.

Published in the United States of America by Oxford University Press
198 Madison Avenue, New York, NY 10016, United States of America.

© Oxford University Press 2016

All rights reserved. No part of this publication may be reproduced, stored in a retrieval system, or transmitted, in any form or by any means, without the prior permission in writing of Oxford University Press, or as expressly permitted by law, by license, or under terms agreed with the appropriate reproduction rights organization. Inquiries concerning reproduction outside the scope of the above should be sent to the Rights Department, Oxford University Press, at the address above.

You must not circulate this work in any other form
and you must impose this same condition on any acquirer.

Library of Congress Cataloging-in-Publication Data
Names: Harbin, Ami.
Title: Disorientation and moral life / Ami Harbin.
Description: New York : Oxford University Press, 2016. |
Series: Studies in feminist philosophy | Includes bibliographical references and index.
Identifiers: LCCN 2015035937| ISBN 978-0-19-027740-6 (pbk.) |
ISBN 978-0-19-027739-0 (hardcover) |
ISBN 978-0-19-027741-3 (ebook) | ISBN 978-0-19-027742-0 (online content)
Subjects: LCSH: Ethics, Modern. | Act (Philosophy) | Orientation. | Feminist theory.
Classification: LCC BJ301 .H37 2016 | DDC 170—dc23 LC record available at
http://lccn.loc.gov/2015035937

For my mom and in memory of my dad—
two of my strongest toeholds

CONTENTS

Preface: Life beyond What One Has Concepts For   xi
Acknowledgments   xxi

1. Being Disoriented   1
    1.1 Contextualizing the Concept   3
    1.2 Disorientation and Family Resemblance   13
    1.3 Methodologies for Interpreting Disorientations and Their Effects   22
        1.3.1 Claims about What Disorientations Are   24
        1.3.2 Claims about What Disorientations Do   25
        1.3.3 Implications of This Account for Moral Motivation and Agency   29
        1.3.4 Implications of This Account for Understandings of Oppression   32
    1.4 Conclusion   34

2. Moral Motivation beyond Moral Resolve   36
    2.1 Identifying Moral Resolve   37
    2.2 Legacies of Resolvism   42

CONTENTS

2.2.1 Resolvism in Accounts of Moral Development	43
2.2.2 Resolvism in Accounts of Moral Judgment	44
2.2.3 Resolvism in Accounts of Moral Failure	49
2.2.4 Resolvism in Accounts of Moral Growth	50
2.3 The Disorientations of Grief	53
2.4 Contesting Resolvism	57
3. What Is Disorientation in Thinking?	65
3.1 Disorientations of Life under Racism	67
3.1.1 Double Consciousness and Awareness of Oppressive Norms	68
3.1.2 White Ambush and Awareness of Oppressive Norms	73
3.2 Disorientations of Learning about Oppression and Privilege	77
3.2.1 Consciousness-Raising and Awareness of Political Complexity	78
3.2.2 Critical Classrooms and Awareness of Political Complexity	83
3.3 The Power of Awareness without Moral Resolve	88
3.3.1 Prompting Epistemic Humility	91
3.3.2 Prompting Resistant Re-identification	93
3.3.3 Prompting Different Relations to Felt Power	95
3.4 Conclusion	95
4. Tenderizing Effects and Acting despite Ourselves	97
4.1 Disorientations of Interruption	99
4.1.1 Illness, Sensing Vulnerability, and Living Unprepared	100
4.1.2 Trauma and Living Unprepared	106

4.2 Disorientations of Ill Fit ... 110
    4.2.1 Queerness and In-This-Togetherness ... 110
    4.2.2 Migration and Living against the Grain ... 114
4.3 The Power of Tenderizing Effects ... 119
4.4 Conclusion ... 123

5. Injustice and Irresoluteness ... 125
    5.1 Resolute and Irresolute Actions against Injustice ... 127
    5.2 Both/and Actions, Heterosexism, and Mass Incarceration ... 131
    5.3 Doubling Back Actions, Implicit Bias, and Colonialism ... 138
    5.4 Building without Blueprints and Post-Industrial Poverty ... 144
    5.5 Conclusion ... 149

6. Disorientation and Habitability ... 153
    6.1 Dismissing Disorientations ... 154
    6.2 Responding to Disoriented Others ... 160
    6.3 Responding to Oneself as Disorientable ... 169
    6.4 Back to the Rough Waves ... 174

Notes ... *177*
References ... *199*
Index ... *221*

PREFACE: LIFE BEYOND WHAT ONE HAS CONCEPTS FOR

When Adorno tells us that only by becoming inhuman can we attain the possibility of becoming human, he underscores the disorientation at the heart of the moral deliberation, the fact that the "I" who seeks to chart its course has not made the map it reads, does not have all the language it needs to read the map, and sometimes cannot find the map itself.

—Judith Butler (2005, 110)

Humans don't just live in a world of breakables; we *are* breakables.

—Elizabeth Spelman (2002, 49-50)

This book is about being disoriented: experiencing serious disruption such that we do not know how to go on. To become disoriented is, roughly, to lose one's bearings in relation to others, environments, and life projects. Experiences of disorientation prompt sustained uncertainty: Who am I now? What should I do? How should I relate to others? As disoriented, we can feel out of place, uncomfortable, uneasy, and unsettled. Disorientations are typically spurred by major life shifts to which we do not know how to respond.

Disorientations are neither straightforward nor rare. They can be triggered by a wide variety of events, from everyday experiences of losing a job, coping with a breakup, or moving across the country, to those as unfathomable as tsunamis, or grief at the loss of multiple loved ones. People describe any number of feelings in such cases: devastation, resignation, or indifference (attempted or actual). What disorientations share is the way they prompt a particular question in response: *How can I go on?*

I will argue in this book that part of moral life is relating to a world where serious disorientations are possible. Moral agents are all the time planning our lives while knowing that they may be disrupted, developing capacities to respond well to such disorientations, and being in relationships with others who are disoriented. Our experiences of disorientation can teach us about how to live responsibly in unpredictable circumstances.

Whenever I have presented, discussed, or even mentioned my work on this topic, people have examples of disorientation to share. Many of those real-life examples have inspired and propelled this book. During early discussions of this project in philosophical contexts, I began to notice that, in addition to a number of common examples, one specific comment came up frequently: *you must be drawing on Susan Brison's work on trauma*. I was indeed engaging with Brison's work (see my discussion of trauma in chapter 4), so this response was affirming and a helpful shared reference point. But when the question started to come up every time I presented anything on the topic of disorientations, I realized something else. Philosophers were inclined to equate disorientations with trauma: they were associating not knowing how to go on with not being able to go on.

Over time, it became clearer to me that philosophers mainly have resources for understanding disorientations as the kinds of experiences that could compromise agency. Against a standard background of understanding moral agency, it is not easy to see how an experience that compromises one's capacities for decisive action could improve agency.

This account of disorientations as an important part of moral life grows partly out of the intersection of two feminist sources: Sara Ahmed's *Queer Phenomenology* and Judith Butler's *Giving an Account of Oneself*. I read Ahmed as giving an account of the power of veering away from compulsory heterosexuality—a power that comes in part from the tenuousness and uncertainty of the move away from straight inheritances. And I see Butler as giving a relational account of identity and agency—who I am and what I can do depends on who I am to others. Others partly constitute who I am, and living with that fact can be unsettling. While neither Ahmed nor Butler prioritizes giving a specific account of the importance of disorientations in moral life, reading these works together was a catalyst. It seemed clear to me that (1) queer disorientations are one important kind of disorientation among many others that can also have significant power; and (2) an agent's not knowing who she is or what to do is in fact a very significant part of responsible agency.

The origins of my interest in disorientations might be traced further back to a common enough philosophical tendency to be intrigued by breaking points in personal identity, where one recognizes the inadequacy or insecurity of one's foundational beliefs—experiences like conversions, crises of faith, or paradigm shifts. The potency of moments like these were distilled first for me by the existentialist tradition: Nietzsche's account of reconciling oneself to the absence of a God, Heidegger's account of becoming authentic in the face of one's own death, Camus's sense of coming to live with the absurdity of one's own existence. As will become clear throughout the book, I am now more interested in some interpersonal dynamics not found in these particular accounts. Still, the significance of these moments has been clear to me since first reading the existentialists.

PREFACE

A number of basic commitments are foundational for my account. One is that disorientations are not rare experiences: rather, they are common and deeply relatable. Though a life free from disorientations may be more attractive, individuals know what disorientations are, because many of us have experienced them or witnessed them in the lives of those we love. It is rare to find someone who cannot identify with having been disoriented. Many of us have experienced grief, a major illness, a crisis of faith, or a paradigm shift in how we see the world. Further, individuals can relate to the idea that disorientations change who we are, and that after disorientations, we are not the same as we were before them. We anticipate that how they change us will be different in different cases. Individuals may not typically use a moral lens to consider the effects of disorientations, but the fact that they are part of the set of important experiences that make us who we are is, I think, uncontroversial.

Another commitment of mine is to the view that understanding everyday experiences matters for understanding moral motivation. Unsurprisingly, processes of becoming morally motivated to act are more complex than simply becoming informed about how to apply a moral framework to a moral dilemma. Yet, much of philosophical ethics makes it look like such situations are the chief area where moral motivation occurs, or at least the area deserving of the most attention. This account of disorientations contributes to a tradition of feminist ethics that highlights the moral significance of everyday practices of relating to other agents and to contexts within which we live. This means that moral action is not only or chiefly something we perform when faced with moral dilemmas, but something that we practice all the time. Looking at common life experiences—whatever we track as the experiences that make us who we are—is an important starting place for looking at motivation.

PREFACE

As I discuss in chapter 1, even if many of us find disorientations relatable, what counts as "disorientation" in the sense I will discuss requires clarification. People use the term to describe everything from quite minor experiences (e.g., forgetting which of several boring buildings the passport office is in), to more major ones (e.g., feeling like life will never be the same after the death of a parent). My view narrows the scope of experiences somewhat, focusing on the major life experiences of disorientation that can make it difficult to go on. As will be clarified in chapter 1, the more minor experiences will not count as disorientations in that sense.

My commitment to getting as clear as possible on *what disorientations are* and *what specific disorientations do* requires understanding disorientations from as many angles as possible. A multidisciplinary approach supports this. First-person accounts (testimony from experiencers) are a very important source of information about disorientations and their effects. I draw on them throughout the book. Philosophical accounts of doubt, confusion, and ambivalence are other important sources. And qualitative and quantitative research in psychology and sociology into how individuals cope with trauma, grief, illness, and oppression provide other important sources. Researchers in psychology are more aware of the power of disorientations than philosophers tend to be, but we will see that there can also be troubling assumptions that limit psychological research on disorientations, and important ways philosophical perspectives can help.

My arguments are situated within a tradition of feminist, naturalized moral psychology. Simply put, I am committed to understanding moral motivation in terms of natural facts, and to contributing to an account of the position of disorientations in moral life that is also informed by empirical work in the natural and social sciences. I pay attention to particulars—particular agents, particular kinds of disorientation (where kinds of disorientations will vary widely), and particular effects of disorientation. Further, I pay attention to the experiences of non-dominant individuals (e.g., racialized, disabled, non-cisgendered people) whose experiences are still often neglected by standard philosophical accounts. I do not make claims about what all disorientations are like, or what all disorientations can do. The phenomenon does not allow for generalizing in that way. Rather, I show how disorientations of different particular kinds have in some cases had different particular effects, and I argue for the *moral benefit* of some of those effects. I argue in chapter 1 that "disorientation" is best understood as a family resemblance concept, which allows for understanding how disorientations can vary as widely as they do, while still being meaningfully related.

As we will see, much of philosophical ethics still privileges decision-making as the chief mechanism of moral action. In other words, when looking for evidence of moral motivation, philosophers still most commonly look to what an agent has decided to do or not do. Moral motivation is seen as successful if an agent comes to a better decision about how to act in some context. If some experience (e.g., feeling sympathy, gaining knowledge about some harm) helps an agent come to better decisions, it is morally motivating. The account of "moral benefit" I employ comes from an understanding of responsibilities individuals have to respond to the needs of themselves, others (human and nonhuman), and their environments. Much of responsible action occurs through the ways individuals relate to each other, and also through the way we confront the harms experienced because of systems of social group-based harm (oppression). I will highlight how, when the effects of disorientations allow us to respond to harmful oppressive contexts, they can be morally beneficial. As will become clearer in chapters 1 and 2, my claims about the morally beneficial status of the effects of some disorientations depend on an understanding of moral motivation as something that extends beyond better decisions about what to do. Moral decisions and moral decisiveness are part of moral motivation, but I will argue that (a) there are ways in which we can be morally motivated in new ways without coming to decide how to act better; and (b) experiences can be motivating without helping an individual decide better about how to act.

The arch of the argument is as follows: in chapter 1, I characterize disorientations and situate my account of what disorientations are in light of other related notions. I offer an account of disorientations as a family resemblance concept and examine the methodological complexities involved in interpreting disorientations. Chapters 2 to 5 then confront a number of assumptions of mainstream moral psychology: that becoming morally motivated means resolving to act differently (chapter 2); that clear feelings are best for generating moral and political awareness (chapter 3); that improved moral action is something we do when we are aware of what we are doing (chapter 4); and that resolute action is the best able to address injustice (chapter 5).

In chapter 2, I survey models of moral motivation in philosophy that have tended to position morally mature agents as those who are able to decide how to act, and experiences as useful primarily through their capacities to help individuals resolve what to do. Within this tradition, emotions have been seen as most relevant for moral motivation when they guide moral judgment: when I feel angry about something, I judge that I ought to confront it; when I feel proud about something I have done in the past, I judge that I ought to do more of that in the future. But individuals are not always able to resolve how to act, and many experiences do not help us do so. I raise the example of the disorientation of grief. If experiences like the disorientations experienced by those in grief do not help individuals decide how to act, and indeed sometimes make it impossible for individuals to clearly judge how to act, then how could such experiences motivate better action? Understanding disorientations as having the potential to generate improved moral practices will require understanding moral motivation as in some cases evidenced by something other than decisive moral judgment.

In chapter 3, I draw on descriptions of experiences of double consciousness, consciousness-raising, and critical education, to consider how the experiences of disorientation at the heart of each in some cases generate new awareness. Disorientations seem to challenge what we know and leave us feeling like we know less than we once did. Yet at the same time, in some cases of disorientation, individuals express gaining new kinds of awareness about the complexity of their social locations, and about the norms that structure their lives. I consider the moral and political significance of such awareness, given that it is not a kind of awareness that helps agents decide what to do.

In chapter 4, I examine how at the same time as some disorientations generate awareness, others disrupt everyday sensuous and affective habits of being embodied, moving in space, and relating to others. In such cases, how individuals should act, how others will respond, what is appropriate, healthy, or normal becomes uncertain. Drawing on further articulations of the disorientations of illness, trauma, queerness, and migration, I investigate contexts where ease and expectation are disrupted, and argue for the moral and political significance of the *tenderizing effects* of disorientations.

In chapter 5, I turn to contexts of injustice to examine how particular kinds of actions can be called for. Against the background of the assumption that addressing injustice requires agents to be determined and decisive, I consider contexts in which acting against injustice can require more multi-directional, questioning, and indeterminate methods. I examine the ways in which, in some specific contexts, acting against injustice can require less decisive action than is often thought. I also examine the role of disorientations in the lives of agents who ought to take such action.

Chapter 6 concludes the book with a discussion of the proper place of disorientations in moral life. The accounts of disorientation the book highlights will show how disoriented individuals come into contact with families of origin, friend groups, political communities, schools, universities, churches, workplaces, and medical and criminal justice systems. If these groups and institutions see all disorientations as best avoided, disoriented individuals face a lack of support, as well as social or institutional isolation. Given that disorientations are common parts of our lives—though they vary widely in kind and effect—which can *motivate* morally better action, I argue that communities and social systems have responsibilities to make disorientations livable for individuals in particular ways.

I will not argue in favor of disorientation for disorientations' sake. Disorientations are not so much good in themselves as they are a reality. The promise of experiences of struggle is sometimes recognized through slogans like "what doesn't kill us makes us stronger." Loosely put, this book advances a more controversial thesis: "experiences and efforts to act can be morally and politically beneficial, even when they make us weak." Throughout the book, I resist tendencies to frame necessary moral or political change chiefly or most importantly in language of transformation. The cases of disorientation I consider are most relevant for the ways they can make individuals more able to inhabit the uncertainties and fragilities of moral life. As I will argue, more than disorientations transform, they tenderize.

There are many more examples of disorientations than those discussed in this book. There are also many more accounts of experiences like disorientations than those I survey—many more in English literature alone. The possible negative effects of disorientations are an important enough reality that I remind readers of them throughout the book. We cannot know in advance which disorientations have the potential to benefit moral agents, and which do not. Disorientations do not always enable moral agency, and it is important not to glorify or over-aestheticize such difficult experiences. They can and do interfere with wholehearted, decisive action. They can paralyze, overwhelm, embitter, and misdirect moral agents. They can unhinge us from positive moral orientations we have lived out in the past. The kinds of disorientation we have experienced in the past can affect our threshold for tolerating them (i.e., how much disorientation we can handle and experience as help rather than harm). Even so, in this book I show that disorientations have potential benefits for action that have been so far under-recognized in moral philosophy, and that the phenomenon of their promise deserves more attention in the future.

ACKNOWLEDGMENTS

So much has made writing this book possible.

Many of the ideas in this book are ones I have presented at conferences and other public venues, where I have received very helpful feedback. I thank audiences at Dalhousie University, the International Association for Philosophy and Literature, the Society for Existential and Phenomenological Theory and Culture, the North American Society for Social Philosophy, the Southwestern Ontario Feminist Philosophy Workshop series, Eastern Michigan University, the Canadian Society for Women in Philosophy, the American Philosophical Association, the Canadian Philosophical Association, the Western Canadian Philosophical Association, the Western Michigan University Medical Humanities Conference, the Mentorship Project for Pre-tenure Women Faculty in Philosophy, the Society for Analytic Feminism, and the International Network on Feminist Approaches to Bioethics.

Parts of this book have been previously published. I first introduced the concept of disorientation and previous versions of some of the cases discussed in chapter 1 (sections 1.1 and 1.2), chapter 3 (section 3.1), and chapter 4 (sections 4.1 and 4.2) in

ACKNOWLEDGMENTS

"Bodily Disorientation and Moral Change," which appeared in 2012 in *Hypatia: A Journal of Feminist Philosophy* 27, no. 2: 261-278. Chapter 2 (section 2.4) is adapted from my article "Prescribing Posttraumatic Growth," which was published in 2015 in *Bioethics* (Early View Online, doi:10.1111/bioe.12164). Portions of chapter 5, and part of chapter 2 (section 2.2) are adapted from an article entitled "The Disorientations of Acting against Injustice," which was published in 2014 in *Journal of Social Philosophy* 45, no. 2: 162-181. All are reprinted with permission.

A University Research Committee Faculty Research Fellowship Award from Oakland University in 2013 allowed me to complete the first draft of this book. Ongoing support from the College of Arts and Sciences, the Department of Philosophy, and the Women & Gender Studies Program at Oakland University has allowed me to present, teach, write, and receive feedback on these ideas, all of which has shaped my thinking.

My students in Philosophy and Women & Gender Studies have inspired me throughout my writing. Many of the texts I discuss here are ones I first taught in courses on ethics, feminist theory, gender studies, and philosophy of emotions, and discussing them in classrooms has brought them to life.

I thank Cheshire Calhoun, Editor of the Studies in Feminist Philosophy Series, and Lucy Randall and Jamie Chu at Oxford University Press for all their careful work and guidance. It has been a joy and a privilege working with them. And I am very grateful to three anonymous reviewers of the manuscript, two of whom I later learned were Lisa Tessman and Elizabeth Brake, and the third of whom remained anonymous, for their generous and insightful comments and suggestions, which had a substantial impact on the book. I also thank Julie Voelck for her work reading and editing the manuscript.

The mentorship I have received from feminist philosophers has been extraordinary. I first began thinking about disorientation

ACKNOWLEDGMENTS

during my doctoral studies at Dalhousie University. While there, Sue Campbell read and reread drafts of everything I wrote, anticipated and helped me through so many kinds of questions, and provided constant, cheerful support. She was an exemplary philosopher and having her as my teacher and friend has been one of my greatest fortunes. Susan Sherwin was a truly generous and trustworthy teacher and mentor to me, and continues to be an unfailing source of steady wisdom, philosophical insight, and deep support. I am so lucky to be able to learn from her. I am very grateful for Margaret Urban Walker's extensive and incisive feedback on earlier parts of these ideas, which has guided and informed the book and my thinking. The efforts of all the people who have built feminist philosophy associations and created, edited, and reviewed for feminist philosophy publications like *Hypatia* and the Studies in Feminist Philosophy Series are fundamentally important for the growth and strength of the field of feminist philosophy, and they have created the space for research like mine.

I have benefited enormously from the work and feedback of Françoise Baylis, Brenda Beagan, Suze Berkhout, Robyn Bluhm, Stephen Boos, Kirstin Borgerson, Samantha Brennan, Danielle Bromwich, Lorraine Code, Margaret Crouch, Peggy DesAutels, Jeff Dudiak, Lauren Freeman, Matthias Fritsch, Michael Garnett, Lisa Guenther, Warren Heiti, Cressida Heyes, Karen Houle, Grace Hunt, Michael Hymers, Ada Jaarsma, Hilde Lindemann, Maureen Linker, Jennifer Llewellyn, Duncan MacIntosh, Doug MacKay, Alice MacLachlan, Joe Millum, Kate Norlock, Naomi Scheman, Greg Scherkoske, Henry Schuurman, Lisa Schwartzman, Şerife Tekin, Marika Warren, and many other excellent philosophers and scholars. At my own institution, I have been very grateful for the support of my colleagues in Philosophy and Women & Gender Studies, and in particular for Phyllis Rooney and Mark Navin, who provided feedback on multiple drafts of many chapters in this book, and Jo Reger, whose advice and encouragement throughout my process of writing have been invaluable.

On a personal note, I am sustained by the presence and care of many people. Jan Sutherland is more than family to me. Alexis Shotwell has been there for me and shaped my thinking in so many ways. The friendship and camaraderie of Rina Mackereth, Jen Hoyer, Erin Fredericks, Ted Rutland, Victor Kumar, Adam Auch, Karen Schaffer, Heather Jessup, Nora Madden, Scout Calvert, and Chris Dixon has made my life rich. My whole family, and especially my mom and dad, to whom this book is dedicated, has my gratitude.

My greatest love and thanks go to Michael Doan. As a philosopher, he has been my closest and most truth-telling interlocutor. I love the way he thinks. As my partner, he has loved and encouraged me without fail. Our life together is orienting.

DISORIENTATION AND MORAL LIFE

[1]

BEING DISORIENTED

On December 26, 2004, Sonali Deraniyagala survived a tsunami. On vacation on the coast of Yala, Sri Lanka, Deraniyagala was staying at a beach hotel with her husband, Steve, her two sons, Vik and Malli, and her parents. The day they were preparing to leave, she noticed a strange tide. What looked at first to be an odd wave quickly turned into brown and gray surges of water, coming onto the beach and toward the hotel. In her 2013 memoir, *Wave*, Deraniyagala writes:

> I grabbed Vik and Malli and we all ran out the front door. I was ahead of Steve. I held the boys each by the hand. "Give me one of them. Give me one of them," Steve shouted, reaching out. But I didn't. That would have slowed us down. We had no time. We had to be fast. I knew that. But I didn't know what I was fleeing from. I didn't stop for my parents.... I didn't shout to warn them. We must keep running. I held the boys tight by their hands. We have to get out. (Deraniyagala 2013, 6)

They reached a vehicle and began to drive away. When the jeep filled with water, Deraniyagala was swept into the wave and shoved through trees and bushes. Eventually coming to consciousness with her head above water, Deraniyagala describes what she saw:

> My eyes couldn't focus. But I saw then the toppled trees everywhere, I could make those out, trees on the ground with their roots sticking up.... This didn't look like Yala, where the ground is dry and cracked and covered in green shrub. What is this knocked-down world? The end of time? (Deraniyagala 2013, 13)

Eventually, the bodies of Deraniyagala's husband, sons, and parents were identified. She was the only one of her family to survive. The first chapter of *Wave* summarizes the day of the tsunami and the weeks that immediately follow. The next eight chapters document Deraniyagala's attempts to survive the years after it.

In everyday usage, "disorientation" can have a number of meanings. People use the word to describe many kinds of experiences, from reaching the top of an escalator, to forgetting one's own name in advanced dementia. By disorientation I mean, roughly, temporally extended, major life experiences that make it difficult for individuals to know how to go on. They often involve feeling deeply out of place, unfamiliar, or not at home.[1] Though they may not regularly be as devastating as Deraniyagala's, disorientations are ubiquitous.

Many experiences can be strange, upsetting, or exhilarating, and they may have implications for agents that philosophers have not thought enough about. Getting lost in a new subway system, or being under the influence of a drug can be experiences with all of these features. But these are not the kinds of experiences I will consider here. It is equally important to emphasize that I am not referring to completely debilitating experiences, like very serious experiences of psychiatric illnesses. The disorientations I discuss are sustained periods of life when we are coping with having been blindsided by major events. To echo the oceanic metaphor from Deraniyagala's

Wave—one used strikingly often to describe disorientations, as we will see—to be disoriented feels like one loses one's footing and is adrift in deep, unpredictable waters. In many such cases, it seems impossible that life will go on. Yet it does, and individuals can be carried along with it. Of philosophical interest to me is what happens to moral agency in these periods of being carried along.

An individual might deliberately pursue or cultivate experiences of disorientation, perhaps because she hopes that disorientations will benefit her in some way. She may go on a religious retreat or enter into a military boot camp with the distinct goal of being shaken out of her habits and everyday life. These and other disorientations can affect individuals in ways they do not anticipate. Even so, it is important to emphasize that the disorientations I discuss are ones individuals *have not chosen*, and in most cases have not seen coming. As I will argue, it is especially when experiences of disorientation exceed one's will that they stand to be morally beneficial in the senses that interest me. Further, as I will show, individuals need not go looking for disorientations in order to be affected by them—they occur often enough as it is.

Where philosophers have discussed experiences similar to disorientations (canvassed below), they have for the most part regarded such experiences as threats to agency and, a fortiori, moral agency. As I will track throughout the book, disorientations have been treated for the most part obliquely, as experiences avoidable and best avoided. Disorientations have appeared in the shadows of philosophical accounts of brighter realities of clarity of thought, strength of will, happiness, and well-being.

1.1 CONTEXTUALIZING THE CONCEPT

Fascination with disorientations comes somewhat naturally to philosophers. Philosophers have considered how disorientations can play a significant role in human experiences of knowing, feeling, acting responsibly, coming to terms with one's freedom, being embodied, and self-identifying. While not always explicitly named as such, disorientations have been of interest to researchers in many sub-disciplines of philosophy: to epistemologists, philosophers of emotion, existentialists, phenomenologists, and personal identity theorists. As we will see, philosophers have discussed disorientations both abstractly, from a third-person perspective, as well as from the first-person standpoint of having experienced them in their own lives. Disorientations are also of interest outside philosophy, and as I will discuss here, particularly for researchers in clinical psychology and medicine.

In the history of epistemology, disorientations have appeared as experiences that prompt inquiry, or that make some kind of question no longer ignorable. In the *Meno*, Socrates is compared to a stingray who stuns, numbs, perplexes, and disorients his interlocutors as part of the process of educating them (Plato 1981 *Meno*, margin 79e-80b). And in the *Phaedo* and the *Republic*, disorientation is a deliberate tactic used by Socrates in the process of *reorienting* his pupils (Plato 1956; 1981 *Phaedo*, margin 89).[2] At other times, disorientation comes from the inquiry itself, from arriving at an impasse or finding oneself having challenged too many basic assumptions to be able to go on. Perhaps the most obvious account of this sort in the history of western philosophy appears in Descartes's *Meditations*, where Descartes deliberately attempts to doubt his perceptions about everything that exists.[3] While arguing for the importance of certain knowledge and justified belief, Descartes provides a vibrant description of the disorientations of having beliefs challenged or of finding we do not know.[4] For Descartes, we see something like disorientations as important but transitory experiences in the course of challenging unsupported beliefs. Since this willingness to view beliefs as challengeable is often seen as an important component of conceptual inquiry, philosophers might be especially familiar with this kind of disorientation. Considering the disorientations of realizing all one does not know, C. S. Peirce writes:

> Let a man venture into an unfamiliar field, or where his results are not continually checked by experience, and all history shows that the most masculine intellect will ofttimes lose his orientation and waste his efforts in directions which bring him no nearer to his goal, or even carry him entirely astray. He is like a ship in the open sea, with no one on board who understands the rules of navigation. (Peirce 1877, cited from 1955, 8)

For Peirce, the process of establishing sound knowledge requires recovering some amount of *orientedness* after being disoriented. More recently, disorientations have been seen to overlap with experiences of confusion, of not feeling able to discern the truth from lies, or to clearly get a handle on concepts.[5]

Within philosophy of emotions, we also see themes of disorientation as particularly pronounced in pragmatist thought, especially in John Dewey and William James's theories of emotion. In "What Is an Emotion" (1884), William James characterizes emotions in something like language used to describe disorientations: emotion is defined as a perception of a *physiological disturbance*. He argues that emotions are perceptions of physiological experiences—when we are in danger, we experience bodily response (e.g., increased heart rate), and our perception of those responses is the feeling (e.g., "fear").[6] According to Dewey's further developed "Theory of Emotions" (1894), emotions are experiences of the world that have three parts: the feeling (e.g., of disgust), the behavior (e.g., recoiling, gagging), and an object with an emotional quality (e.g., an infected wound). From the perspective of an account of disorientation, Dewey's theory of emotions builds on James's in interesting ways: emotions are *disruptions of smoothly functioning practices of rationality and embodiment*. For Dewey, emotional experiences are often responses to disruptive shifts in environmental situation (e.g., encountering a bear in the woods), and such experiences very often result in emotional seizure, where we become *discoordinated*, unable to respond definitively.[7] At the time when Dewey and James were writing, interest in themes of disorientation ran through other texts informed by pragmatist themes, and especially through James's family's writings; William James's father, theologian Henry James Sr., wrote specifically about "vastation," a Swedenborgian term for an experience of terror that was an important stage in a process of spiritual regeneration.[8] And the body of work of novelist Henry James Jr., William's younger brother, is now understood to reflect the disorientations of life in modernity. As Robert Pippin describes them, Henry James's novels are "full of characters who begin their lives as quiet passengers on some busy train of life, and 'wake up' for one reason or another, insist on a turn at driving, and must then decide where to go (where it is worth going) and how to get there" (Pippin 2000, 29). As we will see, themes of disorientation from the pragmatists' approach to emotion have influenced the work of many of their students, including the work of W. E. B. Du Bois, who studied with William James, and who developed an account of "double consciousness" (to be discussed in chapter 3).

Unsurprisingly, many existentialist accounts of freedom and responsibility attend closely to the role of disorientations in agents' lives, and to how coming to terms with one's freedom and responsibility can be disorienting. Heidegger's account of anxiety in *Being and Time* might be read as an account of something very much like disorientation. For Heidegger, when Dasein comes to face itself authentically, it must face its own death as something which belongs to it alone. In the movement toward authenticity, Dasein responds to its inevitable death with anxiety. This anxiety allows for the individuation or singularization—coming to see one's own death as belonging to oneself alone—which is a necessary component of the movement from inauthentic to authentic Dasein (*BT* 240, 250). In Heidegger's terms, "*the state of mind which can hold open the utter and constant threat to itself arising from Dasein's ownmost individualized Being, is anxiety.* In this state-of-mind, Dasein finds itself *face-to-face* with the 'nothing' of the possible impossibility of its existence" (*BT* 265-266, original italics). Interpreting the early Heidegger, Lawrence Hatab explicitly makes the connection between anxiety and disorientation: "Heidegger's notion of authenticity—understood as the tension between socialization and individuation, animated by anxious disorientation and reorientation—has much to contribute to ethics" (Hatab 2000, 77).

Building on Heidegger and others, Jean-Paul Sartre's concept of *forlornness*—the distressing experience of realizing that God does not exist, that there is no ultimate judge of right or wrong action beyond us as individuals—is likewise closely related. In his overall view of emotions, Sartre critically evaluates emotions as often escapist experiences one voluntarily uses to bring oneself ease and avoid facing the reality that existence precedes essence. For instance, Sartre thought that individuals could feel *forlorn* upon realizing that there would be nothing to give meaning to their existence apart from one's own free choices—one might not know how to go on without a god or system of morality. But in some cases, individuals could seize such opportunities to face their own freedom. As Sartre writes in *Existentialism & Humanism*:

> Everything is indeed permitted if God does not exist, and man is in consequence forlorn, for he cannot find anything to depend upon either within or outside himself.... One will never be able to explain one's action by reference to a given and specific human nature.... Nor, on the other hand, if God does not exist, are we provided with any values or commands that could legitimize

our behavior. Thus we have neither behind us, nor before us in a luminous realm of values, any means of justification or excuse.... Man is condemned to be free. (Sartre 1973, 33-34)

Instead of succumbing to forlornness, one could instead come to accept that one has freedom to make choices within the realities of one's situation and is responsible for creating values.[9] To say that one invents values contrasts with *discovering* values. As Sartre writes, "Life is nothing until it is lived; but it is yours to make sense of, and the value of it is nothing else but the sense that you choose" (Sartre 1973, 54). Instead of avoidance and denial, individuals can invent themselves. This is a way to reorient out of the feeling of abandonment, without reference to external landmarks (e.g., God, morality)—one becomes committed to making one's own path. Themes of disorientation can be found even further back in existentialist writings than Heidegger or Sartre: in Kierkegaard's discussions of the religious textual accounts of the "leap of faith," when preparing to kill his son by God's command, Abraham might be seen as having been, at least for a time, disoriented. Even when he *goes on in a certain way* (climbing the mountain, holding the knife), he does not feel sure of what he is doing.[10] Nietzsche's call for individuals to embrace the life-affirming will to power might also be seen as a call that would be, for those able to heed it, isolating, bewildering, and disorienting.[11]

Philosophers of embodiment further track the disorientations of everyday life through lenses of habit and corporeal experience. On phenomenological accounts, disorientations are deeply disruptive to *habits*—to the unthinking ways individuals act and relate to others. Phenomenologists have emphasized how individuals develop patterns in basic ways of sitting, standing, reaching, and pausing, as well as in more complex situations of holding hands, carrying infants, and wheeling wheelchairs. Establishing and practicing bodily habits allows us to feel oriented,[12] and we feel most oriented when we perform movements correctly (Casey 1987, 149-153). Sara Ahmed (2006) starts from considerations of Husserl and Merleau-Ponty to establish how individuals become oriented through practicing habits of movement, action, and interaction. Her analysis of orientation highlights how we are most at ease when our body habits align with those shared by others, and with those others expect of us: "To be orientated, or to be at home in the world, is also to feel a certain comfort. . . . The word 'comfort' suggests well-being and satisfaction, but it also suggests an ease and an easiness" (Ahmed 2006, 134). Practicing bodily habits leads to felt *orientation* by making some embodiments so intuitive we do not (because we need not) notice ourselves enacting them. When something in habitual processes breaks down, our habitual actions are disrupted. When bodily habits are disrupted, we can come to feel disoriented. As Edward Casey (1987) explains:

> The main function of orienting is to effect familiarization with one's surroundings. To be disoriented, or even simply unoriented, is to find these same surroundings unfamiliar, *unheimlich*. . . . In particular, it is not to know which way to go or to turn—which route to follow. Getting oriented is to learn precisely which routes are possible, and eventually which are most desirable, by setting up habitual patterns of bodily movement. (Casey 1987, 151; see also Ahmed 2004, 146-155)

As I will show, though my account considers how disorientations are disruptive beyond the level of bodily habits, understanding how orienting it can be to unthinkingly perform habitual actions will help us understand how disorienting it can be when habits are disrupted—and how new possibilities for action can open up at the point of being disoriented.

Contemporary philosophers of personal identity have further described experiences of disorientation as similar in some ways to feelings of no longer knowing who I am,[13] self-doubt,[14] demoralization,[15] torn choices,[16] and, as I will discuss at length in the next chapter, ambivalence.[17] As I return to in chapter 3, Sandra Bartky's 1990 account of the "double ontological shock" of feminist consciousness-raising also resonates closely with my understanding of disorientation.[18]

In addition to approaching disorientations with some conceptual distance in these different domains, occasionally philosophers have described disorientations in their own lives, in some cases with the hope of drawing out immediate philosophical implications. John Stuart Mill's autobiography is one of the most eloquent examples of this, expressing the complex interrelation of philosophical and personal uncertainty. In the context of a period of serious emotional upheaval, Mill noted that he was partly disoriented by the philosophical realization that reaching the goal of "reforming the world" would not in fact bring him happiness (Mill 2009, 53). As he described it, his distress eroded through everyday experiences of pleasure:

> It is very characteristic both of my then state, and of the general tone of my mind at this period of my life, that I was seriously tormented by the thought of the exhaustibility of musical combinations.... This source of anxiety may, perhaps, be thought to resemble that of the philosophers of Laputa, who feared lest the sun should be burnt out.... The destiny of mankind in general was ever in my thoughts, and could not be separated from my own. I felt that the flaw in my life, must be a flaw in life itself. (Mill 2009, 58)

Mill tried to cope with his disorientation philosophically by developing an account of happiness. He claimed that the best mode of securing happiness would be aiming at some other end (2009, 56-57), and that the most important features of an account of political philosophy would be not a set of model institutions but the principles on the basis of which such institutions should be designed (2009, 64).[19] More recently, Ann Cvetkovich's *Depression: A Public Feeling* provides another example of a theorist's description of disorientation in her own life. Cvetkovich begins the book with a memoir of her own depression and anxiety, carried through years of graduate school and academic life, and then theorizes depression in relation to spiritual process, medicalization, racism, and art. She describes a combination of anxiety and depression much like disorientation when she writes:

> It was a feeling deeply embedded in different parts of my body. Like physical pain, it kept me fixated on the immediate present, unable to think about other things. But it was also dull enough and invisible enough—no blood, no wounds—that I could live with it. I was confused about what to do because I no longer knew how to avoid it or how to imagine it ending. (Cvetkovich 2012, 35)

Like Mill and Cvetkovich, many other theorists have described personal experiences of disorientation in the context of broader philosophical or theoretical projects. C. S. Lewis and Martha Nussbaum have provided accounts of their own grief, Du Bois an account of his double consciousness, Minnie Bruce Pratt an account of her own consciousness-raising, Havi Carel an account of her illness, Susan Brison an account of her own trauma, Sara Ahmed an account of her experiences of queer disorientation, and there are others.

Beyond philosophy, a number of concepts resonate with disorientations in medicine and in psychological research and practice. Experiences much like disorientations are already part of clinical psychology, in some cases positioned as symptoms of mental or emotional disorders. In some cases of physical or mental illness, "disorientation" is the specific term used to describe an individual's lack of awareness of identity, location, and temporal framework. When disoriented in this sense, individuals cannot remember who or where they are, or what day or year it is. Disorientations in the more wholistic sense of *not knowing how to go on with one's life* may overlap more with clinical classifications of depressions, anxiety, post-traumatic stress, alexithymia, dysthymia, or adjustment disorders. In some cases, disoriented individuals certainly experience hopelessness, unhappiness, or fatigue as people often do when depressed. They may experience fear and panic as people can when anxious. They may be avoidant or hyper-vigilant, as with some people who experience post-traumatic stress disorder (PTSD). As in cases of alexithymia, people who are disoriented can struggle to identify their own emotions (Sifneos 1973). Individuals may have long-term difficulty making decisions, and feel chronically low, as in cases of dysthymia/persistent depressive disorder. Difficult events or stresses can trigger anxiety, fear, anger, or sadness and individuals can struggle to adjust, making everyday life and relationships difficult to navigate. But disorientation is not captured well by any of these diagnoses. One can be disoriented by lacking a sense of how to go on, without necessarily being unhappy, anxious, avoidant, unable to identify one's feelings, or low.

While some of the clinical strategies for helping individuals cope with depression, anxiety, and so on may prove useful in helping individuals cope with disorientations (e.g., psychotherapy), I have elsewhere argued for the importance of *not* classifying the kinds of disorientations at issue in this book as themselves mental illnesses.[20] As will be clarified in chapters 3 and 4, disorientations may *accompany* mental illnesses (as they do physical illnesses) while not being mental illnesses themselves,[21] and they may occur completely separately from mental illness.

The disorientations I will describe share features with all of these parallel concepts, but are also importantly distinct. On my view, *disorientations are experiences that make it difficult to know how to go on.* As we will see, there is a gap between the existing philosophical treatments of disorientations—which offer (at best) insight into why these or experiences like them are so debilitating—and the evidence we have for how usual such experiences are, and how significant they can be. The main objective of the book is to address this gap.

1.2 DISORIENTATION AND FAMILY RESEMBLANCE

Though we have begun to see some things that will *not* count as disorientations, still a very large set of experiences are candidates for inclusion in the category. The set of things that can count as disorientations on my view is indeed substantial and diverse. Disorientations can be experienced very differently in different lives, depending on what else a person has experienced and other factors that augment qualities of disorientation in particular lives. Moreover, what causes disorientation will be different in different cases. One event (e.g., a loved one dying) may be disorienting to some and not to others, or disorienting to a person at one time in her life in a way it would not have been had it happened earlier or later. Particular types of events (e.g., being unexpectedly diagnosed with a serious illness) will be disorienting to most people most of the time, but contingencies of a particular life may make such an event less disorienting, or not disorienting at all. As will become clearer in the coming chapters, disorientations can vary widely in kind and degree. Further, some people are more vulnerable to serious disorientations than others (e.g., facing a serious illness without access to healthcare), so how likely one is to face serious difficulties and to become disoriented by such difficulties depends in part on one's identity and social position.

Disorientations can also be unexpected responses to very expected events. Growing, aging, and facing our deaths can prompt significant disorientations as we are forced to confront new patterns of movement or self-care. Individuals might be disoriented when faced with new challenges, as when starting a new job. They might be differently disoriented in new environments, as when reentering a profession after having children. Disorientations might occur upon entering new communities, as in the first year of high school. We can be disoriented when we find ourselves out of step with the practiced life-rhythms of communities, as when we take a leave of absence from work because of illness. Or we might feel disoriented when we are no longer part of institutions, as in retirement after years of working. The fact that we can see such experiences coming does not always make them less disorienting. Common, expected events can trigger disorientations that feel like serious displacement.

On my view, we need to *feel* disoriented in order to *be* disoriented, but being disoriented does not require that we describe what we are experiencing as disorientation.[22] Individuals may only come to view experiences as disorientations in retrospect; many of us tend to view ourselves as "oriented," even in the midst of crises that we recognize after some time as having been severely disorienting. A number of things may get in the way of my seeing myself as disoriented: I may fear being disoriented, I may need to present myself as feeling oriented in order to continue in my life (e.g., to keep my status as good employee or parent), or I may be convinced that wallowing in difficult experiences will only make things worse. In fact, as we will see, the way agents in the midst of serious disorientations are often treated can give them good reason to want to avoid seeing themselves as disoriented. At the same time, as I return to in the final chapter, being able to recognize an experience of our own *as* disorientation can make a difference to the way we experience it.

In the coming chapters, the disorientations I describe are typically just one part of a period in an individual's life—there are other kinds of experiences going on at the same time. For example, in chapter 2 I describe cases where the death of a loved one is disorienting for individuals. Though my focus is on the disorientations individuals experience as a result of the death of a loved one, they are likely having distinct experiences triggered by unrelated events/situations at the same time (e.g., fear of an upcoming meeting with a boss, pride at staying within one's monthly budget), that may augment or be augmented by the concurrent disorientation, while still not being part of the experience of disorientation itself. Likewise, at the same time as they are disoriented, individuals may be having distinct experiences triggered by the same event/situation that prompted the disorientation (e.g., anger at one's siblings for not helping plan a memorial service). Though the distinction between these experiences and disorientations may be more or less murky depending on the particular situation, they can still be distinct.

This raises the question of how to identify or individuate disorientations, when they can be prompted by such diverse kinds of contexts as loss of loved ones, education, oppression, trauma, illness, migration, and queer sexualities. Consider a parallel question in the case of grief. What makes it make sense in everyday life to call all experiences of grief "grief"? We might think experiences of grief all share some feature (e.g., suffering as result of the loss of someone or something significant). Of course within this category there can be significant variation—grief over the loss of one's child is not the same thing as grief over the loss of one's home in foreclosure. Yet, both might meaningfully be described as grief. At the same time, we have standards for understanding what should be allowed to count as grief, and disregarding such standards can generate conflict.[23] If someone takes a parking spot you were waiting for, and you call your experience "grief," a friend might be angry. Such a response trivializes her experience of the death of a loved one. How we describe and categorize disorientations has similar intersubjective implications. How we all describe our experiences matters for how we can each describe our experiences, and how we can each describe our personal experiences matters for our ways of coping with or making meaning of them.

In *Philosophical Investigations*, Wittgenstein offers a "family resemblance" account of how to understand a word by looking at various cases where the word is used and noticing the overlapping features of the word in the multiple cases. Wittgenstein proposes that the meanings of words like "number" and "game" are best understood by seeing how different uses of the word are directly and indirectly related to each other:

> We see a complicated network of similarities overlapping and criss-crossing: sometimes overall similarities, sometimes similarities of detail.... Why do we call something a "number"? Well, perhaps because it has a—direct—relationship with several things that have hitherto been called number; and this can be said to give it an indirect relationship to other things we call the same name. And we extend our concept of number as in spinning a thread we twist fibre on fibre. And the strength of this thread does not reside in the fact that some one fibre runs through the whole length, but in the overlapping of many fibres. (Wittgenstein 2001/P.I. PP 66-67)

As José Medina summarizes Wittgenstein's account of family resemblance, "the meaning of a word is constituted by overlapping similarities rather than by a single defining feature or set of features" (Medina 2002, 212 n. 192).[24]

I want to suggest we understand "disorientation" as a family resemblance concept. Though there is significant variation between different things we call disorientations (like there is significant variation between things we call games), different instances of disorientation are related to each other as are fibers in a rope. Different things we call disorientations in the sense I use the word here have overlapping similarities.

The cases of disorientation I discuss are related to each other in a number of ways, and some are more similar than others. For example, as will become clear in chapter 3, the disorientations of feminist consciousness-raising and the disorientations of critical education can be very similar. Both alter the way an individual relates to her identity, privilege, and oppression, and both can make it impossible to keep acting in the same way. At the same time, each is distinct, depending on particulars of context, who one is, what one's life was like before, what supports one has, and so on. Both these kinds of disorientation relate less directly to the disorientations of grief. The death of a loved one also makes it impossible to keep acting in the same way, but in a very different sense than feminist consciousness-raising or critical education does: an individual disoriented by grief can no longer act as though one's loved one is alive. Grief too can change the way one relates to one's identity, but again in a very different sense than feminist consciousness-raising or education might. For example, an individual grieving the loss of an only child must adjust to being no longer straightforwardly recognized as a parent. Yet there are *threads of relation* that run through these and other cases of disorientation. All the cases I discuss are, roughly speaking, sustained, difficult experiences that make it hard to go on. When I say disorientations are *roughly speaking* "sustained, difficult experiences that make it hard to go on," I am highlighting the senses in which different instances of disorientation can vary significantly even with regards to these specific features.

All the disorientations I discuss are *sustained* in the sense that they are not just passing, momentary flashes of unease quickly followed by a return to feeling fine. Beyond that, the meaning of "sustained" varies. Unlike some classifications of experiences, such as those used in clinical contexts, there is not a minimum time requirement (e.g., six months) that must be met in order for something to count as disorientation, nor a maximum time allowed (e.g., two years) before the experience becomes recognized as a more severe condition. What counts as "sustained" might be indexed to the particular context of disorientation. Disorientations brought about by having some kind of marginalized identity in an oppressive social world (e.g., by being nonwhite in a racist social context or queer in a context of heteronormativity) may last longer than disorientations brought about by a diagnosis of a curable illness, but both count as *sustained*, relative to their context. Different examples of disorientations in my sense can have very different temporalities; some can be gradual, and others can come about more suddenly. Events or experiences that were once disorienting can cease to be disorienting, as when we adjust to the loss of a loved one over time. Experiences that do not at first spur felt disorientation can become disorienting, as when a chronic illness is manageable at first but worsens to the point of disrupting one's life plans. Or we can become so accustomed to difficult experiences, like caring for a dying sibling, that we become disoriented only when they cease. Given that disorientations affect individuals differently, and in most cases, unpredictably, depending on many other factors (e.g., how oriented one's life requires one to be at a certain time), disorientations can also be sustained while feeling different at different points.

Likewise, all the disorientations I discuss are *difficult* in the sense that they add strain to an individual's life, making it less easy than it would be without such disorientation, but the character of such difficulty varies greatly among different disorientations. For instance, the ways in which feminist educational contexts can be difficult for students are not the same as the ways grieving the death of one's child is difficult. Such difficulties are qualitatively and quantitatively different, though it still seems right to call both difficulties—in both cases, life would be easier without them.

And crucially, what it is like to feel that it is *hard to go on* can vary immensely among different cases. All the cases I discuss are cases that stop short of making it impossible to go on, in the sense of making life no longer bearable at all (becoming fatal), and all are cases that pose more than a minor challenge to an individual's capacity to adapt. But it is clear that there are lots of possibilities for difference in the grey area between those two extremes. It can be hard to go on after the disorientation of coming to see oneself as a beneficiary of colonial privilege. But it is hard to go on in a very different sense after the disorientation of experiencing ongoing colonial violence against one's family. Suggesting that these kinds of "hard to go on" experiences could be on a par with each other is not only false but itself violent.

Later on in *Philosophical Investigations*, Wittgenstein writes, "'Grief' describes a pattern which recurs, with different variations, in the weave of our life" (*P.I.* Part II, i). As Naomi Scheman discusses the passage, the question of whether two people are both feeling grief can only be answered through attention to the *details of what individuals say and do,* and to *what those details mean in the context of their lives* (Scheman 2011, 157). The same is true of disorientations—there is significant variation in individual experiences of disorientation, and to know whether two people are both disoriented, we need to pay attention to the details of what they say and do, in the context of their lives.

Given all the variation among the cases of disorientation, it might seem that the cases diverge more than they overlap. Understanding two individuals with diverse experiences as both disoriented may not seem accurate. Part of the project of this book is to make the case for the value of considering even very different experiences of disorientation together—not on a par, but through the lens of thinking about the place of disorientation in moral life.

Note that we can *understand what others are talking about* when they talk about being disoriented, seemingly without much confusion or difficulty. Here, the question of how to understand disorientations is complicated by the fact that, as will be clear throughout the book, sometimes people use different words to refer to what I am calling disorientations. For example, we describe ourselves or others as *being in a rough patch, being shaken up, having lost our way, needing guidance, taking things one step at a time*. Sometimes we do not use any particular term at all, but we know how to anticipate that someone in a particular context (e.g., having just gotten divorced, lost a job, or been diagnosed with cancer) is likely to feel disoriented, and so we talk with or about them from that assumption.

In practice, we might best tell *what we think disorientations are* by looking at our expressions of care and concern for others who are disoriented. When we ask *how someone is holding up*, we are asking, among other things, how she is coping with the disorientation we imagine she might be feeling. And if she answers that *things are going as well as can be expected*, we take that to mean, among other things, that she is coping with not knowing how to go on with her life. We have a sense of what periods of disorientation are like, we know how to recognize when others are in them, and in some cases we know how to recognize when we are in such periods ourselves. (The question of whether we more readily recognize the disorientations of others than we recognize our own is an interesting one that would need other kinds of empirical investigation.) We have ways of evaluating and comparing disorientations, and of evaluating disoriented individuals. Such judgments are expressed, for example, when we recognize how some kinds of disorientations are appropriately more devastating than others, or when we blame individuals for being too shaken up by a minor event, or for wallowing in a period of disorientation. So there is a set of phenomena—disorientations—we treat as related and as meaning certain things for the individuals experiencing disorientations. When asked what disorientations are, we might not have difficulty coming up with what seem like central features of an instance of disorientation. But it turns out that such criteria neither easily fit all instances of disorientation, nor are sufficiently compelling as to motivate us to exclude the instances of ill-fit. There are no necessary and sufficient conditions for something to count as an instance of disorientation.

In sum, I have become convinced that understanding disorientations as a set of widely varying but related experiences does justice to the way we regularly recognize and anticipate the reality of disorientation in the lives of others. Disorientation is often just one part of what we recognize when we recognize others in very difficult periods of life; we can recognize other things at the same time (e.g., injustice, harm, loss, illness). Partly, though, we come to relate to others as in periods when they are likely to feel that they don't know how to go on. Disorientations are ubiquitous, and I aim to offer a philosophical account of them as such.

Further, I will suggest that we gain a better understanding of moral life by treating disorientations as a set of related (while still distinct) experiences. When we look for disorientations among even very diverse kinds of experiences, we begin to see some ways disorientations are concurrent with our development as moral agents. As will be clearer in the coming chapters, treating different disorientations one at a time is necessary in order to clarify the specific effects of disorientations. Different disorientations have different effects.

Having established particular effects of particular disorientations, paying attention to comparisons among disorientations and their effects can help clarify features that different disorientations share. Likewise, it can help us understand how in some (not all) cases different disorientations generate similar effects, or generate distinct effects that are morally beneficial for similar reasons. Attention to the whole set of disorientations (alongside attention to particular kinds of disorientations separately) highlights how, though the particular effects of disorientations are importantly different in different cases, their possibility or moral relevance is largely precluded by a certain philosophical tradition of understanding moral motivation. As a set, disorientations help highlight how much orientedness is taken for granted in characterizations of the best moral agents, and how alternative conceptions of moral motivation are necessary.

My goal is to provide an account of disorientations that does justice to the features even very distinct cases of disorientation share, without obscuring the importance of what keeps them distinct. At various points in the following chapters, I make it clear that what makes particular cases of disorientation distinct can be as or more important to recognize as what makes particular cases of disorientation similar. Different theoretical and political goals can make the differences between disorientations in need of prioritizing.

1.3 METHODOLOGIES FOR INTERPRETING DISORIENTATIONS AND THEIR EFFECTS

This account of disorientation contributes to a tradition of feminist inquiry that aims to do justice to the realities of underrepresented lives. Its focus of attention is not always on *everyone's* reality, but on the under-investigated realities of some people's lives. The account also seeks to hold theories responsible when, by generalizing from some (often dominant) individuals' experiences, they neglect the significant experiences of some others (e.g., as feminist psychologist Carol Gilligan held Kohlberg accountable for generalizing from studies of male research subjects to what is true of everyone's moral development). The possibility of objective knowledge about experiences of disorientation depends on working toward a complex enough account of them to do justice to richly diverse perspectives. The claims I make are challengeable and correctible, by the people who experience disorientations as well as by theorists and scientists.

I understand this book as in part a response to Margaret Urban Walker's call for an "empirically obligated practice of ethics" (2003, 104, 217; see also 2003, xvii, and 2007b, 31) in the specific domain of considering disorientations. One way to work toward this goal is to start from multiple sources, including, as will be centrally important to this text, first-person testimonial accounts, as well as qualitative and quantitative research in psychology, medicine, and social work. My account of disorientations and their morally significant effects weaves together these and other sources, employing a feminist philosophical perspective in order to understand what kinds of information different sources are best able to provide, and how such sources can be complementary in generating a rich and complex account of the phenomenon. Different kinds of disorientations are the objects of different areas of research—for example, some disorientations are extensively studied in clinical contexts, while others are better characterized in first-personal or sociological accounts of queer life or racism. To do justice to both the variation and resemblance among different disorientations, I draw together multiple sources of information. As feminist epistemologists and feminists working in psychology have established, who and where one is makes a difference to what and how one knows; some dominant modes of knowing and reporting about knowledge (e.g., clinical research) often reflect the perspectives of those already working within those institutions, to the neglect of those who are not part of such institutions, or who are not readily studied by them.[25]

Distinguishing four main tasks of the book can help outline my methodology. Each of these parts of the account depends on a variety of sources of information, and a feminist philosophical approach is important in each case. There are in some cases important points of disagreement about how to characterize disorientations or their position in moral life. These raise questions and points for further research in the future.

1.3.1 Claims about What Disorientations Are

A central aim of this book is to identify certain kinds of experiences as disorientations, and to defend disorientation as a family resemblance concept that allows for seeing even very disparate experiences as being relevantly related. In defining disorientations, I am offering a broader view of what disorientations are than has yet existed. As a broad set that includes many quite different kinds of experiences, I draw on a collection of distinct sources to characterize disorientations, including first-person accounts, philosophical accounts, and qualitative and quantitative accounts from psychology, medicine, and social work. I also draw on trauma theory (Herman, Caruth, Brison), anti-oppression theory (Du Bois, Yancy, Pratt), and queer theory (Ahmed, Butler, Cvetkovich) to help characterize disorientations in those domains. Empirical studies from clinical research on experiences of grief, illness, and traumatic stress provide a wealth of information in characterizing how such experiences can be disorienting. Research in social work and sociology on experiences of coming out, racism, consciousness-raising, college education, and migration has also informed my account of the disorienting dimensions of such experiences.

Some of the people experiencing the disorientations that interest me end up in clinical contexts, and others do not. Many of the accounts of disorientations related to oppression, for example, are from people who do not seek help in clinical settings, and/or who do not see their experience as something that would motivate seeking professional help. Some turn to other sources of support, such as religious or political communities. Likewise, some individuals experiencing disorientations become research subjects in sociology and social work, and others do not. Social scientific research gives particularly useful access to the ways those who are being studied because of some other experience (e.g., experiences of living as queer in heterosexist contexts, or as racialized in racist contexts) express being disoriented in that context. Clinical and social scientific research provides part of the picture of what disorientations are, as can first-personal and other accounts.

More than other approaches, a philosophical account of disorientation has the resources to provide accounts of how experiences may reflect characteristics of the world, how such experiences can fit into the structure of agency and responsibility, and how responses to experiences are themselves morally and politically significant. A philosophical account of disorientations can help us better understand ourselves and understand "the good life" as one that may include disorientations.

1.3.2 Claims about What Disorientations Do

In chapters 3 and 4, I show that some disorientations have specific *effects*, that is, that particular disorientations have changed attitudes, capacities, behaviors, and ways of relating to others, in particular ways. I support claims about these effects of disorientations with an interdisciplinary approach, drawing on first-personal accounts (testimony) in various formats (memoir, autobiography, short first-personal accounts) from philosophers, feminist theorists, authors, scientists, medical practitioners, journalists, and others. I also draw on qualitative and quantitative studies in psychology, psychiatry, sociology, social work, and medicine about the effects of disorienting experiences. Such research supports my major claims about what the specific effects of disorientations are in specific cases. Though I do not aim to show that all disorientations of some kind have a particular effect (on my view, not all the disorientations of grief or illness are likely to have the beneficial effects I track), I do show that we have reason (in various forms of evidence) to believe that, for example, the disorientations of illness *have in some cases* prompted capacities for sensing vulnerability. I then employ a feminist philosophical approach to argue for the moral significance of these effects.

To account for disorientations' effects, I draw in part on written first-person accounts of disorientations from a number of different perspectives: people who are experiencing grief, people who become feminist activists, students who encounter radically new perspectives on the world, people of color who face racial segregation, a child of doctors who is diagnosed with terminal illness, a philosopher who survives sexual assault, a queer man whose community faces widespread HIV, an Argentinian immigrant to the United States, people working against injustice, and many others.

I also draw substantially on empirical studies of the disorientations of grief, double consciousness, consciousness-raising, critical education, illness, trauma, queerness, and migration, which offer support for thinking that specific disorientations have specific effects. There have been extensive psychological studies of experiences like the death of loved ones, traumas, serious illnesses, military combat, and natural disasters. As with what I am calling disorientations, these experiences are all understood to seriously compromise stability, and to make it difficult or impossible for individuals to go on. The styles and scope of studies very widely, from in-depth phenomenological or semi-structured open-ended interviews of fewer participants, to online or mailed surveys of hundreds of participants.[26] Studies of the effects of disorientations are performed using measurements of coherence,[27] autonomy-connectedness,[28] self-efficacy,[29] cognitive adaptation,[30] changed world-assumptions,[31] changed outlook,[32] or illness impact.[33]

In characterizing the effects of disorientation on the basis of first-personal and empirical sources, I return to the insights of feminist epistemologists regarding the importance of identity and social position for knowledge. My account of each effect of disorientation is supported by both first-personal and empirical evidence, though a few things are important to note here. In some cases, more attention to the effects of disorientations in a particular area of life has been paid by first-person than by empirical accounts, or vice versa. For example, there is far more empirical research on the disorientations of illness than on the disorientations of feminist consciousness-raising. Further, the goals of particular research programs shape the methodologies of that research. When tracking effects of some event, the goal for clinical research is usually to discover what will restore health, to facilitate recovery, and to establish best practice for treating or interacting with individuals facing such difficulties in the future. Given this, the more generalizable the results of research, the better. Outlier or idiosyncratic experiences are not the focus of such analysis.[34] By contrast, the conclusions drawn about disorientations based on testimonial, first-person (and sometimes second-person) accounts of experiences and effects are not meant to be generalizable.

Critical awareness of the limits of a particular source is always needed. For example, in much of the empirical literature about the effects of traumatic experiences, there is typically an explicit positioning of some effects as negative (e.g., feelings of hopelessness or diminished self-esteem) and others as positive (e.g., feelings of strength or new life priorities). Here I am thinking of the substantial literature on resilience,[35] hardiness,[36] adversarial/stress-related growth,[37] coping,[38] and post-traumatic growth.[39] As such, there is from the start an assumption about the obviousness of some effects being positive and others being negative. A philosophical approach to the empirical literature allows for asking *why some effects of disorientations are assumed to be positive while others are assumed to be negative.*[40] In drawing on the literature in cases where undefended assumptions shape research findings, I approach the research with critical awareness of its limitations. In other words, I have paid attention to the effects of disorientations the empirical literature outlines, while in many cases not endorsing the studies' assumptions about which effects are obviously positive (e.g., increased mastery over one's feelings), versus which are obviously negative (e.g., increased awareness of the uncontrollability of the world).[41]

To be clear, in all cases, I am making the point that a particular kind of disorientation (e.g., the disorientations of experiencing racism) *can* generate one or more particular effect(s) (e.g., prompting awareness of oppressive norms and their contingency) on the basis of evidence that, in some cases, such a disorientation has generated the effect(s). I do not argue that *all* kinds of disorientations are able to generate that effect. In some cases, there are overlaps in the effects different kinds of disorientations can have: for instance, as we will see in chapter 4, some disorientations of illness and some disorientations of trauma have prompted capacities for living unprepared. It may be that there is support for thinking that different kinds of disorientation prompt more similar or overlapping effects than I argue for here. I only argue for the effects of particular disorientations for which there is already clear support. I also do not argue that *all* instances of *that particular kind* of disorientation (e.g., all instances of the disorientations of terminal illness) will necessarily generate that effect.

I remind at various points that it is clear that disorientations can occur without having any positive effects, or they can have very negative effects. It might be that the disorientations of grief or serious illness much less commonly have beneficial effects than the disorientations of consciousness-raising or education. I am only making the case for thinking that particular instances of disorientations in some cases have some effects. Though beneficial effects may not be the norm, we will see support for thinking they are not unusual.

1.3.3 Implications of This Account for Moral Motivation and Agency

Having characterized disorientations and made the case for the ways specific disorientations can have specific effects, I will then make the case for seeing those effects as *morally promising*. Doing so requires clarifying the understanding of moral practice I have in mind, and making the case for how some practices (including many that have not been considered paradigm cases of moral action in traditional philosophical ethics) should in fact count as important parts of what it is to be a responsible moral agent. Here I apply the work of many feminist philosophers who have challenged traditional understandings of the autonomous moral agent and argued for the moral significance of everyday practices of relation.

In situating disorientations and their effects in a broader feminist understanding of moral motivation and agency, I am challenging a number of assumptions that have shaped philosophical ethics.

In particular, I will suggest the need for a reconsideration of the central place given to decisive moral judgments and virtuous character traits. Many ethical frameworks understand moral and political change as centrally involving changes in an individual's moral judgments about what to do. As I discuss at length in chapter 2, multiple strands in ethics and moral psychology demonstrate great interest in how individual agents become able to form moral judgments and act confidently according to them. Taken together, these accounts have implications for what kinds of experiences would appear to *hinder* moral agency: namely, experiences that compromise moral judgment and/or confident action. Secondarily, such accounts have implications for what acting morally is understood to *feel like*. Agents may feel confirmed in the rightness of their actions when they feel decisive, wholehearted, and in control, and concerned about possibly misguided actions when they feel otherwise.

Doing justice to the position of disorientations in everyday lives will require challenging models of moral agency that: (1) identify successful moral agents as those who have well-ordered preferences on the basis of which they act decisively; and (2) identify paradigm moral actions as wholehearted decisions about right and wrong. Much of empirical psychology, like much of moral philosophy, is working from now outdated models of moral agents. Feminist philosophy is particularly helpful in this regard because it has established much richer accounts of relational agency and the moral significance of everyday practices of relation.

Besides accounts that emphasize the importance of decisive moral judgment and action, traditional virtue ethics accounts understand moral action as following from the cultivation of virtuous character traits. On such accounts, agents develop stable, enduring dispositions to act virtuously (e.g., courageously, generously, or prudently), which are expressed in contexts where specific kinds of virtuous actions are called for. These traits are deliberately cultivated by individuals, and learned through interaction with virtuous others. While it might seem that the beneficial effects of disorientations could be best understood as prompting beneficial changes in *character*—a general point to which I am sympathetic, as I will discuss further in the next chapter—it is important to clarify in advance why traditional virtue ethics approaches will not be well suited to understanding the morally beneficial effects of disorientations.[42] The effects of disorientation I will discuss are not properly understood as virtuous character traits. Such traits are typically understood to be *static* (i.e., reliable, unchanging), *enduring* (i.e., once cultivated, they are ongoing), and *global* (i.e., once cultivated, they are available for application in all areas of an individual's life). As we will see, the morally beneficial effects of disorientations I discuss are unlike virtuous character traits in all these senses: they are dynamic; in some cases temporary; and expressed only in select areas of life. Further, virtuous character traits are traditionally understood to be things that individuals can deliberately cultivate, with the help and guidance of others (teachers, parents, etc.). By contrast, the effects of disorientations discussed in the next chapters are not pursued by agents, but unchosen, unwilled effects of experiences many individuals would rather avoid.

Distinguishing the effects of disorientations from virtues is important in order to avoid what I see as a significant misunderstanding of the position of disorientations in moral life. As we will see, disorientations can have odd effects. In the cases I will discuss, they do not strengthen agents, or give them stable dispositions to act well. Rather, in the cases I discuss, they attune individuals to the particularities of an unjust moral landscape in ways that allow them to respond well to it in some ways, for some period of time. In short, the effects of disorientation can do more to shift how individuals interact in specific contexts and relationships than to change what traits individuals possess overall.

As I will suggest in the next chapter, it is partly because of limited visions of moral agents and moral actions that disorientations have gone untreated in ethics for so long.

1.3.4 Implications of This Account for Understandings of Oppression

Throughout the book I situate disorientations and their morally significant effects in an understanding of oppression in two senses: (1) oppressive conditions can cause disorientations; and (2) contexts of oppression can be a location where the effects of disorientation can be especially important. Just as I do to understand all causes of disorientation, to understand the ways oppressive conditions can prompt disorientation I draw on multiple first-person, phenomenological, philosophical, and empirical sources. Here the first-personal sources are particularly important, as often they are best able to give voice to members of marginalized groups. I draw on anti-racist, queer, and migrant accounts especially, which in some cases are from sources that are both testimonial and theoretical (e.g., Du Bois's *Souls of Black Folk*). To understand the importance of the effects of disorientations in contexts of oppression, I draw on feminist accounts of the harms of oppression and of responsibility for anti-oppressive actions. I am making claims about the facts of the moral and political landscape of injustice, arguing that the effects of some disorientations (again, not all, not all the time) can be morally beneficial given these facts, for example, given what kind of action/motivation is required to address these injustices.

In situating disorientations and their effects in a broader feminist understanding of conditions of oppression, I am challenging the idea that social identity is irrelevant for what and how we experience, and I am also challenging tendencies in traditional ethics to overlook the injustices of oppression as morally significant harms in need of address. On my view, considerations of experiences of disorientation must include the social and relational position of those who experience major disruptions. Who individuals are, situated in relationships and structures of power, shapes what disorients them, how they experience disorientations, and what disorientations do in their lives.

As will become clear, who experiences disorientations, how they experience them, and what effects such experiences have are all factors mitigated by social privilege. It matters who one is within power relations of, for instance, gender, race, class, disability, and sexuality. How we experience being disoriented and how such experiences shape us as moral and political agents depends on who we are and who is around us. Even so, as we will see, oppression and privilege can shape our experiences of disorientation in unexpected ways. Many of the descriptions of disorientations changing action discussed in the book (chapters 2, 3, and 4) come from individuals who have often experienced marginalization: women, those who are racialized and medicalized, queers, and survivors of sexual violence. Connections between experiences of oppression and experiences of disorientation are not accidental.

As will become clear, the domain in which disorientations can prompt changed action for the better involves primarily moral practices of relating to oneself and other living beings. Within this domain, many living beings are currently harmed by domination, oppression, and unjust exercises of power in social life. Thus, many cases of changed action for the better described here are ones where individuals confront the harms of oppression and structural injustice—specifically, the harms of racism, sexism, heterosexism, ableism, and other oppressions. Neither all harms nor all responsibilities issue from the need to work against structures of oppression. While this is not the only domain in which disorientations can have positive effects, many of the examples discussed in the book focus here.

A major contention of the book is that when disorientations help moral agents, they do so not primarily by helping us resolve how to act. Real-life disorientations prompt individuals to morally and politically salient changes in action, and especially to new ways of relating to, caring for, acting with, and relying on other people, often apart from those individuals first deciding to do so. Crucially, disorientations can help us act even when we do not reorient. As I discuss in what follows, many feminist and anti-racist philosophers have articulated the ways oppression is perpetuated in large part through unconscious rather than deliberate actions (e.g., micro-inequalities, racist biases, ableist habits, colonialist ignorance). This book focuses on the flip side of that reality. If it is true that unintentional actions (habits, biases, ignorance) often have the power to perpetuate oppression, feminists should also detail the power of unconscious actions to effect anti-oppression.

1.4 CONCLUSION

Disorientations are complex and intriguing. They have been of interest to theorists, writers, theologians, and empirical researchers, but a number of questions about them remain in need of philosophical attention. I have suggested that we should understand disorientations as a set of, roughly speaking, sustained, difficult experiences that make it hard to go on. Understanding disorientations this way, as a set of related, though widely varying experiences is useful. It does justice to the meaning the concept has in our everyday practices of relating to one another while disoriented, and it provides the ground for a philosophical investigation of the moral significance of such experiences. In particular, a feminist philosophical approach to disorientation allows for engaging multiple important sources of information about disorientations and their morally significant effects. Such an approach also allows for attending newly to the ways disorientations play out in individual lives, and how they are different depending on differences in social position.

[2]

MORAL MOTIVATION BEYOND MORAL RESOLVE

> There are moments, most unexpectedly, when something inside me tries to assure me that I don't really mind so much.... I've plenty of what are called "resources." People get over these things. Come, I shan't do so badly. One is ashamed to listen to this voice but it seems for a little to be making out a good case. Then comes a sudden jab of red-hot memory and all this "common-sense" vanishes like an ant in the mouth of a furnace.
>
> —C. S. Lewis (1961, 2)

As we saw in chapter 1, disorientations are a complex phenomenon. They are multidimensional experiences that arise in many different contexts in our lives. Given the intensity of such experiences, it is not surprising that they can have serious effects on our ways of acting. Given their complexity, it is not surprising that the effects might be hard to predict.

In this chapter, I will begin to lay the groundwork for understanding how complicated experiences like disorientations *could* have beneficial effects on moral action, given what philosophers have so far claimed about how experiences can prompt moral change. I will first identify what I see as a dominant assumption that the best evidence of successful moral motivation in an agent's life is *moral resolve*—a combination of knowing what to do, feeling able to do it, and successfully carrying out the required action. I will consider the ways this assumption has narrowed the focus of particular strands of moral psychology, making it likely to be in the background of philosophers' minds as we approach the question of the role of disorientations in moral life. I will then turn to research on the effects of grief to make visible the gap between what philosophical accounts based on moral resolve are able to explain about the effects of difficult experiences and what seem to be morally significant features of such experiences. It will then be possible to establish an account of moral motivation beyond moral resolve, and this will be the foundation going forward for my account of the moral promise of disorientations' effects.

2.1 IDENTIFYING MORAL RESOLVE

A great deal of moral psychology has focused on answering the question of *how to tell that a moral agent has been successfully motivated to act*. The best evidence of successful moral motivation is often seen to be an agent's *deciding* how to act and carrying out that action. For example, if a moral agent encounters a drowning child on the side of the road, the best evidence of her having become successfully motivated to act would seem to be her coming to act: saving the child, or not. The question of whether or not she has in fact acted responsibly or done the right thing comes later. If she acts, outsiders have reason to think she has been successfully motivated.

The processes by which we arrive at such moral actions are diverse. Of course, not all moral actions are as dramatic or discrete as saving a drowning child—many are instead more subtle and ongoing, as are the numerous actions involved in being in friendships or family relationships over time, or the many kinds of actions involved in participating in a workplace or community. Everyday actions of perceiving, communicating with, and responding to others are morally significant—agents can perform such actions responsibly, in ways which demonstrate care and respect, or fail to perform them well, causing neglect or harm. Different kinds of moral action will be the results of different kinds of processes of motivation. To identify what kind of motivational process is at work in generating a given kind of moral action, moral psychologists can pay attention to what may have prompted an agent to develop certain practices or to change actions over time.

In many cases, moral actions are preceded by some form of judgment or decision—an agent judges what she *ought to do*, what she *must not do*, or simply *what to do next*. In the above case, it seems likely that an agent arrives at the moral judgment "I ought to save the drowning child," or just "now save the drowning child," and acts in accordance with that judgment. How she arrives at such a judgment in the first place is a complicated question and has been a topic of great interest to philosophers. As we will see in section 2.2.2, this question still guides much of the research in empirical moral psychology, where many researchers have argued that agents do not typically arrive at such judgments through consciously reasoning about what we ought to do (as some in the history of philosophy have assumed), but rather by quick and automatic intuitions.

In addition to possible variation in what prompts them, moral judgments can also vary in quality: they can be more or less in conflict with other judgments of what action is required. In the drowning child case, it may be that the agent's judgment is not in conflict with any other requirements—it is obvious to her that saving the child is what is required. Other judgments may not be so simple. For instance, an agent may judge that he should put on his own oxygen mask before assisting his child during an in-flight emergency, while finding this conflicts with another judgment about what is morally required (i.e., to protect his child before himself). The agent may act upon the judgment to put his own mask on first, while knowing this judgment is in direct conflict with another.[1]

In addition to the processes by which individuals become motivated to act, agents can feel different ways about the actions they perform—however an individual acts in response to the drowning child, she may feel proud, tentative, concerned, or ashamed of that action or of herself as agent. Some moral judgments may be ones we enact less confidently than others, either because they are in conflict with other moral judgments or for other reasons. In the oxygen mask case, the conflicting moral judgments may undermine the agent's confidence, even as he acts upon only one of his judgments.[2] Likewise, an agent may clearly judge that she must save the drowning child, but do so with fear and uncertainty. So while we might imagine a paradigm case of moral judgment involving the identification of a single moral requirement and confidence in acting upon that requirement, we can see that these features of moral judgments do not always align, and that moral actions can be performed even when they do not. Certainly moral agents can lack confidence and still act upon their moral judgments.

In sum, we arrive at moral actions through a variety of processes, a central one of which is moral judgment, and we can act according to moral judgments without necessarily being confident about our actions. Given how much of our moral life involves becoming motivated to act through the process of first forming moral judgments about how to act, it makes sense that moral judgments continue to be a central focus of studies of motivation. But it is also possible to act morally without first judging how to act in the sense of having a clear sense of what to do next—in some cases, we act without having first decided how we ought to act, or without having formed a judgment about what to do next. Many more examples of such actions will come up in the next chapters, but for now, consider the following kind of case: a close friend tells you he has been diagnosed with multiple sclerosis. You express concern immediately through your body language, your changed way of listening to him, and your words. Over a longer period of time, you respond continually to him, making space for him to talk about his experiences, anticipating, perceiving, and fulfilling his needs, and allowing your relationship to change in keeping with his circumstances. But from the moment of your first conversation, throughout the length of his illness, you do not feel you know what to do—you simply act. When asked, you say you do not know what to do and are just taking the situation day by day. Some might be inclined to understand this as either: (a) a case of not exactly moral actions, but instead just behaviors or habits; or (b) a case of moral actions on the basis of some implicit set of moral judgments—perhaps the judgment that "I ought to help my friend by doing *x, y,* or *z,*" or just "Now do *x, y,* or *z*"—even if you cannot verbalize that judgment when asked. I think neither of these readings does justice to the case. You are acting morally in the kinds of ways described earlier—through everyday actions of perceiving, communicating with, and responding to others—without having decided how to do so. Given the specifics of this case, your capacities for judging how to act may have even been compromised. You do not know what to do, and yet you are continuing to act.

In addition to being actions not based on earlier judgments of how to act, many of the actions discussed in the coming chapters are actions performed non-confidently. It is perhaps unsurprising that lacking a judgment of what to do in advance of acting would compromise one's confidence. Though many of the actions I will discuss in contexts of disorientation are actions performed both without earlier judgments about how to act, and without confidence, it is worth noting again how moral judgment and confidence can come apart: just as in the case of the drowning child it was possible to act on a non-conflicted, clear judgment and nonetheless lack confidence, it is also possible to act without first having judged how to do so in caring for one's friend with MS and still feel some degree of confidence for other reasons (e.g., confidence about one's ability to care for others in general, on the basis of past caring relationships). In other words, the presence of moral judgment does not ensure confidence, and its absence need not preclude it.

I now want to introduce some terminology that will be of use going forward: when a person acts on the basis of a moral judgment about what to do and how to do it, and with feelings of confidence (about the action, herself as agent, or both), I will describe her as acting with *moral resolve*. The dual-meaning of resolve is intentional. When agents know what to do, how to do it, and have confidence, they can *resolve how to act* (in the sense of judging how to act), and they can *act with resolve* (in the sense of acting decisively, with determination, and confidence). In many such cases, an agent has some kind of experience (e.g., feels concern for the drowning child) that helps her formulate her moral judgment, often triggering an intuition about the best course of action. Call this the *resolutionary power of experience*. The experience of concern helps her resolve (judge) how to act and to act with resolve (confidence). By contrast, in the case of the friend with MS, your experience of concern cannot be described as having resolutionary power. It is an experience that motivates action but does not point toward a clear path forward. When a person acts without having first judged how to act, and without feeling confident in her actions or herself, she acts *without moral resolve*. She neither resolves (judges) how to act nor acts with resolve (confidence).

Note that we have already seen middle ground cases here. It is possible to act on the basis of a moral judgment about how to act, while lacking confidence. It is also possible to act without first having judged how to act, while maintaining confidence. And of course there are other possibilities that involve *not* acting, whether or not an agent has formulated a judgment of what to do, and whether or not he is confident. Going forward, my chief interest is in the cases of *acting without moral resolve* (i.e., acting without having judged how to act and without feeling confident). As we will see, action without moral resolve will come up often in the next chapters; in the cases of disorientation that will be discussed, often a disoriented person lacks a judgment of how to act, lacks confidence in their actions and themselves as an agent, but still acts in morally significant ways. The question then becomes: What status do actions without moral resolve have in philosophical accounts of successful moral motivation?

Before establishing how I think moral psychologists should go about understanding moral motivation in cases of *action without moral resolve*, I want to suggest that difficulties in understanding this action are the result of a dominant but restrictive perspective in moral psychology, driven by the assumption that to be morally motivated means that an *agent acts with moral resolve*. As we will see, there is variation in accounts of what gets agents to the point of moral judgment and confident action, and growing attention to the important role emotions play in that process of motivating agents to act, so the process is not always assumed to be entirely based on deliberation or reasoning. Still, whatever gets agents to the point of motivation, that point of motivation is by and large assumed to be evidenced by an agent judging what must be done and how to do it, feeling confident about their prospective action, and enacting it— in other words, acting with resolve.

2.2 LEGACIES OF RESOLVISM

A number of literatures at the intersection of philosophy and psychology take for granted a vision of the best moral agents as those with moral resolve. As will become clear, moral resolve is assumed to be at the heart of moral motivation at every point in an agent's life—from accounts of how children become mature moral agents and how people make moral judgments, to common failures of moral agency, to concrete cases where life events improve how agents act. This pattern of assuming moral resolve to be the best (or perhaps, in some cases, *only*) evidence of successful moral motivation should be understood as what I will call a legacy of *resolvism*; its overemphasis on moral resolve eclipses other significant aspects of moral motivation.

2.2.1 Resolvism in Accounts of Moral Development

Moral resolve is taken to be foundational for moral agency by many philosophical and psychological accounts of moral development. Jean Piaget's psychological theory of childhood moral development has informed much of the philosophical literature on moral development. For Piaget (1932), moral development in children involved a progression from heteronomous morality, where morality is seen as rule-following and immorality as rule-breaking, to autonomous morality, where individuals are seen as mutually establishing meaningful rules by reasoning. Lawrence Kohlberg (1971, 1981) later developed a more elaborate theory of moral development in children that specified six stages of moral maturation. Starting from the least mature stage, moral action is first driven by obedience and punishment-avoidance, then self-interest, then social conformity, then respect for authority, then a perceived social contract, and finally, the highest form of moral maturity is principled ethical action. For instance, when given a scenario asking whether a husband should ever steal drugs needed to save his wife's life, a mature subject would recommend a principled action: perhaps one that allows for all individuals to be given equal respect.[3] Kohlberg's view of moral development privileges what I am calling moral resolve by equating capacities for decisiveness with moral maturity.

Though Kohlberg's understanding of moral development has been important in the subsequent literature in philosophy, it has also received substantial criticisms. Carol Gilligan's (1982) famous critique (see also Murphy and Gilligan 1980; Benhabib 1985) highlights a number of troubling assumptions at work in Kohlberg's account and challenges his approach directly for the way it favors what she argued were more masculine patterns of moral reasoning over more feminine approaches to moral reasoning. Note, however, that while Gilligan shifted the question to how women make moral decisions more often with an awareness of relationship and aiming to best meet the needs of everyone, she did not fundamentally challenge the vision of moral growth as developing capacities for maximum moral resolve. She challenges Kohlberg's assumptions about which factors lead to decision; but the process of decision-making is still central.

2.2.2 Resolvism in Accounts of Moral Judgment

The field of research at the intersection of ethics and empirical psychology is growing and bringing a more sophisticated analysis of the importance of emotions in moral agency. Against the background of rationalist accounts of moral judgment that downplayed or disregarded the significance of emotions, a variety of "dual-systems" models offer understandings of moral judgment as a process partly (and in some cases, largely) dependent on emotional experiences. According to dual-systems models advanced by Jonathan Haidt, Joshua Greene, and others,[4] moral judgments arise from two discrete systems: automatic, unconscious intuitions, on the one hand, and controlled, conscious reasoning processes, on the other. Both systems can be involved in the production of moral judgments, though many accounts show that the unconscious, automatic system in fact produces most of our moral judgments.[5] Many of these accounts have built on Kahneman and Tversky's early research distinguishing intuitive judgments from both perceptual and reasoning processes (1984; Tversky and Kahneman 1971). They developed a two-systems view of judgment, distinguishing intuition (system 1) from reasoning (system 2). As they explain:

> The operations of System 1 are typically fast, automatic, effortless, associative, implicit, (not available to introspection), and often emotionally charged; they are also governed by habit and therefore difficult to control or modify. The operations of System 2 are slower, serial, effortful, more likely to be consciously monitored and deliberately controlled, they are also relatively flexible and potentially rule governed. (Kahneman 2003, 698)[6]

While Kahneman and Tversky's two-systems view aims to describe processes of judgment in general, it has been widely influential in the context of research on moral judgment. Two major proponents of a dual-systems account of moral judgment, Joshua Greene and Jonathan Haidt (2002), have argued for a model of moral judgment according to which moral judgment is generally the result of quick automatic evaluations (intuitions), and moral reasoning is rarely the direct cause of moral judgment. Typically, moral judgments appear in consciousness as a result of quick, effortless intuitions (Haidt 2001, 815). In some cases, individuals then reason in a slow, effortful way about these moral judgments after the fact—we may search for arguments to support the judgments we have already made, or to persuade others to come to hold the judgments we do (Greene et al. 2001; Haidt 2001, 818-819). Post-hoc reasoning can give the illusion of controlled, conscious reasoning processes being the originators of moral judgments more often than they are.

Discussions of *moral dumbfounding* help the clarify dual-system theorists' challenge to assumptions of the centrality of reason in processes of moral judgment. Haidt et al. (2000) describe an example of a case where, when faced with an imagined scenario of consensual, protected sex between siblings, study participants are asked a series of questions about whether such behavior is acceptable, and why or why not. Their responses are evaluated to try to determine what produces, for example, the judgment that incestuous sex between siblings is never acceptable, even when one cannot back up one's judgment with reference to a concern about sexual violence or biological concern about offspring. The point is to show how in some cases, participants make a moral judgment (e.g., that sex between siblings is immoral) without being able to then explain their reasoning. In some cases they can provide explanations after the fact, but ones which do not seem to have formed the basis for their original judgment. In other words, the point of dumbfounding cases is to show that rational deliberation is not the only or primary factor in guiding moral judgment.

Some areas of this work then focus on specifying instances in which reasoning does play more of a role in moral judgment. For instance, in "The Secret Joke of Kant's Soul," Greene argues that deontological moral judgments (e.g., about inviolable rights or duties) are driven by automatic emotional responses, whereas consequentialist judgments are more driven by controlled reasoning processes. On Greene's view, deontological moral judgments seem to be driven by "alarm-bell" intuitions (e.g., we must *never* push the large man off the footbridge). In such cases, an individual has a strong feeling that something must or must not be done, though it may be not obvious how to explain that feeling. By contrast, consequentialist moral judgments do not appear to be intuition-driven in the same way—they take longer and involve some emotion along with some rational cognition (Greene 2008; Greene et al. 2008). This claim specifically counters a Kantian position on moral judgments as not the product of emotions (Greene 2008, 37), as well as contesting Kohlberg's understanding of both deontological and consequentialist judgments as being results of advanced moral reasoning (Greene 2008, 41).

Attention to dual-process models in moral psychology marks an important shift in tendencies of ethical theory to privilege reasoning processes and disregard the potential role of feelings and emotions. We can note, for example, the significance of the shift away from Kohlberg, who endorsed a rationalist model that is still deeply influential in moral psychology today. Dual-systems accounts have opened up possibilities for philosophical work more attentive to the role of intuition and emotion in motivation, and they have been informative for a number of new directions in moral psychology.[7]

Validating the role of emotion and intuition in moral judgment might seem to be a step toward recognizing the problem of resolvism in accounts of moral motivation, since a focus on processes other than reasoning might start to highlight less decisive aspects of moral action. But notice that, even when some parts of this literature suggest that emotions and intuitions should be seen as playing a greater role in processes of moral judgment, dual-systems accounts still emphasize *moral judgments about how to act* (e.g., the judgment that one should steer a runaway trolley to kill one person in order to save five others) as (1) the key end product of both systems (whether produced by intuition or by reasoning), and (2) necessary components of moral motivation.

In this literature, the moral experiences of interest are still "experiences of moral requirements"—in other words, the experience of coming to judge that some action is a responsibility, duty, or obligation. Whether one arrives at it by intuition (as we seem to in most cases) or reasoning, the relevant result of the processes is the moral judgment: *I take myself to be required to do something.*[8] I must steer the trolley to kill one person and save five, I must not push the man off the footbridge, and so on. Even Haidt's somewhat broader characterization of moral judgments as "evaluations (good vs. bad) of the actions or character of a person that are made with respect to a set of virtues held to be obligatory by a culture or subculture" (2001, 817) emphasizes the product of processes of intuition or reasoning as evaluations of actions or character traits. Dual-systems accounts offer more fine-grained and empirically grounded analyses than have been previously available, but their goal is still limited to explaining the phenomenon of the production of moral judgments.

As we will see, other psychological research points to motivational effects of experiences that are not reducible to the production of moral judgments. Dual-systems models are not equipped to explain the processes of experience by which one becomes motivated to act *without having arrived at a judgment*. Such accounts will not be well suited to explain the motivational capacities of experiences like disorientations that fail to generate decisive moral judgments, but in some cases nonetheless motivate changed action. Furthermore, they support the tendency to equate successful moral motivation with the production of moral judgments, which leads philosophers to expect that dual-systems models will be capable of explaining all kinds of moral motivation, and thus that any processes or experiences not well explained by dual-systems models were not examples of moral motivation in the first place. As such, dual-systems models are part of a legacy of resolvism.

2.2.3 Resolvism in Accounts of Moral Failure

Beyond accounts of moral development and moral judgment, accounts of moral failure also demonstrate deeply held assumptions about the importance of moral resolve. Accounts of weakness of will, for example, are centrally concerned with the failure of agents to be able to motivate themselves to act as they know they should.[9] The failure is partly a failure of agents to align the features of moral resolve described earlier: judging what to do, how to do it, feeling confident, and especially to follow through with action. An agent can fail in a different sense if she fails to act with integrity, where lacking integrity can mean lacking appropriate regard for one's role in determining what is worth doing (Calhoun 1995), or failing to stand for one's convictions in an epistemically responsible way (Scherkoske 2010, 2012). An agent can also be seen to fail morally by failing to exhibit autonomy or self-respect.[10] Judgments of the moral failures of others are sometimes described as reactive attitudes to others' failures to know what to do and/or to act decisively; an individual can blame or resent a loved one for failing to know what to do or how to do it, or for dithering or hesitating when moral action is required.[11]

Harry Frankfurt's (1987) account of ambivalence as moral failure is one of the most important examples of associating a lack of moral resolve with moral failure. For Frankfurt (1987, 41–42), successful moral action requires in part reconciling first- and second-order desires and reaching decisions about how to act. According to Frankfurt (1987, 42), decisive selves deal with inevitable internal conflict not by expelling one of the causes of the conflict, so much as by dissociating themselves from whichever desires conflict with the decision they have made. Successful moral agents are thus wholehearted: they are clear on what must be done, how to do it, and they feel of one mind about their role in the situation (Frankfurt 1999,

100). Any less than this is a kind of ambivalence, evidence of moral failure. As such, moral failure is often associated with failures of moral resolve.

2.2.4 Resolvism in Accounts of Moral Growth

Finally, in addition to the standard assumptions about moral resolve that run through accounts of moral development, moral judgment, and moral failure, we find such assumptions in research in clinical and moral psychology about *moral growth*. Returning to some of the literature introduced in the last chapter, research on resilience and growth after psychological distress demonstrates resolvist assumptions in understanding morally relevant aspects of personal growth.

As we saw in chapter 1, empirical psychologists have in some cases paid attention to experiences like disorientations (e.g., adjustment disorders, post-traumatic stress, and others) and have offered accounts of ways such experiences can have both troubling and sometimes positive effects. The substantial literature on resilience, benefit-finding, hardiness, and post-traumatic growth have offered quantitative and qualitative support for thinking that experiences like disorientations in some cases help individuals *grow*. There are multiple senses of growth relevant to such accounts, and some of them are moral senses. For instance, in psychological research into personal growth after difficult experiences, much attention is focused on a capacity of individuals for *meaning-making*—making sense of difficult experiences as part of a grand narrative (e.g., of God's will), or salvaging some benefit out of otherwise destructive events. Often these benefits take the form of new priorities or strengthened determination to cope with life challenges. Some views strongly associate healthy adaptation with self-mastery, and unhealthy adaptation with a failure to act decisively (Livneh 2000).

Many studies explore specifically the relation between intensity of distress and likelihood of growth in the five domains, but there is conflict between findings. Some studies have found that greater distress predicts more likely growth,[12] and others have found that more intense distress makes growth less likely.[13] Stewart et al. summarize the factors investigated in many studies of post-traumatic resilience as follows:

> Many of the factors reported to be associated with, or predictive of, resilience in physical illness were those previously identified in studies of resilience in other forms of adversity—self efficacy, self esteem, internal locus of control, optimism, mastery, social support, hardiness, hope, empowerment, acceptance, determination, personal growth, social support, coping strategies, spirituality, cognitive appraisal, and sense of coherence. (Stewart et al. 2011, 206)

Accounts within this field typically start from assumptions that the healthiest or most mature agents are those who are most autonomous, coherent, in control, and independent. Before a difficult event, agents are autonomous and independent; a trauma or similar occurrence can compromise such autonomy, but in some cases agents are seen as becoming strengthened, more independent, and more capable of self-determination as a result.

In one particular area of such research, Richard Tedeschi and Lawrence Calhoun have developed a research program into "post-traumatic growth" using the term to describe how individuals can grow in five domains following traumatic experiences, developing: "greater appreciation of life and changed sense of priorities; warmer, more intimate relationships with others; a greater sense of personal strength; recognition of new possibilities or paths for one's life; and spiritual development" (2004, 6).[14] Individuals are seen as having grown when they are more able to find benefits, make meaning, create new priorities, feel as though new paths are opening, feel stronger, recognize themselves as survivors, and so on. Those who are seen as having grown in morally relevant ways are those who are, as much as possible, clearer about who they are and what their goals are. Individuals are seen as best able to grow the more they are able to manage their distress (Calhoun and Tedeschi 2012)—to regulate uncontrolled overwhelming feelings, and to develop capacities for reflection on their feelings in light of their life narratives. I have critically evaluated some bioethical and clinical implications of Tedeschi and Calhoun's specific account at greater length elsewhere,[15] but here my goal is only to make the resolvist assumptions of the approach visible. To the extent that individuals become better agents as a result of life experiences, on Tedeschi and Calhoun's view, they do so by *becoming better at deciding how to act*.[16] Implicit in these accounts are resolvist assumptions about what can count as evidence of moral growth—agents who have grown are better able to judge what to do, have a better sense of how to do it, feel more confident in their courses of action, and act. Agents who, following traumatic events, have less of a sense of what to do or how to do it, or compromised confidence in their capacities for action are not seen as having experienced moral growth.

To recap: in many accounts of moral development, moral judgment, moral failure, and moral features of personal growth, we see assumptions about the central importance of moral resolve. As we will see, there are certainly exceptions—most notably, some feminist views that do not make capacities for resolve so central to their understandings of moral agents. But, by and large, moral resolve is seen as a requirement for moral maturity, emotions are seen as generators of moral resolve, a lack of moral resolve is seen as predictive of failure, and agents are seen as having grown when they have developed moral resolve. We could trace the centrality of moral resolve back much further than I have here. What counts as evidence of personal and moral growth is overwhelmingly represented by both psychological and philosophical discourses as decisiveness, commitment, and *resolve*. Yet, while the emphasis on resolve in moral action is dominant in much of moral psychology, it is possible to think beyond it.

2.3 THE DISORIENTATIONS OF GRIEF

To begin to consider moral motivation apart from moral resolve, it helps to investigate cases where we are inclined to say that there are features of moral motivational processes occurring, and nonetheless an absence of moral resolve. For example, consider common experiences of grief.

It is clear that, though it is not always, the loss of loved ones can be deeply disorienting, from the disruption of everyday habits one has developed in relation with the person one has lost, to the sudden need to reconsider one's most substantial life plans. We grieve as social individuals who have typically learned shared narratives from families, communities, cultural, and religious frameworks about what we might or should feel in grief, and about what we should or should not express.[17] In the disorientations of grief, one might feel something like relief at the same time as feeling something like dread and something like guilt, while all remain indeterminate.[18] Grief can cause individuals to reconsider their identities and question who they can now be (Talbot 2002).

Studies of caregivers following the loss of a loved one show that grief can be lasting, making it difficult for individuals to go on for years after loss (Frantz et al. 1998). While the disorientation of grief can continue, making it difficult to know how to live without the person they have lost, people in grief may become more accustomed to being in grief over time. For example, they can become less surprised when they cry, or more expectant of difficulty in talking about their plans (Waldrop 2007). Grief can make it more likely that individuals will have compromised self-worth, will perceive the world as less benevolent, and struggle to understand events as meaningful, and these effects have been found to be more likely the more violent the death of a loved one was (Janoff-Bulman 1989; Mancini et al. 2011). Long after the death of a loved one, individuals in some cases feel fatalistic, lacking in control, and wary of an unpredictable future.[19]

These studies confirm what first-person accounts of grief have also richly expressed: that the loss of loved ones can be paramount to the loss of one's social world and can precipitate a period of dramatic distance from one's practiced ways of being in the world and around others. In *The Year of Magical Thinking*, Joan Didion describes her grief after the sudden death of her husband. As she writes: "Grief has no distance. Grief comes in waves, paroxysms, sudden apprehensions that weaken the knees and blind the eyes and obliterate the dailiness of life" (2006, 27).[20] Grief can feel like antsiness or dissatisfaction, an aversion to sitting with the loss. As Jeannette Walls describes her experience in the months following the death of her father:

> I found myself always wanting to be somewhere other than where I was.... I felt best when I was on the move, going someplace rather than being there.... It took me a while to realize that just being on the move wasn't enough; that I needed to reconsider everything. (Walls 2009, 280)

The feelings one has *about* one's grief add another layer of unsettlement. Even if one has lost a loved one before, different instances of grief are unpredictable, and individuals may feel isolated or embarrassed, wondering whether what they are experiencing is common or abnormal (Bechdel 2007, 48).

Yet both psychological research and first-person accounts of grief suggest that, at the same time as grief can devastate, in some cases it also produces significant effects that some individuals see as beneficial. Individuals can come to relate to friends and family members differently, in some cases with strengthened, more mutually supportive relationships (Davis et al. 2012). For example, some research into the grief of spouses after the death of a child has shown that spousal relationships can be strengthened, with each partner coming to be able to better support the other. In some cases the grief strengthens their other relationships as well and makes them stronger co-parents of their other children (Büchi et al. 2009). Caring for and grieving one's dying partner can be deeply disorienting, while such experiences have also been shown in some cases to bring out new capacities for meeting one's partner's needs, beyond only those directly stemming from the illness (Folkman 1997). A study of individuals a year after the loss of a loved one further supported understandings of grief as motivating improved relationships; participants became more patient, understanding, accepting, compassionate, and in more supportive relationships with family members (Frantz et al. 1998).

Another study of long-term effects of grief is particularly interesting for the ways it reports both effects perceived as negative and those perceived as positive. Examining life changes reported by bereaved spouses and parents four to seven years after the sudden loss of a family member, Lehmen and colleagues (1993) found that effects that were common within a significant group of participants sometimes directly contrast with those found common within another group—grief in some cases caused strengthened spiritual faith in some people, while causing exactly the opposite in others. Participants noted the following effects of long-term grief (listed in order of how many participants reported that effect): increased self-confidence (35%), focus on enjoying the present (26%), shattered life goals (26%), increased acceptance of mortality (23%), greater appreciation for life (23%), increased emphasis on family (19%), increased awareness of life's fragility (15%), social isolation (15%), increased religiosity or faith (15%), increased openness and concern for others (7%), trying to get through each day and not planning for future (6%), and decreased religiosity or loss of faith (5%) (Lehman et al. 1993, 99). The findings are interesting in part because they demonstrate a rich language for the effects of grief. Much more could be asked about what it means to feel "acceptance of mortality" or to "gain awareness of life's fragility." But notice that none of these participants reported increased capacities for forming judgments about how to act. Even so, many of these effects seem nonetheless to be morally significant changes.

Some first- and second-person accounts also suggest that experiences of grief can have beneficial effects. Didion (2006, 74-75) describes how, in grief, she was still able to meet the demands of her ill daughter and felt heightened sensitivity to the experiences of others facing serious illness and grief. Walls (2006, 283), too, describes becoming able to mend relations with her estranged mother, after her father's death. In her memoir *Kitchen Table Wisdom*, physician Rachel Naomi Remen (2006) describes the example of the partner of one of her patients:

> One of my patients, a young businessman with non-Hodgkin's lymphoma, was concerned from the moment of his diagnosis about how his wife would be able to manage both his illness and the possibility of his death. He described her as painfully shy and retiring, fragile even.... Yet as he struggled with difficult chemotherapy, as he lost ground, as disappointment after disappointment led to his premature death, she underwent a remarkable change. It was she who supported him in taking

risks, she who called doctors and other experts all over the country, who took over more and more of his business, learning as she went, who supported and comforted their children. Her courage, in both her personal and her business life, was as awesome as it was unexpected. (Remen 2006, 106-107)

Whether we would explain this woman's experience as Remen does, in terms of the development of courage, or as something else, it seems that this is another case in which experiences of grief can prompt some capacities for action to respond to the needs of others.

We have some support for thinking that, while experiences of grief can disrupt identities, habits, and futures, they also in some cases can change individuals' ways of relating to their own lives and to others. We cannot understand these effects as helping to inspire better capacities for making decisions, or for judging what to do in a given moral situation, because the very same experiences that cause these effects compromise capacities for clear-headedness and judgment. If grief has these effects, how can we begin to understand their moral significance? Note that we have not morally evaluated these effects—that is not yet the goal, as it will be in the cases of disorientation in the coming chapters. The point for now is just to ask what resources philosophical understandings have for noticing anything morally beneficial in the listed effects of grief. Given the clear absence of moral resolve prompted by grief, my concern is that even the *possibility* of moral benefit among these effects will not be noticeable.

2.4 CONTESTING RESOLVISM

I have suggested that there is a dominant resolvist assumption in moral psychology that moral motivation is best evidenced by the presence of moral resolve, involving a combination of judgments (about what to do and how to do it) and feelings (of confidence). Experiences that have the potential to motivate agents in this way are experiences with resolutionary power.

But we can see now that there is a gap between what we have reason to think are moral effects of some experiences—for example, the ways that grief can make people more able to meet the needs of others—and what moral psychology has been keen to see as the best evidence of moral motivation (i.e., moral resolve). As I will show in the coming chapters, most of the effects of disorientation fall in this gap. Without a philosophical framework for understanding how experiences can have morally significant effects without generating moral resolve, many experiences beyond disorientations are likely to be insufficiently understood. Beginning to consider a non-resolvist account of moral development will give philosophers a better chance of understanding the effects of these experiences as morally beneficial, even as they do not help agents resolve how to act and act with resolve.

As we have seen, I am committed to a non-resolvist account of moral motivation according to which moral judgments are one among other markers of successful moral motivation. Other markers of having been motivated fall under the umbrella of "having been moved," for instance, coming to act, expect, or attend differently as the result of some experience.[21] If disorientations are to be understood as in some cases motivating action without moral resolve, empirical investigation of markers of moral motivation other than moral judgments will be required.

Some experiences *fail* to help agents judge what to do and how to do it, and fail to inspire confidence in such agents. Other experiences *actively compromise* capacities for judging what to do and how to do it, and actively compromise confidence. In other words, some experiences fail to generate moral resolve, and others actively compromise moral resolve. Both kinds of experiences may also fail to prompt, or actively compromise, capacities for action. But, crucially, both kinds of experiences may fail to generate or actively compromise moral resolve, *while still prompting action*.

In making the case for the moral promise of experiences lacking resolutionary power, one might make two possible claims: (1) a weaker one, that moral action in some everyday cases requires capacities apart from those of moral resolve, and that disruptive experiences can help us develop such capacities; or (2) a stronger one, that moral action in some everyday cases requires capacities the development of which may be facilitated in contexts where moral resolve is compromised (i.e., required capacities might include those of *failing* to judge what must be done, or *not* clearly knowing how to do it, or *lacking* confidence). In the coming chapters, I defend both claims. I will suggest that both the *non-resolutionary effects* and the *anti-resolutionary effects* of disorientations can be morally beneficial. These claims are compatible and fully consistent with the understanding that moral resolve (judging what to do and having confidence as agents) remains an important part of much of our moral lives.

Feminists have long suggested that the vision of moral life which equates moral action with an agent making a decision, choosing between two options, each of which has relatively predictable consequences, is not likely to tell us everything about the complexities of moral agency. Many feminists have elaborated conceptions of agents as relational, in the sense that they fundamentally exist in, and are conditioned by, interdependence with others (Koggel 1998; Sherwin 1998). In contrast with some views of agency, relational theorists (Mackenzie and Stoljar 2000) have established a nuanced view of how all capacities for agency are relational: no proper acts of knowledge, judgment, memory, decision, and so on, can happen without relational development (Code 1991; Meyers 1997; Friedman 2000; Campbell 2003). Perhaps most troublesome about the dominance of resolvism in ethics and moral psychology is the way such models make the primary locus of agency the *individual who judges*, and make the truly strong moral agent seem to be the individual who *judges for herself*. As such, my challenge to resolvism builds on feminist challenges to the primacy of the individual agent as fully in control of (and therefore responsible for) her own and only her own actions.

In addition, as we have seen, my view is building on the work of feminists who have understood moral action as involving such everyday practices as thinking, communicating, forming relationships and planning, as well as judging moral situations, holding ourselves and others responsible, and working for political change (Walker 2007b, 10). Our ways of acting with other living beings are clearly morally weighty, though everyday practices of communication and relationship building have been largely overlooked by some traditional accounts of moral agency. Many aspects of the moral landscape are fairly clear to us. It is my responsibility to not steal someone else's wallet, to not behave rudely toward others, and to keep an eye out for cyclists on the road. Other responsibilities I have to care for, support, and prevent harm to others, and in general to act responsibly with respect to my own needs and the needs of others, are complex and not always so easy to explicate. Relationships among individuals are always shaped by power dynamics, difference, and systems of injustice. Relationships within systems of injustice introduce a set of responsibilities that might be seen as subtle, complicated, or difficult to respond to. In challenging resolvism, my view articulates a feminist ethics of everyday practice, by emphasizing changes in actions in interpersonal realms structured by power relations and injustice, where such changes in action can occur without moral resolve.

By directly initiating non-resolvist understandings of moral motivation, some areas in feminist moral psychology have challenged presumptions of control, showing how agents can be unluckily responsible for harms and failures in unchosen circumstances. Considerations of moral luck have attended to the ways not only individual actions but indeed entire lifetimes of moral development can be outside individual control (Nagel 1979; Williams 1982; Card 1996; Walker 2003, 26). Not only actions and omissions, but also responses to the luck of their circumstances are morally significant for individuals. Other feminist accounts have directly confronted the equation of moral action with wholehearted commitment (Calhoun 1995, 2009), offering a vision of the possibility of flourishing lives in the absence of deliberate goal-oriented commitment. I take my characterization of the non-resolvist dimensions of moral motivation to be working alongside these challenges to ideals of moral agents as successful only when committed and in control.

In chapter 1, I contrasted my discussion of disorientations' effects with a traditional virtue ethics approach to understanding the development of virtuous character traits. Some of my concerns with traditional virtue ethics approaches have been articulated in other feminist accounts which seek to retain a focus on character, while attending more to dimensions of power, oppression, and domination than traditional virtue ethics accounts have. My account of the moral significance of some effects of disorientation is thus also informed by recent feminist engagements with character theory, including especially Lisa Tessman's account of burdened virtues in liberatory struggles, and Robin Dillon's articulation of critical character theory. Tessman (2005) has offered a critical revision of a eudaimonistic virtue ethics with an insistence on the need to attend more to the position of virtues and vices as produced and practiced in contexts of domination and oppression, and with the suggested addition of a new category of virtues. *Burdened virtues* are traits that help individuals survive or resist oppression, even while such traits can be "burdened"—that is, can have costs for the individual who possesses them, in some way preventing her from flourishing (Tessman 2005, 4). Feminist attention to virtue ethics is helpful, according to Tessman (2005, 5), because anti-oppression struggles must work in part to transform the characters of selves shaped by oppressive structures, as well as changing the structures themselves. More than a revisionary account, Dillon (2012, 84) introduces "critical character theory" as an intended replacement for traditional virtue ethics. While in traditional virtue ethics, the central focus is on individuals' traits rather than on actions, institutions, or practices (Dillon 2012, 84), critical character theory takes power as a central organizing concept (85) and focuses on seeking liberation through understanding character in contexts of oppression and domination (86). I am thus following Dillon's explicit rejection of many of the aspects of traditional virtue ethics: while virtue ethics has positioned character traits as static, isolable, and fixed, critical character theory instead understands character as "fluid, dynamic, and contextualized" (2012, 105). Dillon (2012, 104) also rejects the traditional idea that virtues are the result of individuals' deliberate life choices, arguing instead that character is nurtured and shaped socially, through relational interactions and social institutions. Her view can be read as making way for an analysis of disorientations' effects. As she writes:

> A feminist critical theory ... would insist on carefully examining ... the social conditions that make characters more or less resistant or amenable to change. This would connect with the feminist attention to the interrelatedness of humans and to conditions of dependency, vulnerability, immaturity, incapacity, and disability.... We should also take seriously the possibility that there might be distinctive virtues that develop through or are called for in circumstances of psychic disunity. (Dillon 2012, 102, 101)

My account of disorientations' promise is partly an articulation of the ways such circumstances of psychic disunity can prompt shifts in how individuals relate to the social world. In the coming chapters, I show that feminist accounts of relational autonomy, everyday moral practices, moral luck, and flourishing beyond decisiveness can be mobilized in support of a much-needed non-resolvist account of moral motivation. Further, we will see that the ways disorientations can be beneficial without generating, or sometimes by compromising, moral resolve are indexed to particular moral contexts. That is, what makes non-resolutionary or anti-resolutionary effects beneficial is different in different contexts of action, and there are many contexts where moral resolve remains appropriate and useful. Disorientations can have effects on agency by making agents more aware of morally salient features of the social world (chapter 3), as well as by making agents more adaptable to the unpredictable moral landscape (chapter 4). The ways disorientations can be beneficial often have to do with the value of more tentative, sensitive, and less sure-footed ways of being.

Thankfully, disorientations are not necessary for improved moral action in all cases: persons in many cases come to act better without being disoriented. Moral resolve is an important part of moral life, as are experiences with resolutionary power. Disorientations will not even be sufficient for improved moral action in all cases, since persons can become disoriented in debilitating ways that impede their action. It is true, after all, that grief and other disorientations can, as Didion notes, "derange the mind" (2006, 34).[22] Frankfurt's account of the importance of wholeheartedness and preference-ordering for action is intuitive for this reason. In many cases an agent who acts wholeheartedly will be better off than one who faces perpetual turmoil of will.[23] The main goal of this chapter has been to make room for the claim that experiences like disorientations *may* be morally productive, *even when* they fail to generate, or directly compromise, moral resolve. What I am challenging are tendencies to focus on moral resolve as the sole or most important process of moral motivation and the only indicator of moral growth, and tendencies to see experiences as only morally helpful when they have resolutionary power.

[3]

WHAT IS DISORIENTATION IN THINKING?

The Meditation of yesterday has filled my mind with so many doubts that it is no longer in my power to forget them. And yet I do not see how I shall be able to resolve them; and, as though I had suddenly fallen into very deep water, I am so taken unawares that I can neither put my feet firmly down on the bottom nor swim to keep myself on the surface. . . . I shall continue always in this path until I have encountered something which is certain, or at least, if I can do nothing else, until I have learned with certainty that there is nothing certain in the world.

—René Descartes (1971, 102)

There is no orientation to bringing something into being if there is no awareness of something lacking in a situation. The lacks, as we have seen, may be due to what has happened in the past, to injustices in the present, to the deficits and discomforts associated with being alive at a particular time and place. They may be due to unreflectiveness, to the incapacity to interpret lived situations.

—Maxine Greene (1988, 22)

We have begun to understand how experiences like disorientations could be morally promising even if they were to fail to generate decisive action.[1] In the last chapter, I argued that experiences can change action beyond their "resolutionary power." Experiences can help us act even when they fail to help us resolve what to do, and sometimes by directly compromising moral resolve. Recognizing the limits of resolutionary power opens the door to considering how disorientations—experiences that do not seem to generate moral resolve, and in many cases clearly compromise it—might nonetheless be morally productive.

In this chapter, I turn to specific disorientations and begin to advance the case for their moral promise in the first sense that interests me. I will show that some disorientations can prompt individuals to gain *new awareness* in politically and morally important ways, even when they still do not prompt moral resolve.

To support my claims about the potential moral promise of disorientations in the coming chapters, I pay attention to many different contexts of disorientation. Some of them have been of interest to feminists already, and for good reason. Disorientations can result from experiencing and recognizing the harms of, for example, anti-immigrant nationalism and gender-based violence (as I will continue to discuss in the next chapters). Here, I start with some other disorientations that have been of great interest to feminists—the disorientations of experiencing some harms of oppression and the disorientations of experiencing oneself as privileged. Looking at familiar cases of experiencing racism, experiencing white privilege, feminist consciousness-raising, and critical education begins to reveal the importance of disorientations for generating awareness. Feminists have reflected a great deal on experiences of racist oppression, white privilege, consciousness-raising, and anti-oppressive education. Though they have already recognized the power of some experiences of being harmed by racist or sexist oppression, or of coming to see oneself as privileged, for generating awareness and action, they have not yet sufficiently recognized the role of *disorientations* in that process. In this chapter, I clarify the significance of that role.

In sections 3.1 and 3.2, I make the case for seeing how the disorientations that can be part of experiencing the harms of racism, white privilege, consciousness-raising, and feminist education in some cases prompt specific kinds of awareness of oppressive norms and their contingency, and of political complexity. What I mean by awareness (as opposed to new beliefs or new knowledge) will become clearer as we go on. I then argue that these kinds of awareness can be politically and morally beneficial, still without helping us resolve how to act.

3.1 DISORIENTATIONS OF LIFE UNDER RACISM

A great deal of work in feminist and social epistemology has considered how individuals come to be aware of racism, of the particular harms one has experienced under racism, and of the ways individuals benefit from white privilege. Philosophers of race have investigated epistemic dimensions of experiencing racism. For example, they have developed research into the ways people of color can experience what W. E. B. Du Bois termed *double consciousness*, namely, seeing oneself through two perceptions simultaneously: through one's own positive self-perception (e.g., as citizen, valuable human, worthy of respect), as well as through the negative perceptions of racist others (as black and therefore less valuable, less worthy of respect). Philosophers of race have also clarified how anti-racist knowledge can be produced and transmitted to combat the deliberate forgetting of racist histories. The ways racism infuses social relations can be so common as to become taken for granted, certainly for those benefiting from white privilege in such relations, but also for those directly harmed by them. As such, the task of creating philosophical accounts of how individuals gain awareness of racism has been challenging—especially given the extent to which philosophy as a discipline delegitimizes philosophy of race and anti-racist epistemologies.

Feminist philosophers have paid close attention to what it is like to experience racist harms for many reasons, not the least of which being the desire to gain as full as possible an understanding of *what the harms are* in order to support and clarify how we should work together to eradicate the systems that produce them. *Experiencing racism*—experiencing harms of racist norms as a person of color, or experiencing racial privilege as a white person living in racist contexts—has already been seen as important both epistemically and motivationally. Such experiences may teach individuals at the same time as they propel them. But more remains to be said about how such experiences have these effects, and further examination reveals that disorientations can be more important parts of these experiences than have yet been realized.

3.1.1 Double Consciousness and Awareness of Oppressive Norms

The experiences of people of color living in conditions of racial domination, discrimination, and violence are not uniform—what one experiences depends on the contingencies of one's circumstances—but it is clear that racism deeply shapes the psychological and physical experiences of people of color. As noted above, one facet of the experience of being racialized in white-dominated societies that has been widely documented and described is the phenomenon of *double consciousness*. A person of color may experience double consciousness by coming to see themselves partly through positive self-perception (as someone who belongs, is equally valuable, and trustworthy) at the same time as through the racist perception of a white person (as Other, inferior, and dangerous). The individual becomes unable to hold only a positive self-perception, but instead always partly sees themself as a dominant other does—an object to be feared, exploited, or dominated.

Empirical studies detail how individuals can experience double consciousness as a result of racist perception in many areas of life. For example, black individuals have been shown to develop double consciousness as a result of racial profiling in shopping malls or by police.[2] Black university students who may have already internalized negative stereotypes about their inability to succeed throughout childhoods can come to see themselves critically through the eyes of university educators and peers.[3] Black and Latino workers partly see themselves through the negative stereotyping of employers.[4] Double consciousness can make it difficult or impossible to hold a clear, unified vision of oneself and the world. When racialized individuals come to internalize racist perspectives and to see themselves as racist others see them—for example, as criminal, unintelligent, unreliable—it means that a person moving toward a goal (a trip to the mall, a college degree, a job, or promotion) must resist the constant pressure to give in to what those around assume: that failure is the natural trajectory of a racialized individual. In other words, the double consciousness that results from racism can make it difficult to develop a sense of oneself as valuable and successful, and it can make it difficult to orient oneself toward goals or make progress toward them. The experience of double consciousness can make it difficult to go on.

At the same time, it seems that through some experiences of racialized double consciousness, individuals begin to notice that there are social norms constricting the way individuals and institutions function. In experiences of confusion, anger, and discomfort, some racialized individuals become aware of how normal it is to be profiled, attacked, or mistrusted while black.[5] For example, black university students can feel constantly out of place in an environment where their blackness stands out.[6] These experiences in some cases crystallize awareness of the specific ways white, affluent students see them. As one study emphasizes, students can realize that they are seen as urban and poor, criminals, dangerous, undeserving, lazy, likely to be on welfare, less intelligent than white students, violent, and sexually promiscuous.[7]

When a black university student experiences double consciousness—seeing herself partly through the eyes of a white student—the black student observes in some cases how she is failing to adhere to racist *norms*, for example, that it is normal for a white student to attend an Ivy League college but abnormal for a black student to attend. The discomfort of seeing oneself as black through white eyes in some cases clarifies racist norms and one's position within them. The *normal* shopper is white, so a black person does not belong at this store. The *normal* university student is white, so a black student does not belong at university. Living with double consciousness can be disorienting because it is a constant reminder of the ways one does not belong. It can make it hard to go on, to continue attending university, or to continue in one's job, and so on. Black university students come up against the norm that only white students can succeed, and they are thrown back. It is disorienting to come up against racist norms and be thrown back, but in some cases this experience also makes it clear where the norms are. In some cases, it generates awareness of the power of the norms one is coming up against, that get expressed through the fearful or suspicious perspectives of dominant others.

A racialized individual might alternatively gain awareness of racist norms through a different kind of disorientation—the strangeness of being treated as though one *does* belong, after having grown accustomed to constantly being unwelcome. It can be very

WHAT IS DISORIENTATION IN THINKING?

disorienting to suddenly be seen as *trustworthy*. Vernon Andrews (2003) offers a reflexive auto-ethnography of his experience as a black academic conducting research in various countries. Having gotten used to seeing himself through the lens of white people in the United States, he travels to New Zealand and describes the following interaction with a stranger who offers him a ride:

> I squeezed my large frame into the front seat and rode down the hill with him to my destination as we talked rugby. On the ride I had the amazing experience of lightness. I was experiencing trust by another individual who had white skin but did not know me. Call me deprived, but I had never experienced this level of trust and confidence from a white stranger in America.... I actually said to myself, "Why does this man trust me? Doesn't he know that I am a black man?" (Andrews 2003, 69–70)

In such cases, one can gain awareness not only of the norms that exist and the ways they oppress, but also of their contingency, that *they could be otherwise*.

W. E. B. Du Bois's own account of double consciousness in *The Souls of Black Folk* (1903) demonstrates the sense of awareness that interests me here. He analyzes his early experiences of racism growing up in Massachusetts in the late 1800s, which would shape his experiences as a black man for the rest of his life. He describes one childhood memory as the basis of his account of double consciousness:

> I was a little thing, away up in the hills of New England.... In a wee wooden schoolhouse, something put it into the boys' and girls' heads to buy gorgeous visiting cards—ten cents a package—and exchange. The exchange was merry, till one girl, a tall newcomer, refused my card,—refused it peremptorily,

with a glance. Then it dawned on me with a certain suddenness that I was different from the others; or like, mayhap, in heart and life and longing, but shut out from their world by a vast veil. (Du Bois 1996, 16)

In this quick exchange, the girl identifies Du Bois as black, in opposition to her whiteness. It is a shock to Du Bois, and he instantly sees himself as the girl sees him: as less worthy than she is. He identifies the resulting experience of double consciousness as the duplicity of being both same and different, "an American, a Negro; two souls, two thoughts, two unreconciled strivings; two warring ideals in one dark body" (Du Bois 1996, 17).[8] Du Bois (1996) describes the feelings of double consciousness as conflictedness (5), a lack of effective strength (6), being weighed down or handicapped while needing to run (9), despair (9), and helpless humiliation (10).[9] Du Bois describes how oppressive identification—the simultaneous identification and marginalization as "other"—introduces a tension between who one wants to be (someone who "sits with Shakespeare"; Du Bois 1996, 90) and who one is allowed to be. Seeing oneself through two visions at once makes for a lack of ease and a struggle to proceed in making plans and relating to others. In other words, double consciousness, as Du Bois identifies it, is a kind of disorientation.[10]

As in the cases of the black citizen, black university students, or Andrews's experience in the stranger's car, the disorientation of seeing himself partly through racist understandings allows Du Bois to gain awareness of how inconsistent racist norms are. Du Bois comes up against the racist norm that white kids only play with white kids, and he is thrown back. Through the next years of his life, some white people see him as a qualified employee, while others see him as a servant; some political figures see him as a comrade, others as a threat. Du Bois becomes able to interpret his experiences of racism as partly the uneven enforcement of contingent norms—he sees that such norms do not exist identically everywhere, and that they are not evenly enforced. The experience of punishment whenever Du Bois does something that does not fully conform to norms is also what makes it possible to gain awareness of them—it is what keeps them from fading into the background of what is natural.

The disorientations of double consciousness in some cases have the capacity to generate awareness of oppressive norms and their contingency because they are, in part, acute experiences of tension between one's survival and the persistence of those oppressive norms. By "oppressive norms," I mean norms that generate implicit expectations about what kind of actions by people and treatments of people in social groups are acceptable, and harm individuals that deviate from the norm.[11] There are norms about the ways people perceived as white, upper middle class, straight, or healthy should be respected when entering a restaurant, shopping for a computer, or buying a pregnancy test. These norms are connected to the ways people perceived as nonwhite, poor, queer, or ill are more likely disrespected or treated as suspicious in the same locations. Of course, there are exceptions to the norms that hold much of the time: a salesperson may not follow *every* black teenager around his store. But norms are the kinds of things that structure action much of the time, often without individual actors needing to put conscious effort into following the norm. As we have seen, racist norms in some cases become explicit through disorientations, as a rule one did not know existed becomes explicit when one gets punished for breaking it.

3.1.2 White Ambush and Awareness of Oppressive Norms

It is possible to "experience racism" in a very different sense than as someone harmed by it—namely, by coming to experience oneself as *white* in a world that privileges white people. Coming to recognize one's whiteness is in some cases disorienting in ways that also generate awareness of racist norms. Linda Martín Alcoff calls this "feeling white." As she writes, "'feeling white,' when coupled with a repudiation of white privilege, can disable a positive self-image as well as a felt connection to community and history, and generally can disorient identity formation" (2006, 206).

A white person may not ever recognize white privilege, even as she benefits from it daily. Of course, much keeps individuals from recognizing white privilege. Even so, any number of situations can prompt a white person to recognize her whiteness. She might travel somewhere where her whiteness makes her a minority. She might move out of a predominantly white neighborhood. She might enter a relationship with a person of color.[12] It can be disorienting to recognize whiteness as a major part of one's identity in any of these contexts. Beverly Daniel Tatum (1997) describes an experience of "disintegration" as an important step in the generation of anti-racist identity:

> This new awareness is characterized by discomfort . . . at the disintegration stage, White individuals begin to see how much their lives and the lives of people of color have been affected by racism in our society. The societal inequities they now notice directly contradict the idea of an American meritocracy, a concept that has typically been an integral part of their belief system. . . . Responses to this discomfort may include denying the validity of the information that is being presented, or psychologically or physically withdrawing from it. . . . If the individual remains engaged, he or she can turn the discomfort into action. (Tatum 1997, 98–99)

In any context, being called out by another who wants me to recognize the significance of my white privilege can be very disorienting.

Some situations make white privilege abundantly clear, and in these contexts white individuals might still be in denial about the fact that they are privileged. The disorientations that can be involved in recognizing white privilege parallel what George Yancy has called *white ambush*. For Yancy, white ambush happens when white people experience a "surprise attack" of becoming aware of our own racism. As he describes it, white ambush is "a form of attack that points to how whiteness ensnares even as one tries to fight against racism" (2008, 229). To illustrate a case where white ambush could have happened productively but did not, Yancy describes an experience of his own: he was riding an elevator alone with a white woman and experienced double consciousness, for a moment seeing himself through her eyes, as a frightening black man (2008, 5). Later on, Yancy describes the elevator ride to his students, and one white student responds by refusing to believe Yancy's description, refusing to believe that the woman in the elevator had in fact feared him. The student calls Yancy's read of the situation "Bullshit" (Yancy 2008, 227). By responding to Yancy's description of his own experience of racism by further undercutting his authority, denying that he could be telling the truth, the student embodies more dimensions of white dominance and racist superiority, while not recognizing that she herself was also enacting racism.[13] Yancy's point is that the student *could have*, but did not, experience white ambush. The student could have, but did not, become aware that it was her own white privilege that made it feel normal for her to call Yancy's claim bullshit. Being white in racist society is typically orienting.[14] White people are not encouraged to recognize race as a distinct part of our identities. As I read them, experiences of white ambush are excellent examples of how white individuals can also be disoriented by recognizing how our whiteness makes us more trusting of our own perceptions than of the perceptions of people of color, and makes it seem acceptable for us to discredit the claims of people of color. The disorientations of white ambush can prompt awareness of contingent racist norms that we are helping to perpetuate.[15]

The claim that the disorientations of experiencing racism can generate awareness of the oppressive norms and their contingency needs careful qualification. Racism is not always disorienting (for either those harmed or benefited by it), the disorientations of experiencing racism (either in the sense of double consciousness or white ambush) do not always prompt awareness of contingent oppressive norms, and such disorientations are not the only path to such awareness. For those most harmed by racism, such disorientations can instead generate emotional numbing or mental illness,[16] and for those who have white privilege, as we have seen, such disorientations can simply generate increased resistance to recognizing white privilege.[17] However, in some cases experiencing racism *can* be disorienting in ways that generate awareness of oppressive norms and their contingency.

This is not to suggest that double consciousness and white ambush are on a par—experiencing racism as a person of color is harmful, and experiencing white ambush is not. Nor could pointing to ways in which double consciousness can generate awareness redeem experiences of racialization in white-dominated societies. The fact that such experiences do not have exclusively negative effects does not give us reason to value experiences of racist harms overall. Rather, my goal here is to do justice to the state of affairs as they are. It is a fact that being harmed by racist norms and experiencing the accompanying disorientation in some cases can generate awareness of oppressive norms and their contingency. Clarifying how experiencing racism may involve disorientations that can prompt such awareness is relevant for understanding how to support individuals who experience racism. It also has implications for studies in feminist and social epistemology of the epistemic position of those who experience racism—particularly those who are directly harmed by it, but also those confronted by their role in perpetuating it. Note that so far we have established only that awareness is in some cases generated by these disorientations, and not yet what role such awareness might play in anti-racist action. I return to the question of the moral and political significance of this awareness at the end of the chapter.

3.2 DISORIENTATIONS OF LEARNING ABOUT OPPRESSION AND PRIVILEGE

Feminist epistemologists have paid close attention to the role of consciousness-raising and feminist education in universities and beyond. Processes of coming to feminist consciousness (e.g., understanding one's own experiences of sexism in light of widespread experiences of sexism) and processes of feminist education (paying attention to oppressive structures as a subject matter that requires attention) are important for the development of motivation to address oppression. But *how* the development of such consciousness and learning are motivational is sometimes assumed to be obvious, when it is in fact more complex. Clearly, as a result of successful feminist consciousness-raising and education, participants and students should learn histories they did not know and facts about current effects of oppression, and they should begin to think about how to conceive plans of action to counter such oppressions. I take it that these goals shape much of what we do as feminist educators and organizers. In addition, though, participants in consciousness-raising groups and students should also gain a broader level of *awareness* about the complexity of social landscapes structured by oppression and privilege, and understand their place and role in such structures. Students or individuals might not have been able to connect the dots about various harms experienced by people of color, or by people in poverty, or by people with disabilities, and make sense of them as various facets of racist, classist, or ableist oppression. As a result of participation in consciousness-raising groups or classrooms, they should be able to critically and creatively see how these harms relate to one another and to other systems of domination. Such awareness means not just knowing that systems of oppression exist, but also becoming able to anticipate them in action, including in contexts outside of those one has already studied.

There remain questions, though, about how such awareness of political complexity is generated by consciousness-raising and critical education.[18] I want to suggest that it is not only the gaining of information and building of relationships that generates such awareness, but also that feminists and organizers should see specifically the *experiences of disorientation* that can be triggered by such groups or classrooms as part of what generates such awareness. Seen from one perspective, whatever disorientations one experiences in the process might be positioned as a side effect of the real goal: becoming oriented toward action. But, as I will suggest, we have reason to think the function of disorientations in processes of feminist awareness-raising and motivation is more than to reorient.

3.2.1 Consciousness-Raising and Awareness of Political Complexity

In the consciousness-raising groups of the 1960s, many individuals experienced major shifts in their understanding of their social roles and relationships. In the context of the women's movement, consciousness-raising groups were groups of (primarily) women who gathered to discuss their home, relationship, and workplace experiences. Consciousness-raising groups were in many cases characterized by uncomfortable discussions, during which participants encouraged each other to recognize both the ways they were experiencing oppression and the ways they had benefited from privilege. Groups made efforts to address interpersonal conflicts and experiences of anger.[19] Experiences of unease, discomfort, and fear were thus not merely accidental features of participation in such groups, but expected, meaningful components of efforts to confront internalized oppression. Participation in the groups also sometimes triggered major shifts in women's lives. In some cases, marriages ended, women became alienated from their families, lost custody of their children, and lost or left their jobs. Beyond replacing specific old beliefs (e.g., that husbands should have the right to demand sex with their wives) with specific new beliefs (e.g., that forced sex is not acceptable in any relationship), participants in consciousness-raising groups in some cases experienced the uprooting of whole systems of belief. Participation in consciousness-raising groups often made it unclear how to go on with one's life, how to live without long-standing relationships, and how to orient oneself toward new communities and kin. Deeply held assumptions were shown to be unfounded.

In some cases, the disorientations of having one's deep assumptions uprooted have been shown to produce what sociologists have called "moral shock": when an unexpected event or piece of information outrages a person in a way that directs her toward political action.[20] Consciousness-raising groups often had the explicit intention of creating free spaces where emotional expressiveness was fostered and where individuals could experience moral shocks together.[21] In experiencing "moral shock," individuals in consciousness-raising groups began to generate a critical perception of their experiences and behavior.[22] The work of disorientation occurs in part when the security of grounding assumptions is challenged by consciousness-raising groups. Individuals were in some cases disoriented, and such disorientation in some cases prompted the realization that there were such taken-for-granted assumptions in the first place, and that those assumptions were (despite all appearances) non-permanent. I see challenges to these assumptions as the beginning of awareness of political complexity. Such an awareness of political complexity allows for recognizing the sometimes unexpected ways structures of oppression play out in new circumstances. In other words, it is an awareness of political complexity that does not simply institute a new seemingly permanent set of assumptions.

Attending to other ways in which disorientations in sexist and other oppressive contexts can prompt awareness, feminists have considered experiences of *gaslighting*, named after the 1944 film *Gaslight*, starring Ingrid Bergman and Charles Boyer. In cases of gaslighting, individuals are made to question the trustworthiness of their own perceptions, memories, and judgments, making them increasingly filled with self-doubt. In the film, Boyer has murdered Bergman's aunt and married Bergman only as part of his plot to find and steal her deceased aunt's hidden jewels. He intentionally creates conditions that will make Bergman question her own perceptions, for instance, telling her that the gaslights she sees flickering repeatedly are not actually doing so, and that it must be her imagination. Bergman loses confidence in her own capacities for perception and understanding and is filled with fear that she might in fact be losing control of her mind. Such experiences can clearly be disorienting—as Paul Benson describes the premise of the film: "Boyer's scheme is to reduce Bergman to a state of such apparent confusion and disorientation that she will be unlikely to realize what he is up to" (1994, 655). Elena Flores Ruíz has recently reflected on experiences of gaslighting of women of color in professional philosophy, who regularly experience what she calls "normalized alienation" and "professional estrangement" (2014, 197–198). As in consciousness-raising groups, in some cases, experiences of gaslighting are disorienting in ways that generate awareness of political complexity, raising for individuals, sometimes for the first time, awareness of deliberate attempts to discredit their perspectives. As Ruíz describes:

> After hearing the increasingly lengthening scrolling narratives of women of color in the profession of philosophy who dwell, whether briefly or constantly, in this sense of puncturing self-doubt, it finally hit me: Amigas, sisters, we're being gaslighted, predominantly by the somnambulatory policing in the form of normative practices and tacit methodological assumptions in mainstream philosophy.[23] (Ruíz 2014, 201)

The experiences of gaslighting can be unsettling, while also prompting new awareness: it is not that *my* perceptions cannot be trusted, it is that they are vulnerable to being made to look untrustworthy by dominant others. One becomes aware that these and other psychological manipulations could result from oppressions in the future, and that there are additional strategies needed in order to identify psychic results of oppression in oneself.

As a result of the disorientations of consciousness-raising, individuals in some cases have come to understand that the world is not as it has seemed. The requirement that women become mothers is not based on a legitimate claim to women's natures as caregivers. Sex within marriage is not something to which a husband has a right. Individuals can come to recognize that what was once taken for granted about women's lives was in many cases a result of sexist oppression. So, individuals in consciousness-raising groups can experience what Sandra Bartky (1990, 18) has called a *double ontological shock*: the realization that what is happening is not the same as what seems to be happening, accompanied by an inability to tell what is happening at all. On Bartky's account, as on mine, periods of double ontological shock are not experiences that are eventually replaced by more orientedness as one becomes truly feminist.

The experiences can persist.[24] Note, however, that while Bartky argues that the suffering of double ontological shock can be *counterbalanced by* a growing sense of solidarity with other feminists, she does not suggest that it is the disorientation itself that generates awareness. I am making a distinct point, that not only are the disorientations or double ontological shocks frequent features of feminist consciousness-raising, they are in some cases integral to the development of the awareness of political complexity for which many feminists hope.

It is not uncommon for first-person accounts from feminists in consciousness-raising contexts to explicitly discuss experiences of disorientation. In "Identity: Skin, Blood, Heart," Minnie Bruce Pratt describes her own disorientation in consciousness-raising and the awareness of political complexity she gained as a result. Having experienced protections as a white, educated, married, Christian-raised mother of two, when Pratt began participating in feminist consciousness-raising groups, came out as lesbian, and separated from her husband, she describes experiencing disorientations on a number of levels. At the same time as she lost custody of her children and many of the protections of hetero-marriage, she discovered more about her white family's history in legacies of racism and colonialism in the US South. The compounded disorientations of these simultaneous shifts were difficult for her to bear:

> I lived in a kind of vertigo: a sensation of my body having no fixed place to be: the earth having opened, I was falling through space. I had had my home and my children taken away from me. I had set out to make a new home with other women, only to find that the very ground I was building on was the grave of the people my kin had killed. . . . *I was implicated in the doing of some of these injustices, and I held myself, and my*

people, responsible, what my expanded understanding meant was that I felt in a struggle with myself, *against* myself. (Pratt 1984, 35-36)

Pratt experienced many of the central features of disorientation—uneasy, without sure footing, and unsure what to do with her life into the future.[25] She had not previously known of the complexity of the political landscape, that she had benefited from the invisible safety nets as a straight, white, upper class woman. Through her experience, she comes to see such nets everywhere—maintained by racism, heterosexism, religious dominance, classism, and sexism. Specifically, Pratt's disorientations generate her awareness that the political landscape *was the kind of thing* that could feel firm and unnoticeable one day and shaky and visible the next. Unlike experiences that uproot one particular belief and transplant another in its place, the disorientations of consciousness-raising in Pratt's case reverberated beyond whatever specific facts were being challenged. The effects of such disorientations are open-ended. They do not delimit how much of one's understanding may be shaken, or how much awareness will be gained.

3.2.2 Critical Classrooms and Awareness of Political Complexity

"Critical classrooms" might be broadly construed to include any educational context that challenges students' deeply held assumptions about politics, history, justice, responsibility, or relationships. Paradigm examples include feminist classrooms, classes in gender studies, LGBT studies, or race studies. Critical classrooms can introduce new understandings of history (e.g., of local civil rights struggles), new concepts (e.g., "colonialism"), and new sources of information (e.g., media sources beyond the mainstream). As in consciousness-raising contexts, the more our everyday lives and practices are based on taken-for-granted understandings, the more likely we are to be disoriented when they are challenged. Classrooms that engage students in discussions of feminism, critical race theory, anti-colonial theory, and queer theory are likely to be disorienting in the sense that interests me. That is, they can make it difficult for students to know how to go on. Students can feel particularly uncomfortable focusing centrally on experiences of women or people of color.[26] Like in consciousness-raising contexts, critical classrooms can be disorienting when they uproot deeply held assumptions about whose histories and ideologies can be trusted, and when they do not directly transplant a new, permanently trustworthy root system of assumptions. After critical classrooms, students may leave relationships, change careers, alter habits of buying clothing, eat, travel, and clean differently, stop or start participating in some religious communities, or relate differently to health care systems.[27] In such moments of disorientation, fundamental blind spots about the actual experiences of women and dominated groups can be revealed—for instance, the assumption that "I would surely know if I were *myself* sexist or racist" can be uprooted.

    I think of undergraduate and graduate students I have had in my own classrooms. One student from a Philosophy of Sex and Love class I taught stands out for her description of feeling disoriented. In class, we were discussing a section in Ahmed's *Queer Phenomenology*, where she discusses how being queer in heteronormative social contexts can feel like being left-handed in a society built for right-handed people, a constant stretching to meet tools that do not fit. At the front of our lecture hall, two students described what it was like to reach to use desks that were not built for them; a right-handed desk for a left-handed student, a left-handed desk for a right-handed student.

WHAT IS DISORIENTATION IN THINKING?

Being queer, as Ahmed says, can lead to repetitive strain. After the class, a quiet student came from the back of the hall to speak with me. She identified herself as queer and said that Ahmed's example and description had "hit her like a soundwave." I thought about her description through the rest of the course. It seems the "soundwave" experience indicates something about feeling overwhelmed: a student finds herself bowled over by a new understanding in a way that carries meaning *with and beyond* her experience. That is, she learns in a way that both resonates with what she already knows and reverberates beyond it, pointing toward all she does not know. It resonates with experiences of hers that she had not yet even identified as needing consideration, and indicates experiences of others she has not known existed.

Studies of feminist pedagogy have begun to analyze the political import of moments of discomfort in classrooms.[28] In moments where students express discomfort, often in the form of hostility, teachers might even focus the class's attention on the discomfort, giving students time to consider why they are feeling uncomfortable and to explore their own hostility.[29] Megan Boler has characterized a *pedagogy of discomfort,* which "invites students to leave the familiar shores of learned beliefs and habits and swim further out into the 'foreign' and risky depths of the sea of ethical and moral differences" (1999, 181).[30] As Boler explains, disorientations in critical classrooms can generate awareness not in the sense of a new, permanent set of assumptions, but in the sense of a capacity to anticipate political complexity:

> Once engaged in the discomfort of ambiguity, it is possible to explore the emotional dimensions and investments—angers and fears, and the histories in which these are rooted. We can explore how our identities are precariously constructed in relation to one another, so that to suggest change may feel like a

threat to our survival. . . . Learning to live with ambiguity, discomfort, and uncertainty is a worthy educational ideal. (Boler 1999, 198)

I agree with Boler that part of what disorientations can allow for is awareness of political complexity and unpredictability. Unlike Boler, I have characterized disorientation as something not so much deliberately pursued as unexpected and coped with, and as something that could become part of experiences of learning in ways that surprise even those educators who would view it as useful.

Disorientations in critical classrooms can generate awareness of political complexity that extends beyond the replacement of select false beliefs (e.g., colonizers and indigenous communities have coexisted peacefully) with true beliefs (e.g., processes of colonization have been and continue to be deeply harmful to indigenous communities). Experiencing such disorientations can allow for the generation of awareness of political complexity in the sense described in consciousness-raising contexts: an awareness that allows for recognizing the sometimes unexpected ways structures of oppression play out in new circumstances. "Soundwave" experiences of education can be disorienting because they do not provide all the information needed or specify what action is called for. Rather, they point toward all the information we may not even yet know we need. I have seen my own students disoriented by learning that as cis-women, they also experience privilege in a world where a gender binary is the norm.[31] In this case, the awareness disorientations generate is not "that there are other ways of being gendered" but "that my position in the political landscape means that I know about only some of what people live with." It is a kind of awareness that I think is not uncommon in feminist classrooms. Students can feel like they arrived in educational contexts simply aiming to learn more about, for example, women's lives and histories, and leave feeling dislodged from what they had once taken for granted.[32]

In the cases of both feminist consciousness-raising and critical education, we have seen that for individuals to lack awareness about political complexity means, at least in part, that they lack awareness about systems of oppression. They lack awareness about layers, currents, and patterns of social violence, dominance, and vulnerability that repeatedly harm people because they are not sufficiently white, manly, rich, able, straight, or otherwise independent. I am suggesting that we have reason to think it is not only or primarily the *content* of what individuals realize or learn in such contexts that generates the ability to see and anticipate how systems of oppression work. It is their experience of disorientation while learning it—the moral shocks experienced by women in consciousness-raising groups, the feeling of double ontological shock Bartky describes, Pratt's feeling of vertigo, the discomfort experienced by students, or my student's soundwave.[33] Individuals in these cases are disoriented by the uprooting of their deepest assumptions. This experience of being disoriented by having our deepest assumptions uprooted can generate awareness of political complexity. Such awareness goes far beyond understanding just my own life, from being just no longer knowing what to expect (e.g., what does it mean that a woman might not receive equal pay for equal work), to a different set of expectations (e.g., coming to expect that systems of employment will regularly harm certain people, in ways beyond what I alone can anticipate). As such, feminists and educators should understand the disorientations people experience in these contexts not as unfortunate side effects, but actually as very important pieces of prompting awareness. It is the dizzying feeling of not knowing how to go on itself that can generate an awareness of the political landscape being more complex than one person alone could know. That particular feature of experiencing one's deepest assumptions as not only uprooted but as *unexpectedly uprootable* means that in the future, taken-for-granted assumptions may not be so easily treated as potentially permanent things that one could reliably generate alone. The awareness of political complexity such experiences can generate is not merely a new orientation. It is a different way of relating to my own (and others') tendencies to be oriented by certain belief systems, and a new capacity to treat assumptions as fundamentally questionable.

Of course, the disorientations of learning about oppression and privilege in critical classrooms do not always generate awareness. Students' discomfort can manifest in resistance to the material discussed. And though disorientations may not be the only things capable of generating such awareness, I have argued that they are clearly among the things capable of doing so. Even as feminists have recognized that disorientations can accompany consciousness-raising, or as teachers and scholars have noted the existence of disorientations in classrooms, what disorientations can generate has until now been under-theorized.

3.3 THE POWER OF AWARENESS WITHOUT MORAL RESOLVE

So far we have seen that in some cases, disorienting experiences of double consciousness and white privilege have generated awareness of oppressive norms and their contingency. And in other cases, we have seen that disorienting experiences of learning about oppression and privilege in consciousness-raising and feminist classrooms have generated awareness of political complexity. It may seem to go without saying that heightened awareness of oppressive norms and political complexity is likely to lead to more responsible action than less awareness. Yet, in these cases,

WHAT IS DISORIENTATION IN THINKING?

I want to suggest that the actual results of these kinds of awareness are complicated. Note that there is an important difference between the examples of awareness I am highlighting here and other examples of productive awareness that may come to mind. Some kinds of awareness make it obvious how to act (e.g., when I became aware of my strawberry allergy, I stopped eating strawberries). The awarenesses generated by disorientations in the cases I have described are not likely to be of this kind, for at the same time as the awarenesses are generated, *individuals are still disoriented*. The generation of awareness does not override their deep uncertainty about how to go on. Black men in shopping malls or black university students gain awareness of racist norms, but they do not necessarily gain awareness about how to confront them. Du Bois gained awareness of how racist norms apply unevenly in different locations, but he did not automatically know how to protect himself or his children within them. Participants in feminist consciousness-raising groups and students in critical classrooms gain awareness about the political complexities of oppression and domination, but that does not make them feel any more certain of how to proceed. Seeing the promise of the kinds of awareness described here requires re-envisioning what awareness can do apart from helping individuals resolve how to act.

To back up and make the contrast clear, note that in some second-wave feminist consciousness-raising groups, group leaders often saw the success of consciousness-raising as riding on the creation of a lightbulb moment, or *reorientation*. In her famous 1971 article, "The Housewife's Moment of Truth," Jane O'Reilly describes one such moment:

> Click! A moment of truth. The shock of recognition. Instant sisterhood.... The click! of recognition, that parenthesis of truth around a little thing that completes the puzzle of reality

in women's minds—the moment that brings a gleam to our eyes and means the revolution has begun.[34] (O'Reilly 1971)

When understandings of oppression "click" into place, they can *reorient us*, bringing pieces of information together into a framework by which they confirm each other.[35] "Click" experiences can indicate that I have found my experience (e.g., of what I did not know before to call sexism) clearly reflected in another person's account, leading to a powerful feeling of recognition and, sometimes, a clear sense of what to do next. Such reorientations could lead to some new and important kinds of moral resolve. As I noted in the last chapter, decisive action is in many cases very productive. However, the participants in consciousness-raising groups or classrooms I have discussed here seem to lack this "click" of reorientation.

Note that I have been suggesting that disorientations generate awareness in a way that parallels what Alison Jaggar (1997) has argued "outlaw emotions" can do. On Jaggar's view, marginalized individuals often experience outlaw emotions in response to expressions of dominance, as when a person of color feels angry when a racist joke is told, or a woman feels fearful when a man teases her in a sexual way. Such outlaw emotions are not experienced by everyone, but particularly by those harmed by oppressive norms, and they can be "necessary to developing a critical perspective on the world," insofar as they can "bring to consciousness our 'gut-level' awareness that we are in a situation of coercion, cruelty, or injustice" (Jaggar 1997, 397). Although disorientations do not as easily fit into standard emotion categories like anger or fear, they can prompt awareness of oppression somewhat like outlaw emotions do. But *unlike* outlaw emotions, disorientations are not always experienced directly in response to oppression, and they do not typically direct individuals toward any course of action (e.g., to new theoretical investigations of racism, or actions to stop racist jokes). Further, as I discuss at length in the next chapter, unlike outlaw emotions, disorientations are sometimes morally productive without generating awareness at all.

If the awareness generated by some disorientations does not help individuals resolve how to act, what is its moral and political promise?

3.3.1 Prompting Epistemic Humility

One way in which awareness of contingent oppressive norms and political complexity can be morally or politically productive even without generating moral resolve is by allowing individuals to relate differently to others and themselves as knowers. Unlike awareness gained by "clicks" that feel like the corrective acquisition of new and more reliable knowledge, awareness generated by disorientations can make a person more aware at the same time as making them feel less conclusive. As in the case of students learning about oppression and privilege for the first time, awareness generated of political complexity in this way can have the effect of making us aware of our epistemic unreliability, or of the likelihood that since we were so unaware once, it could easily happen again. Disorientations can generate awareness of one's own epistemic fallibility. Having an awareness of myself as more epistemically frail or flexible than I might have thought can be an important part of awareness about my position in complex social relations. One can gain awareness at the same time as feeling less secure in the awareness one has had. As disoriented, I am more likely to develop awareness of how what I notice and how easily I know are related to how settled I feel in my identity as a knower, and how readily I feel I am capable of acting on the basis of my knowledge. While epistemic humility might seem to be a *virtue*, as I noted in chapter 1, it is not a trait in the sense of interest to traditional virtue ethicists. It is not stable or ongoing, it does not necessarily become available for application in all areas of one's life, and it is not deliberately pursued.

The persistent ignorance of socially privileged knowers about systems of oppression and harms experienced by oppressed groups has been shown to be not merely a lack of knowledge about the right facts, but a carefully maintained denial of the epistemic authority of oppressed individuals (Fricker 2007; Mills 2007). As Alison Bailey describes it, "White ignorance is a form of not knowing (seeing wrongly), resulting from the habit of erasing, dismissing, distorting, and forgetting about the lives, cultures, and histories of peoples whites have colonized" (2007, 85). The moral significance of the awareness disorientations can generate should be understood in large part in terms of the ways it can shift practices and habits of knowing and relating to other knowers. The awareness disorientations can generate can develop epistemic humility in a sense that parallels what Medina (2013) has called "sensitivity to insensitivity."[36]

Disorientations are a set of experiences that are not yet being considered in the growing literature about implicit bias. Part of what I am suggesting is that gaining new awareness of racism, sexism, and other oppressions can require complicated experiences, that are more like "soundwaves" than "clicks"—perhaps these can be generated by deliberate engagements with, for example, implicit bias testing, though I think it is significant that the cases of disorientation I consider here are more wholly disruptive of multiple dimensions of persons' lives, and that is an important part of their power.

An individual might be disoriented after being made aware of what she has failed to know because of a failure to notice (e.g., the experience of a mixed race person who looks white to others; Alcoff 2006; Sullivan and Tuana 2007). As a result, she might then be more likely to anticipate limitations in her processes of understanding, for example, in thinking that a person's race can only affect their experience when it situates them as a "visible minority." Further, she might be more inclined to think humbly of herself, for example, to acknowledge how much her position as a "reliable knower" depends on contingent social circumstances and her level of education; to recognize how her only possibility for more accurate knowledge requires that she depend more on the knowledge claims of others. Finally, she might act more tentatively on the basis of other things she thinks she knows (e.g., the gender of a stranger), because she has learned that she has harmed others on the basis of mistaken understanding in the past.

When such awareness is gained, it means that individuals can tread more cautiously in communicating about and acting on the basis of understandings of the world. Having experienced these disorientations, we may become more accustomed to revisiting and revising what we thought we knew. Our habits of knowing change, altering both the content of what we know (i.e., we pay more attention to less obvious parts of the world, and to how they change) and the way we gain such knowledge (i.e., we may come to trust new sources and question others). Awareness of oppressive norms and political complexity may not result in moral resolve—in the cases we have seen, it has compromised felt certainty about how to act. But experiences of disorientation can compel acting in some contexts with a background of epistemic humility—drawing our attention to the fallibility of knowers and the shifting landscape of all we need to know.

3.3.2 Prompting Resistant Re-identification

A second way in which such awareness can be morally and politically productive is by allowing individuals to relate differently to their histories and communities of origin. As we have seen, part of what it means to gain awareness of the oppressive norms and political complexity is to gain awareness of *who one is* within such norms and landscapes. Black students, workers, and citizens come to see themselves partly as racist others see them. Individuals in consciousness-raising groups and students in critical classrooms gain awareness of who they are within sexist, racist, and heterosexist social worlds. After the loss of her community, children, and home, Pratt gains awareness of her identity as coming from a racist town, racist family of origin, as a queer mother experiencing sexism and heterosexism, and as a white woman working with feminists and women of color against racism. As such, these disorientations generate awareness of political complexity that locates who one is within oppressive systems and oppressed and/or privileged communities. An individual gains awareness that one is part of some social groups, not only those one would choose to be, and not part of other social groups, even if one would want to be. Such awareness is an awareness of the way people identify one another, and of the fact that one's identifications are not up to oneself alone. Others are not always correct in their ways of identifying us, but we also do not get to identify ourselves alone apart from others (even others who are intentionally or unintentionally harming us).

Particularly for members of privileged groups, the awareness these disorientations have generated could facilitate what Sue Campbell has called "resistant identification" (2014, 114–132), that is, coming to see myself as identified with my community or communities of origin, and thus as partly responsible even for the actions of those with whom I would rather not identify. Resistant identification can occur when identifying wholeheartedly with one's community of origin feels impossible, perhaps because of the ways my political commitments conflict with theirs, but wholly disidentifying from them is also impossible because of the ways communities of origin shape our identities, and because of how we share responsibility for the ways their commitments continue to shape the world. For the members of privileged groups who have gained awareness in the cases I have described, such awareness can open up promising possibilities for resistant re-identification as a member of those groups, and as jointly responsible for what they have done and will do.

3.3.3 Prompting Different Relations to Felt Power

A final way in which such awareness can be morally and politically productive is by allowing privileged individuals to relate differently to feelings of power. Gaining awareness of oppressive norms and political complexity can feel disempowering: "who am I to do anything about this?" Such powerlessness can be morally beneficial insofar as it can keep individuals from bold or hasty action in any direction and can make the necessity of action-with-others impossible to ignore. It can also challenge tendencies a privileged individual might have to associate feeling aware with feeling powerful and in control. Ways of relating to feelings of power may shift, as people recognize they have better understandings of injustice, even if they feel they lack power to enact change as individuals. As I return to in chapter 5, acting while feeling powerless may turn out to be effective in some contexts of injustice.[37]

3.4 CONCLUSION

I have been building a case for recognizing how disorientations can have effects on action partly through prompting shifts in individual awareness. The awareness generated by disorientations is unlike the "click" of reorientations, and unlike "aha" moments. Gaining such awareness is more like the experience of a soundwave—coming to awareness that resonates and points far beyond what I had known to look for, and far beyond what I know. Through disorientations, I can gain awareness of the contingent oppressive norms and political complexity. A number of dimensions of my life might need to change, but I may not know how. Individuals like Pratt, Du Bois, and the students I have discussed do not feel wholehearted in Frankfurt's sense discussed in the previous chapter, since the kinds of awareness they have gained are of political contexts, normative structures, and their own identities as even more complicated and fraught than they had imagined. There is not always, or often, an obviously best course of action in such cases. The awareness they gain can prompt epistemic humility, resistant re-identification, and different relations to felt power, none of which can be understood as virtuous traits of individuals, but all of which can be promising in moral landscapes where individuals cannot work against injustice in isolation, cannot dis-identify from communities of origin, and must cultivate new power relations.

Individuals who have been disoriented in the senses discussed can become in some cases more likely to understand themselves as one among many knowers, subject to limitations and open to change. They have known themselves to be limited and have seen the need to change epistemic commitments before. I return in chapter 6 to the question of how concrete contexts of consciousness-raising and education might be better structured to anticipate and support the kinds of (non-resolvist) awareness that disorientations can generate. For now, my point is that experiences of disorientation should be of central concern to anyone who cares about becoming more aware of structures of oppression and one's position within them.

[4]

TENDERIZING EFFECTS AND ACTING DESPITE OURSELVES

Moments of disorientation are vital. They are bodily experiences that throw the world up, or throw the body from its ground. Disorientation as a bodily feeling can be unsettling, and it can shatter one's sense of confidence in the ground or one's belief that the ground on which we reside can support the actions that make a life feel liveable. . . . The body might be reoriented if the hand that reaches out finds something to steady an action. Or the hand might reach out and find nothing, and grasp instead the indeterminacy of air. The body in losing its support might then be lost, undone, thrown.

—Sara Ahmed (2006, 157)

I am sitting in a high-ceilinged room in the Royal Hawaiian Hotel in Honolulu watching the long translucent curtains billow in the trade wind and trying to put my life back together. . . . There has been an earthquake in the Aleutians, 7.5 on the Richter scale, and a tidal wave is expected. In two or three minutes the wave, if there is one, will hit Midway Island. . . . My husband watches the television screen. I watch the curtains, and imagine the swell of the water. . . . We are here on this island in the middle of the Pacific in lieu of filing for divorce.

—Joan Didion (2009, 133)

As we have begun to see, paying attention to experiences of disorientation illuminates the complexity of moral and political motivation. In chapters 2 and 3, we saw that collapsing all the dimensions of motivation into an overly pared down model of reflection and decision can neglect the moral significance of whole swaths of experience that fail to motivate in the expected or preferred ways. In chapter 2, I made room for seeing that experiences could help individuals act morally even if they failed to help them resolve what to do, and perhaps by directly compromising moral resolve. In chapter 3, we saw that in some cases, disorientations prompt awareness without individuals coming to resolve how to act, and I argued that such awareness can be morally beneficial.

In this chapter, I turn to the ways disorientations change action and ways of being in the world, still not through helping individuals resolve how to act, and without even making individuals more aware. Attending to the somatic and affective dimensions of disorientation will help highlight how habits of interaction can shift when an individual feels deeply uneasy in an environment. As we will see, lacking ease can shift ways of being in the world, and this can lead to subtle but significant shifts in the practices that make up moral lives.

Building on the accounts of the disorientations of grief (chapter 2), consciousness-raising, critical education, double consciousness and white ambush (chapter 3), here I introduce specific examples of when illness, trauma, queerness, and migration can be disorienting. As in the cases of earlier examples, there are substantial feminist literatures on illness/medicalization, trauma, queerness, and migrant experiences. For the most part, the focus has been on the harms associated with each, particularly for members of marginalized groups. The significance of disorientations in each kind of experience remains to be seen. Of course, illnesses, traumas, coming to embody queerness, and migration are very different kinds of experiences. Thankfully, queerness and migration are not always experienced as introducing threats, and depending on the severity and social responses to illness and trauma, such experiences may not be disruptive in all areas of life. Yet these experiences are all often disorienting in senses of *disrupting habitual ways of being in the world*. All these experiences can be deeply disruptive to one's own future, daily routines, and can disrupt individuals' ways of relating to others and to their own futures.

In sections 4.1 and 4.2, I consider each kind of experience and offer support for thinking that the disorientations that can be part of illness, trauma, queerness, and migration have in some cases prompted particular *tenderizing effects*. In the third section, I argue for the moral and political significance of these effects.

4.1 DISORIENTATIONS OF INTERRUPTION

Many of the examples of disorientation that run through the book are examples of individuals becoming disoriented when life has not gone according to plan. Unexpected events regularly throw a wrench into one's plans for how one's day-to-day life would go, as when I lose my voice the day I need to give a talk, or when traffic is delayed the morning I need to be at work early. These kinds of minor interruptions can be irritating without being disorienting. When more substantial events occur, one is likely to be disoriented, as when a company downsizes and one's job no longer exists, or when a hurricane destroys one's neighborhood. Such events would not be disorienting were it not for the fact that individuals typically have some combination of hope and expectation about how the immediate future will go, and, at least to some extent, we build lives around such hopes and expectations. Though we know that the thing one hopes for and expects (e.g., that our company will continue to employ us, that natural disasters will not strike us) is not fully within one's control, we still regularly act on the basis of such hopes and expectations.

Individuals often structure lives around the hope/expectation that they and their loved ones will be *healthy* and *safe* from harm. We live with the knowledge that illness and violence are possibilities, but we move forward in the hopes that we will not face them. Even though we know that they are possible, we can still be deeply disoriented when we suddenly face them in our own lives or in the lives of those dearest to us.

4.1.1 Illness, Sensing Vulnerability, and Living Unprepared

No matter how much one knows that serious illness is a possibility, coming to face it oneself or in the life of a loved one can be deeply disorienting.[1] Illnesses can radically alter one's current life without being life-threatening. Diagnosis can be both orienting and disorienting. Patients note how it can be a relief to have an explanation for one's symptoms, even if the diagnosis introduces new questions and uncertainties. Being diagnosed with a serious illness can introduce radical changes in day-to-day life and a very different way of relating to one's loved ones. Illnesses can introduce the need to pay attention to our own or others' bodies more than usual, to care for them differently, or to stop using them in ways we have done unthinkingly in the past. More visible physical illnesses (or visible side effects of treatment) can draw unwanted attention, questions, or concern; less visible illnesses can be isolating and can become objects of disbelief or stigma.

Serious illness can alter one's identity in more or less dramatic ways. It can be very difficult to come to identify as *a sick person*.[2] Illness almost always necessitates new kinds of interdependence—the person who is ill typically comes to rely on loved ones and care providers differently. Being ill can mean no longer being able to work, to drive a car, to care for other people in the same way, or to structure one's schedule as one likes. If an individual has been a very independent person, as is expected of adults in general, acceptance of one's growing dependence on others can be very difficult. Illness also almost always requires a slowing down and easing off—more rest is needed and less constant activity is possible. Suddenly one can no longer just power through work days, run from one activity to the next, or spend all of one's energy.

In the case of terminal illnesses, individuals can experience the disorientation of facing their own mortality or the mortality of those around them.[3] Such illnesses can make the near and long-term futures uncertain. Individuals can ask: What will my life look like in a month? How will I afford to support myself and my loved ones? How do I feel differently about my current life in light of my prognosis? Does it make sense to keep doing what I am doing, even if I may not live as long as I thought? Serious illness inevitably alters life plans, as when individuals give up on a desire to have kids, pursue certain careers, or opt to uproot and move across the country to be closer to supportive family members.[4] When illness becomes a reality for me or someone close to me, it is likely to make it difficult to know how to go on. It may not be obvious how being sick will fit into the overarching narrative of one's life.[5] And in any context without a secure health care system, serious illnesses will introduce fears of how one will ensure medical care, or how one will survive without it.[6]

The disorientations of facing illness can have negative implications for one's day-to-day life and one's relationships. Upon diagnosis, a person or caregiver may become absorbed in her own experience, less able to attend to the needs of others. Attending to one's own needs may become at least a full-time job, or even a fixation. Additionally, one might become overwhelmed with fear of future events. Decisions about how to ensure the best medical care, whether or how to continue working, or how to plan for the ongoing needs of one's family members may become engrossing. For some people, serious illness may present as one of the first times where life has not gone according to plan. Deciphering how to make plans in the face of the wholly unplanned might trigger serious anxieties and deep-seated insecurities.

There are times, however, when the disorientations of illness can produce effects beyond self-concern and fear of the future. In some cases, they have generated capacities for *sensing vulnerability*—both one's own and that of others. Clinical psychologists have paid a great deal of attention to the psychological dimensions of being diagnosed with serious illness, so there is now a substantial literature in clinical psychology about how being diagnosed with, or caring for someone diagnosed with, a serious illness can be deeply disorienting, and in ways that can have specific effects. Through confronting illness, individuals in some cases have been shown to experience increased awareness of the needs of people with disabilities.[7] In other cases, individuals struggling with the implications of their illnesses for their own lives have experienced heightened sensitivity to the pain and suffering of others.[8] Significant changes in day-to-day life following cancer treatment (e.g., the loss of capacity to work or eat) have been reported to make individuals' own vulnerabilities stand out, and shifted relationships to allow for feeling more deeply known by others.[9] Caregivers of people with serious illness in some cases have also reported sensitivity to vulnerability, in the sense of becoming responsive to the suffering of others in treatment.[10] Sensitivity to vulnerability in these senses means not only becoming more sensitized to when others may be experiencing the same difficulty they themselves or their loved ones have experienced in illness, but a more general heightened sense of how vulnerable all persons are, having been in some cases taken aback by the fact of one's own vulnerability.

In highlighting how experiencing the disorientations of illness can prompt increased sensitivity to vulnerability, I am noting a difference between what it means to develop *increased sensitivity to vulnerability* and what others might describe as *sympathy* or *empathy*. It is not just that people who experience the disorientations of illness become able to feel sorry for others who are suffering or to recognize another's feelings as being similar to what they themselves have experienced. Rather, it can happen that individuals, in the process of facing their own serious vulnerabilities, come to have heightened sensitivity to others' vulnerabilities to the same or other unpredictable events.

The disorientations of illness can trigger an awareness of vulnerability that extends beyond instances of seeing one's own vulnerability or that of other patients one meets. In *The Cancer Journals*, Audre Lorde describes her experience of cancer testing, diagnosis, and surgeries, describing how cancer "knocked her for a loop" differently at different times. Her experience of her own vulnerability to illness and death triggered new ways of sensing the vulnerabilities of other women's bodies, and her experience of feeling isolated confronting the illness as a black lesbian feminist triggered new senses of the vulnerabilities of other women to facing extreme difficulties alone (Lorde 1997, 28). She felt her own vulnerability to shortened life, to being seen as an untouchable and not worth even investing time in (49), while coming to note with new clarity that "we have always been temporary" (52). Lorde notes that there was a period of serious disorientation, from the time of the biopsy that found malignancy in her breast, through the time of recovery after mastectomy. But it is during this time that her journals document a growing sensitivity to a particular kind of vulnerability of herself and others—the vulnerabilities of women with cancer in a sexist society. As Lorde articulates it, "it is in this period of quasi-numbness and childlike susceptibility . . . that many patterns and networks are started for women after breast surgery that encourage us to deny the realities of our bodies which have just been driven home to us so graphically" (1997, 41). The text considers this vulnerability from the perspective of both promise and threat: as Lorde reads it, the moment of vulnerability of serious illness can be a politicizing moment for women to recognize their own power and connectedness with other women. But the vulnerability can also be a moment where, in her terms, "Cancer Inc." tries to step in and provide false security to women through the promise of prosthetics, reconstruction, and the ability to go on with their past lives, almost *more normally* than they had before. So the sensitivity to vulnerability Lorde describes reaches beyond the vulnerability of individuals, to a politicized sense of the vulnerabilities of whole groups.

The disorientations of illness have been chronicled in numerous first-person accounts, many of which emphasize the serious shifts in identity that the disorientations of illness can prompt. Accounts from professionals, including medical practitioners, clarify how unsettling it can be to no longer be on the side of "the healthy ones."[11] Physician David Servan-Schreiber was diagnosed with brain cancer at thirty-one years old and proceeded into treatment, a relapse, and further treatment. Servan-Schreiber endures a number of strange shifts, many due to the contrast between the ease of his life as a professional and the complexity of his life as a patient. After the cancer diagnosis, he describes feeling out of place, on the other side of norms of medicalization. Once he is treated as an object, as no longer a trusted expert, and by people who seem confident but have no reason to be, he feels acutely how such "normal" practices do not make things easier for everyone. Yet he also describes increased sensitivity to both his own vulnerability and others' (Servan-Schreiber 2008, 23).

In addition to (in some cases) generating increased capacities for sensing vulnerability, the disorientations of illness have also produced what I would describe as an *ability to live unprepared*. In this sense, the disorientations of illness in some cases make individuals less emotionally attached to an assumption that they could or should be able to control or plan for any eventuality. In other words, the disorientations of a wide variety of kinds of illness have prompted a qualitative shift in the ways some people relate to the impossibility of adequately preparing oneself for whatever might happen.

In the cases of a number of kinds of chronic (and in some cases life-threatening) illnesses, individuals have been shown to experience a significantly lowered sense of the controllability of the world.[12] Confronting one's mortality for the first time has been found to drastically alter one's sense of being prepared for the future.[13] In some cases, individuals with serious illness have been found more likely than those without serious illness to view life events as random, and less likely to seek a deeper meaning behind their experiences. The disorientations of illness have been shown to "permanently threaten perceptions of invulnerability."[14] Facing serious illness, some individuals describe "relinquishing their sense of control" and surrendering to the fact that their future is out of their hands.[15] Some people who are not facing illness themselves, but caring for ill loved ones have also been shown to experience a shift in their assumptions about the controllability of the world, and in their need to feel in control of the future.[16] So both some individuals who are ill, and some who care for ill others, have been shown to experience disorientations that have prompted a different capacity for living unprepared.

Philosopher Havi Carel writes of her own experience of being diagnosed with lymphangioleiomyomatosis (LAM): a rare, fatal lung disease affecting adult women.[17] For Carel, the young, fit, careful child of two physicians, the diagnosis of a chronic, untreatable, and eventually fatal illness was like being blindsided.[18] She calls the diagnosis her "ten-year life sentence." Carel begins to relate to her future as not one for which she could have adequately prepared. She writes:

> In my pre-illness days I made plans and wanted the usual goods life offers us . . . to be healthy, to be happy, to be safe. After I became ill, these wishes began to seem grandiose . . . Did I really expect all that? . . . All the usual rules that governed my life—that trying hard yields good results, that looking after yourself pays off, that practice makes perfect—seemed inoperative here. It was the first instance, for me, of unconditional, uncontrollable failure. (Carel 2008, 31, 63)

Through the disorientation of her illness, Carel becomes less assured in her own plans, at the same time as able to continue without such assurance. The disorientation of serious illness compromises Carel's ability to move boldly in the direction of particular goals or aspirations, but she becomes more able to live tentatively in an unpredictable period of her life.

4.1.2 Trauma and Living Unprepared

Just as we hope that we will be free from serious illness, so too we hope no one we love will be a victim of violence. Depending on who and where we are, violence may be a common part of everyday life—rates of sexual violence against women on university campuses and elsewhere are alarmingly high, violence and bullying in schools is commonplace, violence is a regular part of military life, and violence is a leading cause of injury and death for men of color in the United States. Though we know violence is possible, and more likely depending on who we are, we hope for the protection of those we love. When one is the target or victim of violence, it can seem impossible to trust the world or those in it. Since we can never fully prepare for it, the trauma of violence is often disorienting.[19] Psychologist Judith Herman describes the disorientations of trauma as follows:

> Traumatic events overwhelm the ordinary systems of care that give people a sense of control, connection, and meaning.... Traumatized people feel utterly abandoned, utterly alone, cast out of human and divine systems of care and protection that sustain life. Thereafter, a sense of alienation, or disconnection, pervades every relationship, from the most intimate familial bonds to the most abstract affiliations of community and religion. (Herman 1992, 33, 52)

Surviving severe trauma requires serious emotional, physical, and cognitive work, and ongoing traumas or lack of resources can preclude individuals from having the opportunities to pursue the work required. All these steps can involve disorientation, and all the more so when communities restrict expressions of traumatic experiences or fail to recognize individuals as traumatized. Given that many serious traumas are still not regularly recognized as such, it can be particularly disorienting for those who have experienced trauma to face the possibility that they are suffering from post-traumatic stress disorder (PTSD) in a social environment that fails to recognize their pasts as traumatic, and/or fails to acknowledge responsibility for creating contexts where violence is likely to occur.[20]

The disorientations of traumas have different effects on individual lives. In some cases, they are wholly debilitating. Traumas can trigger mental as well as physical illnesses (e.g., PTSD or Complex PTSD). The aftermath of traumas can make lives completely unlivable and have been the cause of many deaths. At the same time, much of the literature discussed in chapter 2 on resilience, hardiness, and post-traumatic growth has aimed to investigate ways in which some individuals cope with the lasting harmful effects of trauma. There are reasons to be cautious about generalizing about the effects of traumas across great differences, and those cautions bear repeating here. Who one is, what kind of trauma one has experienced, and what kind of supports one has in recovery can all make a great difference to which traumas are possible to cope with, and which are not. It is neither possible to say that the disorientations of trauma are uniformly debilitating nor that they are uniformly beneficial.

Though trauma in all cases harms the individual who endures it, in some cases, as with some disorientations of serious illness, the disorientations of trauma generate *capacities for living unprepared*. Traumatic experiences in some cases fundamentally alter individuals' perspectives on the controllability and benevolence of the world. Some adults who have experienced a serious traumatic event become more likely to believe that chance determines life outcomes and to perceive themselves as living in a non-benevolent world.[21] As a result of the disorientations of trauma, in some cases individuals see themselves as having become able to cope with ongoing threat of violence,[22] and as now living with a disrupted sense of coherence.[23] Some individuals who survive trauma report coming to accept the fact that they have never been in control of their lives, that they are fundamentally insecure.[24] These senses of becoming able to cope with one's inability to control or guard against future unpredictability, ongoing possibilities of violence, and of coming to accept one's insecurity are all parts of what I am terming "capacities for living unprepared."

The ability of some disorientations of trauma to generate these capacities is also described in some philosophical and first-person accounts of trauma. For example, Susan Brison has given an account of being brutally attacked, sexually assaulted, and left for dead. Through the disorientation of her traumatic assault and recovery, Brison comes to live unprepared in the sense I have described here. She describes feeling that the world is uncontrollable, and that she will be unable to manage what may come. As she writes:

> Even those who are able to acknowledge the existence of violence try to protect themselves from the realization that the world in which it occurs is *their* world and so they find it hard to identify with the victim. They cannot allow themselves to imagine the victim's shattered life, or else their illusions about their own safety and control over their own lives might begin to crumble. . . . I have no story to tell about how such violence won't happen to us. . . . None of us is *supposed* to be alive. We're all here by chance and only for a little while. The wonder is that we've managed, once again, to winter through and that our hearts, in spite of everything, survive. (Brison 2002, 9, 120-123, emphasis added)

As a result of disorientation, Brison feels overwhelmingly that the world of violence is *her* world, and one for which it is impossible to prepare.[25]

The fact that some disorientations of illness and trauma have the effect of generating sensitivity to vulnerability and capacities for living unprepared does not mean all (or even most) of the disorientations of illness and trauma produce these effects—the goal has been to outline the reasons for thinking *some do*. We know for certain that not all disorientations (i.e., beyond those of illness and trauma) prompt these developments, and in some cases experiences of illness in particular prompt the exact opposite effects, including social isolation or wishful thinking about one's possibilities for controlling future events.[26] Further research is required to investigate what factors about individuals, experiences, or social contexts could make it more likely that some disorientations of illness would prompt such developments, rather than exclusively compromising one's well-being.[27]

4.2 DISORIENTATIONS OF ILL FIT

Distinct from the disorientations of having one's life and plans interrupted are the disorientations of having an identity and a way of being that is a *poor fit* with other people's lives and plans. There many ways to fail to fit in, such as being the only sibling who never goes home for the holidays or being the only person who does not eat meat in one's group of carnivorous friends. One can be an outsider in some ways, while remaining an acceptable insider (still a sibling, still a friend) in others. Some major failures of fit make one less likely to fit in at all, such as being the only person in the office to celebrate Eid, or the only woman in a church group to be unmarried. These and other failures of fit can be justifications for complete exclusion from the social life of a community—one does not speak the language, or one is disabled in a way that others do not understand. Outsider status can be disorienting even in minor cases, but the more stringent the exclusion, the more disorienting it may be.

4.2.1 Queerness and In-This-Togetherness

Experiences of queer desire and queer identification have their own associated disorientations, and more than illness or trauma, ones that can include excitement and exhilaration at the same time as fear and uncertainty. First experiencing and recognizing queer desire can be disorienting, especially if one has little experience with queer sex, relationships, or culture. Coming to perceive non-hetero relationships as possible can be exciting, while one can nonetheless feel tentative about pursuing them. The threat of homophobia can make it difficult to know how to be openly queer. It can be unclear how to come out as queer within straight families, where the expectation of compulsory heterosexuality has been clearly communicated.[28]

Transitions from mostly straight to mostly queer identities can be disorienting,[29] as can coming out in college,[30] or in workplaces.[31] Queers can worry about losing relationships with loved ones after coming out to them or can worry about job loss.[32] Although ideally more joyful and exciting, coming to experience oneself as queer and coming out within mostly straight families and communities can also be disruptive in ways similar to illness and trauma. Living with the threat of anti-queer discrimination and violence can make it difficult or impossible to feel comfortable in social situations.[33] Being queer in a context where it is not safe to be publically out is likely to be difficult and disorienting in compounded ways—not only in the sense of having the experience of being out of step with norms of sexuality and more at risk of violence for being so, but in the additional sense of having to feign straightness to others.[34] Being queer makes one more vulnerable to harm on multiple fronts—to homelessness, health disparities, and imprisonment. Queers who are also lower class, disabled, and/or racialized can face interlocking harms.[35] The specificities of geography, class, and race can make a real difference in how possible it is to feel comfortably queer. Being out in particular work contexts (e.g., the military) can introduce additional levels of institutional heterosexism.[36] Overall, given the way dominant narratives of healthy, successful lives and futures assume straightness, it can be unclear what it means for queers to have a future.[37]

Even given these difficulties, we have reason to think some disorientations of queerness have the potential to generate an effect distinct from capacities to *live unprepared* and *sense vulnerability*, as generated by the cases of disorientation described above.[38] Specifically, the disorientations of queerness have in some cases prompted what we might call, roughly, *capacities for in-this-togetherness*. Capacities for in-this-togetherness mean simply increased capacities for acting as though one's well-being is partly conditioned by or tied up with the well-being of others. In some cases, as a result of the disorientations of queerness, queers have become more interested in LGBT social/political issues, more able to question traditional heterosexual norms, more involved in LGBT organizations, and able to experience more positive relationships with LGBT people.[39] In other cases, queers report that the disorientations of coming out led them to become committed to developing consciousness of stigma,[40] or to become involved in queer collective action, including commitments to become more informed and to educate others about heterosexism.[41] In other words, in some cases, the disorientations of being queer have politicized individuals in the particular sense of becoming collectively minded.

The disorientations of coming out and queer life cannot be understood apart from the disorientations of being part of a community threatened by pervasive social ignorance. How disorienting it can be to be queer is directly correlated to the strength of heteronormativity. It is the persistent assumption that heterosexuality is *normal* and all other kinds of sexuality are *deviant* that makes it still disorienting and disruptive to be queer. There are norms of health and invulnerability that contribute to making illness and trauma disorienting too, but most of us also think illness and traumas are contrary to well-being in senses that extend beyond social norms of health and invulnerability. There is nothing intrinsically harmful about queerness, and there is nothing intrinsically disorienting about queer life. It is heteronormativity and the persistent assumption that queerness is unnatural that makes it dangerous to be queer, and it is in part the social contexts that make queerness dangerous that also make it disorienting. So the disorientations of being queer are interconnected with the disorientations of learning that one is in an endangered community. It is this, I think, that makes sense of how the disorientations of queerness in some cases generate capacities for in-this-togetherness.

Queer responses to the acute AIDS crisis of the 1990s demonstrate clearly how some of the disorientations of queerness prompted capacities for in-this-togetherness. What I have described as the disorientations of queerness—the ways that being queer can make it hard to know how to go on—are related to what Deborah Gould has called *queer ambivalence* (i.e., simultaneous attachments to heteronormative society and failure to fit within straight worlds). As a result, queers feel both shame and pride, anger and a desire to keep the peace (Gould 2001, 141). As Gould has tracked in her research on ACT UP and queer movements of the 1980s and 1990s, queers have experienced what I described in chapter 3 as *moral shock:* they realize that queers as a social group are under attack, that their survival depends on collective resistance.[42] Diagnoses of HIV in queer men in some cases triggered them to see their own health and well-being as bound up with the collective health of others (Mansson 1992; Schwartzberg 1993). From his own interviews with gay men during the years of widespread HIV and AIDS, Frank Browning quotes Reed Grier as saying the following:

> You no longer necessarily look at another gay man as a sexual object, but as a brother, as someone who's in this together with you, someone who has gone through this thing with you, someone who is facing the same issues of mortality, who is there to be cared for, cherished, nurtured, someone to be intimate with.... There is a qualitative shift in the nature of the

relationships between men in this city in the age group who've gone through this. (Browning 1993, 131-132)

At such points, queers have experienced in-this-togetherness as facing near certain death, and fighting against it, together. The disorientation involved in being queer in a heteronormative world in some cases has made individuals feel only able to go on together.

4.2.2 Migration and Living against the Grain

Experiences of migration across state borders may be experienced as hopeful or joyful movements *toward* welcome futures, but in many cases are also or instead experienced chiefly as departures *from* conditions where one is not welcome or where various needs are not meetable. In many cases, the decision to migrate is reluctant, or not a decision at all; individuals would not choose to leave countries if it were not necessary. The growing number of migrations of climate refugees, individuals escaping state or social violence, and migrations to secure seasonal work all fall into this category. Such migrations can bring with them not only the challenges of making one's way in a new landscape, but also the threat of being newly identified as an "outsider." So while in some cases migrations can be exciting or enjoyable—especially for those most privileged individuals who have the liberty of choosing them and are easily able to establish legal status in their new countries—in many more cases, migrating is disorienting.

Migrants may be called to make their identities explicit at any time, to prove their right to be present. Being called out as migrant can harm people in unpredictable ways, depending on their location of origin, their level of privilege, and the judgments of the particular locals that call them out. Those who are not able to secure a formal right to be present may need to avoid many circumstances where they may be forced to identify. Even documented migrants may feel they never fully know what to expect in a place that is not their own. Subtle understandings about, for example, how to interact with bureaucracies, governments, and police may never become clear. All in all, it is harder for migrants than citizens to know how to anticipate what one will need to afford, where one will be allowed to travel, and what dangers one might face. Migrants regularly face the disorientation of not knowing what to expect. Facts citizens find obvious may not be obvious to migrants, and it can be embarrassing or impossible to ask for clarification. Migrants can be disoriented not only by the loss of familiar surroundings and communities, but by the imperative to integrate into new environments, while being continually positioned as foreigner, and often also as unwelcome, unworthy, or dangerous. Migrants are faced with the task of making themselves at least somewhat at home while not at home—a task that is often disorienting.[43]

There are a number of senses of ease that can accompany being a citizen in one's own land. María Lugones has outlined four senses of being at ease: being a fluent speaker, agreeing with all the norms, being with those I love and those who love me, and having a shared history with those around me (Lugones 1987, 12). In some cases, the disorientations of migrating, of having lived within some set of social relationships and practices, and then coming to need to survive as a foreigner within significantly different social contexts have meant that people maintain a slanted stance within norms of, for example, productivity, health, and family, always partly not fitting comfortably within them. Echoing earlier discussed language of "moral shock" and "double ontological shock," migrants can experience not only culture shock upon arrival in new contexts, but also "role shock" (Minkler 1979), not knowing who they are to those new people around them. For Lugones, stereotypes of what it means to be Latina mean that she embodies an ambiguous position between what others expect of her and what she is. As she writes:

> As Latin-American I am an ambiguous being, a two-imaged self: I can see that gringos see me as stereotypically intense because I am, as a Latin-American, constructed that way but I may or may not *intentionally* animate the stereotype or the real thing.... This ambiguity is funny and it is not just funny, it is survival-rich. (Lugones 1987, 13-14)

Accustomed to the disorientations of migration, Lugones is not surprised to feel out of place in different "worlds."

In chapter 3, I discussed the potential of some disorientations to prompt individuals to become *aware of oppressive norms and their contingency*. I want to suggest we have reason to recognize a distinct phenomenon in cases of the disorientations of migration. Some disorientations of migration can generate ways of *living against the grain of norms*. When a migrant's position within norms is made insecure—for example, when he is suddenly no longer a "citizen in his own land," his ways of relating to norms of citizenship can subtly or dramatically shift. He can experience the sort of shift that happens when something we have leaned on as permanent or fixed suddenly is no longer completely secure. A chair turns out to be on wheels. One leans on it less confidently, and is more timid about its presence—one no longer expects it will always be there, and begins to figure out ways to not need it. Living partly against the grain of norms is related to the point about awareness of contingency from the last chapter—there, some disorientations made it possible to become *aware* that norms are contingent rather than necessary. Here, disorientations can make it possible to *live with* oppressive norms as though they could be otherwise. Living against the grain of norms means embodying non-normative relationships, practices, and ways of being in ways that do not easily or immediately succumb to the force of social norms.

The connection to one's past home (also no longer available as a home) means that a migrant may never feel fully absorbed in the new social context.[44] This is partly what Sara Ahmed has described as the condition of "melancholy migrants."[45] The disorientations of migration—persistent uncertainty and unease within their new social contexts—can allow individuals to maintain a position of ill-fit within the norms (including oppressive norms) of the communities they have entered and to maintain their position in a way that shows it is possible to survive without fully embracing or enforcing such norms.[46] Migrants can have structures of family and kinship relations that do not fit into heteronormative visions of nuclear families and gendered households.[47] They may not easily secure the work they are qualified for, or sometimes even "employment" in standard senses of paid labor, but can manage to provide for their own and others' needs.[48] Migrants may not be recognized as deserving of political voice or power but they can be leaders in shaping and envisioning political projects and the work of transforming communities.[49]

Living against the grain of norms is partly related to what Gloria Anzaldua (1987) has called *mestiza consciousness*. The main distinction I am drawing is that, while her conception is focused on how individuals become able to *see* in a mixed way, the capacity to live partly against the grain of norms may occur alongside heightened awareness of contingent oppressive norms, but the two can also exist apart.[50] It is possible, in other words, to be disoriented by migration in the sense described here, and to simply come to live in a way where one's kinship relations do not fit cleanly in understandings of normal family, where one is not "productive" by normal standards but is still creating the conditions needed for survival, where one is not "political" by normal standards but is still envisioning and exercising sovereignties in one's community. All this may or may not be accompanied by what was described in the last chapter as awareness of the contingency of oppressive norms. In other words, the disorientations of migration can prompt a way of failing to fit within norms, without also enabling one to recognize or describe the norms that fail to fit.

While some disorientations of queerness generate capacities for in-this-togetherness, and some disorientations of migration generate capacities for living against the grain of norms, not all do. The disorientations of queerness and migration in many cases have obvious negative effects. They can make the processes of developing queer identities and relationships confusing and challenging. Disorientations can feel isolating in contexts where queers already have insufficient support, and in some cases can contribute to suffering, mental illness, and feelings that life is no longer worth living.[51] Migrants can experience compromised physical and mental health as a result of the strain and risk of major migrations. The stress of migration, lack of access to health care, and lack of access to resources that would support health (e.g., food, security, safe water, preventive care) predict worse health and high mortality rates for migrants.[52] It can prove impossible to acclimate to new lives without the support of families and home communities.[53] For example, some Latino/a migrants now living in the United States navigate precarious conditions of housing, work, health care, and relationships,[54] and some have been shown to be at risk for illness and hopelessness.[55] As in every case of disorientation I describe, the effects of disorientations that are positive are realities in some (though not all) individual's lives. They do not, and could not, outweigh the ongoing harms against queers and migrants.

4.3 THE POWER OF TENDERIZING EFFECTS

We have now seen that, in some cases, experiences of illness, trauma, queerness, and migration are disorienting, and in some such cases, the effects of such disorientations are not exclusively negative. I have been arguing specifically that the disorientations of illness have in some cases generated capacities for living unprepared and sensing vulnerabilities. The disorientations of trauma have in some cases also generated capacities for living unprepared. The disorientations of queerness have in some cases generated capacities for what I have called in-this-togetherness, and the disorientations of migration have generated capacities for living against the grain of norms. While we have begun to anticipate how the effects I have tracked could be beneficial, the case for the moral and political importance of the effects remains to be made, especially given the claim I have been making since chapter 2, that their main benefits will not be found in the way they help individuals resolve how to act.

Simply put, capacities for sensing vulnerabilities, living unprepared, in-this-togetherness, and living against the grain of norms all involve a shift in individuals' ways of relating to complex, deep-seated norms, habits, and expectations. It is not obvious what the importance of sensing vulnerabilities, living unprepared, in-this-togetherness, or living against the grain of norms would be if not for deeply rooted habits of *not* responding to vulnerabilities, of assuming preparedness, of practiced individualism, and of the irresistibility of oppressive norms. These habits of ignoring, assuming, practicing, and going-along-with correspond to the expectation that I and others will take care of ourselves, that I should act as though I am in control, that I am alone in facing harms, and that it is okay to go-with-the-flow of norms. Such habits and expectations are morally and politically devastating. They naturalize ignoring others in need, acting as though one is in full control of outcomes, pursuing one's own good as though it is not bound up with the good of everyone, and complying with norms that harm many because they benefit a few. Because of their character as habits and expectations, they are not easily recognized or dispensed with—no single decision would suffice to stop practicing them.

What gets tenderized by the particular disorientations discussed here are practices of easily embodying the habits and expectations individuals have learned, shared, and firmed up in the past. The language of changing habits and changing expectations helps us understand what is required to allow for these shifts—getting below the level of individuals' decisions, to the level of unlearning. When expectations are unsettled, individuals can come to embody social norms and practiced habits of interaction differently, in ways more responsive to the ways the fragility, relationality, and non-ideal realities of the world affect lives. When habits and expectations are tenderized, one's practices become more pervious to the actual, if unexpected, needs of those around one.

We can understand the moral significance of these tenderizing effects perhaps best by recognizing the important roles *habit* and *expectation* play in moral and political life. Expectations structure much of one's ability to move through the world.[56] Expectations make up a significant part of interpersonal lives and are an important part of how individuals can feel at home or excluded from social worlds. If my expectations for my life are regularly in contrast to what others around me expect for my life, my expectations will be unsettled. As Campbell explains, for dominant identities, "unmet expectations can . . . cause deep anxiety and an inability to know how to negotiate now unfamiliar environments" (1999, 229). Although in some cases unmet expectations can prompt greater awareness of political realities, such anxieties may instead provoke defensive emotional reactions, pushing dominant individuals to hold their expectations even more firmly. Members of dominant groups often experience more ease within their social worlds than those people they dominate, but being at ease is always a matter of degree—especially because individuals do not always possess dominant characteristics in all domains at the same time. The power of the tenderizing effects I have outlined is in part the power to disrupt expectations—and, potentially to also disrupt *one's desire to re-establish new expectations*.[57] In other words, the tenderizing effects that result from some disorientations of illness, trauma, queerness, and migration can not only deplete our feelings of ease in having expectations of control over our lives, but also reduce the extent to which we feel that having such control or ease would align with being ourselves.

In coming to live unprepared, sense vulnerability, relate to others as though we are in-this-together, and live partly against the grain of oppressive norms, individuals demonstrate shifted expectations. To maintain the expectation that one could be fully prepared for the future, invulnerable, independent, or at ease within norms in a world of unpredictability, vulnerability, interdependence, and harmful norms is to be in denial. Tenderized expectations more accurately reflect the actual conditions of oppressive society and prepare individuals to function well within conditions of unpredictability, vulnerability, and interdependence in their work going forward.

Note that none of the tenderizing effects I have tracked here—coming to be able to live unprepared, sense vulnerabilities, experience in-this-togetherness, and live partly against the grain of norms—prompts moral resolve. These experiences do not help individuals conceive of and implement a plan of action. It is not that Brison, for example, offers her son, her students, or other survivors of sexual violence more optimistic or insightful vision of the future. Instead, she embodies a hesitant, resistant, and tender position within the current conditions, which she carries into her research, teaching, ways of parenting, as well as into her way of working within her university and living in her town. What at first seems to Carel to be her failure to manage her own risk and enact her plans seems later more like having succumbed to the uncertainty of health that had existed (for her and everyone) all along. These experiences do not make individuals decisive about how to address a problem. Unlike the cases of disorientation discussed in chapter 3, they are not even experiences that clearly make individuals aware of a problem. Rather, the effects of these disorientations partly prompt shifts in ways of being through *compromising* moral resolve, including the push to determine what one must do. Being tenderized leads to capacities to relate to vulnerable others more gently and generously and to exercise one's powers more reluctantly. As such, being tenderized is also not like the cultivation of virtuous character: one does not come to possess stable traits like courage or temperance. Rather, one comes to relate to others and a moral landscape in more tentative, dynamic ways that can change in keeping with changes in that landscape. Changed actions and ways of being that are outgrowths of fundamental uncertainty about one's position in the world might be understood as action despite one's inability to act decisively. This can be *acting despite oneself*. The tenderizing effects of disorientations, which I have argued prompt subtle but deeply important shifts in relation, can go unnoticed if the only markers of moral progress are seen as conscious, decisive actions.

Eventually, individuals who experience the tenderizing effects of illness, trauma, queerness, or migration might gain awareness and pursue action against injustice. These individuals might become aware of problems, including the needs of people with rare illnesses, the prevalence of sexual assault against women, the harms of heteronormativity and living with HIV, and the experiences of migrant workers of all classes (and especially of the poorest). These individuals sometimes decide to act against those problems.[58] My point in tracking the tenderizing effects of theirs and others' particular disorientations is to note that one might not only act differently following disorientations, but may also experience a qualitative shift in relating to the future, one's own vulnerability, and one's interdependence. Having experienced tenderizing effects of a disorientation, an individual might be more likely to pursue actions with some degree of trepidation, softness, and fatigue, and better able to tolerate a lack of certainty about how to go on.

According to Judith Butler, crucial to becoming able to resist oppressive norms—for example, norms of people as having certain kinds of bodies (and not others), or of people as having certain ways of being gendered (and not others)—is recognizing the ways individuals continue to survive even when they come up against the edges of what is considered normal. Where norms rub up against and restrict what they can do, such individuals show where the norms need to change. The fact that they continue to live with bodies or ways of being gendered that challenge what it means to be a person or gendered, means that such norms do not have the final say over what living beings can do. Speaking of gender norms in particular, Butler writes, "There are humans, in other words, who live and breathe in the interstices of this [gendered] binary relation, showing that it is not exhaustive; it is not necessary" (2004, 65). Those tenderized by disorientations of illness, trauma, queerness, and migration are also living proof that life beyond norms of immunity, invulnerability, straightness, and state-sanctioned citizenship is possible.

4.4 CONCLUSION

As we have seen, when experiences of illness, trauma, queerness, and migration disorient individuals, they do so for very different reasons, and the tenderizing effects I have described occur in only some of those cases. The fact that in some cases disorientations prompt the tenderizing effects of living unprepared, sensing vulnerability, developing capacities for being in-this-together, and for living partly against the grain of norms does not promise that such shifts will always be beneficial. Disorientations can be unbearable when they are too all-encompassing, when they occur at particularly difficult times in our lives, when they occur too often, or when they last so long as to be exhausting. In other words, the tenderizing effects can go too far. As I will argue at length in chapter 6, the promise of disorientation is contingent; it depends not only on how we experience it, but also on what initiates it, how we make sense of it, and how environments and communities respond to us as disoriented. Social and psychological conditions that position disorientations as livable and valuable are part of what can make disorientations promising.

[5]

INJUSTICE AND IRRESOLUTENESS

> We must move toward the future lacking a clear-cut blueprint of what is to be done and shedding a dogmatic sense of the eternal truth but carrying with us a shared sense of the awareness, values, methods, and relationships necessary to navigate these uncharted waters.
>
> —Scott Kurashige (2012, 21)

> A certain amount of pain, the knowledge about vulnerability and pain, is actually useful. It forces one to think about the actual material conditions of being interconnected and thus being in the world. It frees one from the stupidity of perfect health, and the full-blown sense of existential entitlement that comes with it. Paradoxically, it is those who have already cracked up a bit, those who have suffered pain and injury, who are better placed to take the lead in the process of ethical transformation.
>
> —Rosi Braidotti (2006, 249)

We have seen that disorientations have in some cases played an important role in shaping the way individuals act for the better. In chapters 3 and 4, I presented cases in which disorientations of double consciousness, white ambush consciousness-raising, critical education, illness, trauma, queerness, and migration have had specific effects that I argue are morally promising. In addition to suggesting that philosophers should pay more attention to disorientations, not only because they are ubiquitous and interesting, but also for their surprising moral potential, I have been building a case for the significance of seeing unchosen, non-deliberate actions as undeniable parts of moral life. At this point, I want to shift the focus from *individual agents who are disoriented* to *moral contexts within which disoriented (and non-disoriented) agents act.*

Recall that all my arguments for the moral promise of the effects of disorientation have been premised on the claims I defended in chapter 2: that though the majority of moral psychology and ethics treats "moral action" as synonymous with "decisive, conscious, deliberate, intentional action," there is a need for more attention to the moral promise of experiences that motivate different kinds of awareness or ways of being in the social world, *even when such experiences do not help us decide how to act.* My account of the promise of disorientations relies on a non-resolvist account of moral agency—that is, an account of moral action that considers the moral promise of *non-deliberate and non-decisive actions and ways of being,* instead of only considering deliberate and decisive actions as having the potential to be moral. I have made the case for why and how disorientations can generate certain kinds of awareness and tenderizing effects that can be morally valuable, even when these experiences still do not help us know how to act, because they change how we are and how we relate to others. We have seen how these changes can be valuable in a number of kinds of moral contexts, including contexts of injustice.

In this chapter, I start from a question in the spirit of non-resolvism about what kinds of action can be required for acting against certain kinds of injustice. While many contexts of injustice demand resolute action—action that is purposeful, decisive, confident, and unwavering—I want to suggest they do not always. *Irresolute* actions can be called for.

In the first section, I will outline what would make a particular action irresolute. I will then introduce three kinds of irresolute actions against injustice and make the case for why they should be seen as effective in addressing certain kinds of injustice. Finally, I will argue that we need to understand the importance of *irresolute action against injustice* in order to further understand the position of disorientation in moral life.

5.1 RESOLUTE AND IRRESOLUTE ACTIONS AGAINST INJUSTICE

New injustices are constantly being brought to our attention—those arising in our own communities might seem particularly pressing, while those more distant might require more advanced attention to understand and counteract. Injustices occurring very close to home might include violence against women, poverty, attacks on reproductive rights, policies that threaten public education, or the exploitation of fast-food workers. These kinds of injustice are common, widespread, and ongoing. To address these kinds of harms, individuals might decide to take on regular volunteer hours at a women's shelter, to donate money or goods to a community food bank, to raise awareness about reproductive health through organizing events, to gather signatures on a petition to resist school closures, to boycott certain restaurants, and so on. In addition to long-standing injustices, new pressing harms appear all the time, and individuals work together to respond. When an individual learns about the devastating and disproportionate number of people of color in prisons in the United States and comes to understand the harms of mass incarceration, she might decide to organize a group to read and discuss Michelle Alexander's *The New Jim Crow*[1] or to run a book drive for donation to prisoners.[2]

When a heterosexual woman comes to understand the ways queer friends are harmed by a state's refusal to recognize same-sex marriages, she might vote for the party with the most progressive commitments in favor of same-sex marriage.[3] Upon learning for the first time about the Indian Boarding School System in the United States, and about the legacy of poverty, trauma, and illness that is ongoing, an individual might write letters to municipal or state politicians to protect a free clinic for indigenous people in her community that is threatened with closure.[4] When a citizen learns that 38% of people in Detroit are living in poverty, and that tens of thousands in the city have had their water shut off for being unable to afford rising water bills, she might donate money to organizations that are helping people access water.[5]

Over time, a person's involvement in a particular effort may deepen and she might become more involved in more sustained action against injustice. She might learn more about injustices in prison and police systems, and decide to do whatever she can to raise awareness about stop and frisk practices harming men of color or to lobby for changing mandatory minimum sentencing given how the "war on drugs" punishes the poorest and racialized offenders.[6] She might volunteer to contribute time and money to the Human Rights Campaign's fight for marriage equality in her state.[7] She might attend local hearings of a Truth and Reconciliation Commission into the Boarding Schools.[8] She might create a nonprofit organization that supports the development of urban gardens and local food production.[9]

All of these are actions that individuals can take from various sources of concern for justice. Though agents will often realize that prioritizing some projects will mean not being able to devote as much attention to others, they may feel confident that they are, in some way, contributing to the goal of addressing the injustices in their communities. These actions have effects that in many cases successfully meet important goals—prisoners have access to more books, clinics stay open, police officers may become more cautious about violent action, and same-sex couples may gain marriage rights. Even when actions do not meet their goals quickly or at all, they can have positive side effects, such as building relationships, raising consciousness about the possibilities of confronting unjust systems as ordinary citizens, and so on.

Recall discussion in chapter 2 of the importance of some kinds of moral resolve. In some cases where what I ought to (or ought not to) do is obvious, lacking resolve would be odd: What should be confusing about whether or not to steal someone else's wallet? In other cases, lacking resolve could be even morally reprehensible: Who would hesitate to do everything in their power to prevent hitting a child who dashes in front of their car? Some kinds of actions against injustice are similarly sufficiently clear that it would be odd or reprehensible for agents to be anything but resolute about them. For example, when someone asks an eligible individual to sign a petition with the goal of raising the wages for fast-food workers,[10] where doing so would have the potential to help a great deal of workers approach a living wage, and where we know that in many cases the only benefit of such low wages is extra corporate profit, I think it is obvious that he should resolutely sign the petition. Of course, even in this case, not all people will agree that he should do this, or that he should prioritize this over other actions (e.g., attending protests, boycotting the corporation, or supporting unionization efforts). But at least most people who share this understanding of the context of employment, the needs of workers, and the injustice of exploitation would agree that to be irresolute about whether or not to sign the petition would be odd and potentially troubling.

At other times, however, the complexities of a situation complicate decisions about how to act. Feminists might be among the many agents familiar with contexts where it is hard to feel sure about how to act. We may try to create romantic and kin relationships that do not reproduce or reinforce sexism, even when it is not entirely clear how to do so. We may try to hold each other responsible for expressions of racism and ableism, even while it is not entirely clear what supportive relationships of holding each other accountable should look like. In common feminist language, it is difficult to develop tools for dismantling "the master's house," and all the more difficult the more we know we still partially benefit from its protection.

Think further of cases where agents might commit to joining or leading an action against injustice and later realize they did not know what they were doing. For example, philosopher-activist Dr. Grace Lee Boggs arrived in Detroit in the 1950s as a Marxist committed to joining the struggles of autoworkers. She describes how, upon arrival, she immediately recognized that her expectations were not in touch with the reality of the actual difficulties in the area.[11] Boggs's realization—that she had been preparing to enact a solution to problems other than the ones that actually existed in Detroit—led her to hold off and learn from existing movements in the area. Just as the above kinds of decisive actions are likely familiar to feminists, similar roadblocks to decisive action as Boggs experienced might be familiar. The problem is not what one assumed it would be. Plans for addressing injustice that worked in other contexts may not work where we are now. One's role is suddenly unclear. In such cases, acting decisively (or telling others how to act decisively) has the potential to do harm. I want to suggest that paying more attention to a variety of features of some contexts of injustice reveals something important about what kinds of actions can be effective within them. These are contexts where *irresolute actions*—actions performed without sureness of self—may be called for.

5.2 BOTH/AND ACTIONS, HETEROSEXISM, AND MASS INCARCERATION

Consider how, in some contexts, addressing injustice can require working toward conflicting goals at the same time. Think of a black woman in a white and male-dominated workplace who believes that it is important that she (and other women in the future) be present, so she wants to stay in the workplace as a forerunner. At the same time, she knows that by being there, she functions as a token minority worker—someone others can point to as evidence that they are a diverse, inclusive, or welcoming workplace. As such, she is brought to meetings with clients and shareholders as proof of the office's progressive character. Beyond the many everyday ways that the workplace is likely to be taxing or exhausting, she may be conflicted about her role in standing in the way of outsiders recognizing the persistent sexism and racism within the workplace. She may decide to stay but to do so while feeling conflicted.[12]

We can see further conflicted directions of action in other contexts of justice. While some individuals have responded to the injustice of heteronormative legal systems by working in one direction (e.g., to work with the Human Rights Campaign), other agents have understood marriage as only one kind of goal. Marriage rights are important for many reasons in the United States, where marriage is currently the access point to, among other things, parental rights, health insurance, immigration, and inheritance protection. In states where same-sex marriage rights have not been available, queer individuals have been at much greater risk than married hetero individuals of lacking health care, having their children taken from them, and of being denied the state support available to heterosexual couples through taxes and other credits. All of these harms are over and above the fundamental failure of the state and other citizens to recognize their commitments and spousal relationships as valuable and worthy of support. But at the same time as the same-sex marriage movement has grown, some other queer activists have argued that gaining rights for only those same-sex couples who marry ought not to be the focus of a queer movement. Instead, they have argued for the need to recognize the many other needs of particularly low-income queers and trans people of color, and that what should be given priority is securing access to health care, employment, housing, parenting rights, and protection from state and other violence for all queers, regardless of marriage status.[13]

The goals of fighting for same-sex marriage rights and fighting for access to basic rights for all queer (with particular concern for the most vulnerable low-income queer and trans people of color) might be in tension in more than one sense. For one thing, focusing on one goal will *neglect* the other goal; limited resources, time, or attention might make it so that the choice to focus on one goal means the other goal will not be accomplished as quickly, if ever. Almost any pair of political goals might be in tension in this sense. Paying attention to one cause means less attention is available to be paid to another. But these particular goals might also be in tension in another sense. Pulling toward one goal will *pull against* the other goal, making it not only as of yet unaccomplished, but actually harder to accomplish. Only some goals will be in tension in this second sense. The fight against heteronormativity in the law may be one of them.

Recall Claudia Card's argument against marriage and motherhood (1996). Card noted the important distinction between things the state is unjust to deny to some citizens (which marriage rights certainly are), and things citizens should fight to achieve (which marriage rights are not). The example of slavery helped make the point. In a slave-owning society, if women were denied the rights to own slaves, because of the belief doing so would pervert the institution of slavery, women would be as capable of owning slaves as men, but *it would not follow that women should fight for the right to hold slaves*. Likewise, fighting for same-sex marriage might be seen as reproducing the deeply flawed institution of marriage, which has serious problems (e.g., it makes it likely that bad relationships will be preserved and prevents those abused by spouses from being easily able to leave). Card focuses on how fighting for same-sex marriage would give queers the option (and the "consequent pressures") to get married, despite the real risks of doing so. While the state and other institutions use marriage to provide some benefits to all those who are married, marriage also is dangerous for everyone, and particularly for those married individuals who are most dependent (those with less income, whose immigration depends on marriage, who rely on their spouse for health insurance or care, etc.). As she wrote, "had we any chance of success, we might do better to agitate for the abolition of legal marriage altogether" (Card 1996, 15).

But recall also that Cheshire Calhoun (2003) has argued for a distinct position on the same issue. On Calhoun's view, same-sex marriage is important to fight for, not for some of the commonly cited reasons (for equal access to benefits of marriage or as a route to breaking down sexist gender roles within marriage). Instead, same-sex marriage is worth fighting for because marriage currently constitutes the pre-political foundation of society—families are built on it, and values are passed on through it. Because marriage has the political status of sustaining civil society, to deny queers access to it is to qualify only heterosexuals for the creation and maintenance of civil society.[14]

Gaining access to marriage would give married queers access to many more rights, but continuing to fight for access to rights through marriage gives legitimacy to the practice of using marriage as that access point. It accepts rather than challenges the institution of marriage, so long as more of us can gain access to it, and pulls against the goal of creating better institutions, capable of meeting the needs of everyone. The goals of fighting heteronormativity either through gaining same-sex marriage rights or through directly addressing harms against lower class queers and trans people are in tension in both of the above senses. Prioritizing one means less attention for the other; and pulling in one direction risks pulling against the other (achieving marriage equality might lessen the pressure on states to secure goods for other queers).

Though the injustices of mass incarceration are distinct in many respects from the injustices of heteronormativity, we can see in prison activism a similar tension between efforts to work for different goals. On the one hand, many people (both inside and outside prisons) are working to improve prisoner access to things that would make life in prison less dangerous, debilitating, and life-threatening. For example, incarcerated men and women have worked, in some cases in collaboration with others outside prisons, to ensure health care is received by prisoners who need it,[15] create better access to university education,[16] and provide for aging and ill prisoners at end of life.[17] At the same time, in other cases, those concerned with prison justice have argued that focusing on building institutions within prisons to make the lives of prisoners more livable ought not to be the goal of those concerned with addressing the injustice of prisons—the goal, instead, must be *no more people in prisons*.[18] They have argued, for example, that harm reduction in prison will alleviate the pressure to agitate for changing tough-on-crime legislations that vastly over-incarcerate especially men of color, to fight for early release, and eventually to abolish the prison industrial complex. While privilege has protected some communities from direct harms of prisons, and made it seem like prisons benefit and protect them, in fact prisons make life worse for everyone, and the expansion of the prison industry destroys communities and future lives in ways that make the world less safe for us all (Davis 2012).

Much more would need to be said to flesh out all the current goals of queer and prison activism. I have raised only select goals to highlight a structural quality that I think these contexts share. In these and other similar cases, the tension between goals might be between efforts to reduce harm in current unjust institutions, while at the same time working to create new just institutions. That is, they are examples of people acting in ways which simultaneously aim at different goals: to show that black women are able to succeed in a workplace while also bringing awareness to ongoing sexism and racism there; to ensure legal protections for queer couples while also meeting the needs of all queers; to reduce suffering for prisoners while working to end mass incarceration. It might be *a fact about some contexts of injustice* that working for justice within them requires responding to conflicting calls to action. We might call such responses to conflicting calls "both/and" actions. In some cases where there are in fact conflicting calls to action, both/and actions can be useful. So the question is: In which cases can both/and actions be useful? And what kind of action is able to help work toward *both* same-sex marriage rights *and* recognition for the personhood and needs of non-married queers, or *both* harm reduction in prisons *and* prison abolition?

To answer the first question about how to determine when both/and actions can be useful, note that I am describing an objective feature of some contexts of injustice where both/and actions can be possible and productive. To help clarify this point, consider three kinds of medical cases. In Case 1, a patient has symptoms of what appear to be two medical conditions in need of treatment, when in fact there is only one underlying problem, and it is curable. In Case 2, a patient has two medical conditions, and health care providers must choose to cure only one of them, knowing that whichever they choose will mean the other does not get addressed. In Case 3, a patient has two conditions and the full treatment for either condition will exacerbate the other and cause the patient to suffer; but it is possible for health care providers to gradually address both conditions, slowly improving the patient's quality of life. This may mean that it takes much longer for the patient to get relief, and that complete cures may be ultimately unavailable, but these treatments are the best option available and will be a success if the patient can eventually improve on both fronts.

There are contexts of injustice that parallel each of these kinds of cases. In the first kind of case, agents are called to do only one thing (e.g., to support fast-food workers in raising the minimum wage), even if it *seems* to them that they need to be working toward other goals at the same time (e.g., keeping costs low for corporations so they do not remove their businesses from the area). These are cases where agents may misdiagnose the injustice, and attempt to perform both/and actions, but where there are not actually conflicting calls to action that make such both/and actions appropriate or useful.

In the contexts of injustice that parallel the second kind of medical case, there is a clear moral dilemma, and an agent must prioritize one action over another. To take a simplified scenario, imagine an agent can either attend a protest rally calling for the indictment of a police officer or can attend his regular volunteer hours at the social-justice oriented after school program. Because he cannot be in two places at once, and because both tasks require his physical presence, he cannot do both. The agent might decide to prioritize one goal, having decided that it is in fact the more important goal, and act accordingly: for instance, he might decide that it is most important to meet his regular commitment at the school, and work resolutely toward that goal, consistently prioritizing it over this and other opportunities for public protest. He might take himself to have resolved the dilemma. Alternatively, he might decide to prioritize one goal and work resolutely toward that goal (e.g., meeting his regular commitment at the school), in full knowledge that this will mean failing to meet the other equally important moral requirement (participating in the public protest), and thus be acting confidently, while still seeing himself as failing morally. The literature on moral dilemmas has attended to both of these options, with debate about whether moral dilemmas can be resolved (as in the first case, where one option is judged to be more important), or whether there are dilemmas that are genuine and irresolvable (as in the second case). I agree with Tessman (2015) and others who have argued that there can be genuine moral dilemmas, where agents must choose between two incommensurable options, and thus inevitably fail.

Notice now that, in both these kinds of cases, resolute action is possible and called for. Agents are either called to perform the one action that is called for, or to choose between two actions that are called for. My point here is that, in some cases, another kind of action is possible and called for, which roughly parallels the treatment in the third medical case: by acting *irresolutely*, one can tentatively pursue multiple goals that are in tension with one another. Contexts of injustice like that of heteronormativity and mass incarceration might be like this.

To answer the second question about how such both/and actions can be effective, we can first note that both/and actions are irresolute because an agent cannot wholeheartedly decide to act in conflicting ways. Both/and actions are internally ambivalent: an agent pursues actions that work toward separate worthy goals at the same time. These goals are in tension with one another, such that an agent is in some sense actually acting in tension with herself. To be sure, these goals are more general than the above dilemma of the man who cannot be in two places at the same time. The goals are more temporally extended, and in conflict at a more general level.

For example, an agent can work to make marriage less heteronormative, while at the same time fighting against the relevance of the institution of marriage. As Calhoun's view anticipates, this might mean fighting for marriage rights at the same time as fighting for reducing the central role of marriage relations in structuring civil society. Or, an incarcerated agent can work in prison palliative care programs, caring for dying prisoners, while writing and teaching about the need to dismantle prison programs that cover up the most severe harms of incarceration.

In sum, conflicting calls to action do not exist in every context of injustice, agents may or may not correctly diagnose their existence or absence, and both/and actions are not always useful in response to them. It is much more common to have to choose between possible courses of action in response to injustice, and perhaps even more common to be presented with obviously best strategies in response to injustices (even if such solutions are frightening or unattractive). My claim is just that both/and actions are in some cases useful, and that they are good examples of irresolute actions against injustice. Where conflicting calls to action do exist, and where both/and action is possible and productive, holding a "both/and" perspective is likely to involve more conflicted, trepidatious action, but can lead to action that does justice to the coexistence of important goals that are in tension.

5.3 DOUBLING BACK ACTIONS, IMPLICIT BIAS, AND COLONIALISM

Beyond both/and actions, other responses to injustice involve practices of returning to phenomena again and again, with a critical eye to correcting injustices as they appear and cultivating more just practices. Such practices involve not a one-time action but a committed retreading of the same ground, correcting injustices that have been present (and perhaps even corrected) before, but that continue to arise. In academic hiring contexts, for instance, feminists might remind themselves and their colleagues of the realities of implicit bias, and the need to construct hiring environments that evaluate candidates as much as possible by their fit within hiring criteria, minimizing what research shows are tendencies to privilege candidates from more dominant groups.[19] Because biases typically have impact through unconscious rather than conscious actions, part of the task is becoming aware of how, even with the best intentions or claims to objectivity, feminists themselves may have tendencies of judging candidates from more dominant groups more charitably. These tendencies cannot be unlearned easily—it requires constant vigilance and installing external checks and balances (e.g., standardizing interview questions) to try to work against injustice in academic hiring.

In contexts of combatting injustice against indigenous communities in North America, we have already seen some kinds of effective resolute actions against injustice—for example, fighting the clinic closure, or attending Truth and Reconciliation hearings. But given the complexity of colonial legacies in North America, and the persistent failure to acknowledge our colonial past, it is not surprising that more complex action is also called for. Similar in this respect to contexts of bias in philosophy (while distinct in many others), some colonial contexts may require practices of returning to the same ground to correct injustices and cultivate more just practices.

Some of the actions indigenous individuals have described within their own communities demonstrate this kind of process, and First Nations groups have called for non-indigenous individuals to act in ways which also return to the same ground to correct injustices over time. Processes of decolonization advocated by some indigenous scholars and movement leaders in some cases prioritize living in balanced relationships with others and the land, and creating ways to ensure that language, histories, and practices are alive within indigenous families and communities. Indigenous organizers and theorists describe diverse strategies for decolonizing, and some describe the importance of process, including processes of strengthening indigenous history, language, and practices of sovereignty.[20] These are not processes that involve non-indigenous individuals, though they may be ones settlers can support in external ways.[21] Much of what indigenous scholar/activist Leanne Simpson describes as *indigenous resurgence* begins from practices of strengthening individual senses of connection with generations of strong indigenous communities. Resurgence is not described as a movement toward a defined goal. It is instead a constant process, and a movement toward the creation of new ways of building justice for indigenous communities, against the background of colonialism as a still present condition of North American society, industry, and politics. As Simpson describes it, "living in the right way as individuals sets in motion influences and impacts that are impossible to predict" (2011, 144). Many deliberate, direct actions must be taken to end the further seizure of lands and harms to communities. But Simpson characterizes the indigenous leaders that have influenced her the most as "reluctant leaders" (2011, 121), who lead by empowering others to make decisions, make mistakes, and learn.[22] Processes of resurgence allow for the growth and affirmation of indigenous capacities and power.

For non-indigenous settlers, acting responsibly to decolonize requires following the leadership of indigenous groups. Identifying as *settlers* in the first place involves a practice of coming to open ourselves up to recognizing settler privilege. Being committed to decolonizing means becoming able to recognize colonial habits of perceiving ourselves and others as "rightful owners" or "those who belong here." Doing this involves something partly akin to the practices of recognizing implicit bias—it requires a practice of continual self-evaluation with a commitment to correcting injustices and cultivating more just practices of relating to indigenous communities. Such processes are not straightforward, in part because they are not ones with an end-date.[23]

Some goals of decolonization can be realized. Stopping the extinction of a particular indigenous language,[24] conducting an investigation into the rising numbers of missing and murdered aboriginal women,[25] or making sure indigenous communities have access to safe and secure drinking water[26] are all worthy goals that indigenous individuals and settler allies are fighting for. While there are many obstacles that make it difficult to achieve such goals, they are clear goals that can be met.

Certainly anti-colonial justice will never be reached in the sense of restoring pre-colonial relationships. But perhaps, even setting aside any goal of restoring pre-colonial order, a decolonized future is also not one that can be achieved. The destruction of indigenous lands, knowledge, families, and sovereignty cannot ever be fully rectified, because people, knowledge traditions, languages, the health of lands, and the original possibility of trusting, respectful treaty relationships have all been lost and cannot be recovered intact. New anti-colonial realities are important goals, but they cannot fully recover from the legacies of settler dominance and attempted cultural genocide of indigenous groups. Settlers may not ever decolonize our ways of being. So long as settlers continue to benefit from the legacy of colonialism as we currently do in countless ways—starting from the use of land and resources that were seized by force—we and generations to come will never *not* be responsible. For settlers in anti-colonial social movements, the goal is not only supporting indigenous resurgence but decolonizing our own ways of thinking about nationalism, history, property, resources, state governments, immigration, and so on. Settlers might be called to challenge our own colonial thinking on many levels, all of which can require ongoing reminding and re-correcting. Such challenges might come in the form of asking open questions about the experiences of indigenous communities; for instance, why might it in fact make sense for an indigenous community to refuse to acknowledge the authority of the state?[27] Why might indigenous students in fact deserve full financial support in attending universities? Why might an indigenous community in fact have rights to natural resources that settlers do not? Why might an indigenous community in fact need to maintain their own school system? In other words, settler allies can go some way toward decolonizing—but we should not act from the expectation that our ways of thinking and acting will ever be decolonized.

The case of efforts to correct implicit bias, and the efforts of settlers to decolonize, are examples of a kind of "doubling back"—treading the same ground over and over, where that ground is all the time changing, and we regularly confront injustices as they show up in new and (sometimes) unpredictable ways. "Doubling back" action against injustice is not resolute movement toward a goal, but a constant questioning and challenging of unjust tendencies, and cultivating capacities to hear challenges from others. It is irresolute, precisely because it starts from having destabilized the expectation that one's own judgment is likely to be the best. "Doubling back" is an effort that starts from suspicion about, for example, what parts of colonial relations settlers think of as natural or inevitable. The efforts of settlers to decolonize are "doubling back" actions when they follow the leadership of indigenous people, continually challenge colonial habits of thinking, and adjust to new understandings.

In the same way as there are facts about contexts of prison injustice that make both/and action valuable in such contexts (there are in fact goals that are in tension), there are three main features of some contexts of injustice that can make doubling back action valuable.

Psychological features of a context of injustice might make doubling back action useful. It may be useful in cases where individuals are likely to have psychological habits that make it difficult for them to recognize or work against an injustice (e.g., implicitly trusting the claims of white philosophers more than those of philosophers of color). *Epistemic features* of a context of injustice might further make doubling back action useful. In any case where agents will not be easily able to recognize what would count as justice (e.g., what would count as actual justice in academic hiring), checking and rechecking in with a critical eye to recognizing persistent injustices can be the best way to work toward a goal we do not yet know. And/or *metaethical features* of a context of injustice might make doubling back action valuable. In a case where there is an absence of clear success or, in fact, no state of affairs that would count as responsibilities having been discharged, cultivating open-ended practices and processes of gradually less unjust action might be the best goal. The case of colonial injustice might be an example where all three features are in play. The first two features seem to certainly hold. It is difficult for settlers to recognize the harms of colonialism in everyday life and to know what would count as a decolonized society. The third needs some further consideration: it may be that there is no state that would count as anti-colonial justice having been achieved, while we can recognize states of gradually less colonial injustice.

Doubling back actions are likely to be useful in contexts of injustice with these psychological, epistemic, or metaethical features, and are especially likely to be useful in contexts where all are present. In colonial contexts, doubling back means settlers reminding ourselves that tendencies will continue to pull us toward dominating indigenous groups, thinking that we know best about how to re-establish First Nations and settler relations, and protecting the resources we have gained through colonialism. Constant questioning and an ongoing willingness to have settler assumptions challenged may not be decisive action to decolonize, but it can be effective action given the particular responsibilities we have to decolonize. Practices of doubling back are effective in that they are practices of remembering our place in colonial legacies, and hearing indigenous groups' voices telling us about aspects of the past we have ignored.

None of this is to say that resolute actions will not also be called for in addressing implicit bias or North American colonialism, only that they will not be all that is called for. Of course, it would be more straightforward to become experts at following moral rules (e.g., to follow the rule of holding only direct offenders responsible, punishing the church and state officials that ran the Indian Boarding Schools) than to confront the reality that the harms of colonialism may never be gotten over. We can hear the *desire* for straightforward solutions in settler statements of hope that some kind of reparation or settlement will one day be "enough" to finally "put the history of colonialism behind us" (Regan 2010, 20), or to close the "sad chapter" of colonialism in a nation's history.[28] But being willing to contribute to decolonization efforts only when they are clear to settlers, or only when they have a good shot at accomplishing a recognizable goal—in other words, insisting on acting only once we have resolved how to act—will in some cases fail to challenge our colonial mindset of thinking that settlers know best and that the harms of colonialism are solvable on our own terms.

5.4 BUILDING WITHOUT BLUEPRINTS AND POST-INDUSTRIAL POVERTY

In addition to "both/and" and "doubling back" actions, I want to consider one further kind of irresolute action against injustice. Consider contexts of injustice where institutions have reliably failed members of oppressed groups. For example, think of a university campus where sexual assaults are endemic, graduation rates of low-income women students are low, and queer students complain of homophobia in classrooms. In attempting to create a women's center on a university campus, for example, agents may know what needs the center aims to meet, without having a clear sense of how to build such an institution. They may not know how to set boundaries around who is welcome in leadership positions in the space, how to prioritize projects (e.g., establish child care for university students with children, or establish the first queer pride event on campus?), or how to establish governance and decision-making procedures. They may start from the general goal of creating a non-sexist space to support women on campus, but the specifics of what that space should look like may only develop over time.

Other contexts of injustice provide examples of multiple institutions failing members of oppressed groups concurrently. Contemporary cases of post-industrial urban poverty provide clear examples of such compounded harm. When work becomes scarce, many lives can be endangered. Health care can become even less accessible; homeowners can be threatened by foreclosure; in some areas, basic utilities, education, and food security may be threatened; and neighborhoods can become vulnerable to restructuring at the hands of outside speculators. Of course, many kinds of responses to these contexts are possible and different positions on a political spectrum suggest different courses of action. There are questions of whether more reliable state control of resources (e.g., education or basic utilities) should be the goal, and, at the same time, concerns about trusting particular governments, particularly when in cases of financial crisis, democratically elected officials are at risk of being replaced by unelected Emergency Managers. In addition to the resolute efforts to respond to the needs of those in poverty already discussed (e.g., donating water, developing urban food production), some actions against injustice in these contexts work to build systems that it is not yet clear how to build.

One strand of action happening in post-industrial contexts, and particularly in urgent cases where the health and survival of individuals is at risk, is a move for strengthened self-determination and the capacities of individuals to provide for themselves. In this vein, people are working to build institutions to meet the basic needs of communities, without having from the beginning a clear sense of all that will be required in order to do so. They are working together to envision and enact alternative ways of meeting everyone's needs for education, work, health care, community safety, food production, and housing, without relying on systems they have learned are not reliable. Following Scott Kurashige, quoted in the epigraph of this chapter, we might understand these as actions that aim to "build without blueprints."

For instance, in Detroit and other post-industrial cities, individuals have faced extreme poverty and, in many cases, have no real option of leaving to find work elsewhere. Working against the injustice of this context requires, to put it simply, confronting a system of social organization that makes it each individual's private responsibility to manage their own risk and take care of their own, or else be seen as undeserving of life chances. It also means challenging these systems often without having been raised to believe that another way of relating to others could be possible. Action against injustice in these contexts requires challenging the systems of social organization on which many of us still rely (including systems of property that say an individual deserves whatever she can earn), and from which the most privileged of us benefit greatly. Having challenged the systems we have relied on, we will need to build new ones.

In Detroit, community organizations committed to creating caring communities have started schools focused on place-based education, alternative possibilities for work and production, community-based approaches to preventing and responding to violence, substantial initiatives to produce healthy food that will stay in communities, and programs to defend homeowners against eviction.[29] Community groups have sought guidance from other organizations, from the history of effective social movements, and from social and natural sciences investigating solutions for living in contexts with scarce resources. They have prioritized the process of building new frameworks and relationships capable of meeting everyone's needs. All these efforts can be understood as expressions of "prefigurative politics," where, as organizer and sociologist Chris Dixon has clarified, the core idea is that "*how* we get ourselves to a transformed society (the means) is importantly related to *what* that transformed society will be (the ends). The means *prefigure* the ends" (Dixon 2014, 84–85).

Such efforts exemplify irresolute action insofar as there is no formula to follow for meeting everyone's needs, and perhaps not even a clear sense of all the needs to begin with. Possible solutions will be attempted and revised, and they will be better the more revisable they are. Consequences of such actions will not be fully predictable. Ideally they will be solutions that can change and grow as the needs of communities change over time, and that can connect with and mutually support other plans for meeting needs. For example, educational systems should be compatible with health care systems, and these should work together to meet needs as efficiently as possible, but it is unlikely that all the complexities in building such systems will be clear to agents before they make mistakes and learn from them. Indeed, action that aims to build new social systems without a blueprint will likely be best the more it is open to becoming multipurpose and revisable. The way that these new systems eventually will be devised to meet everyone's needs may be as yet unclear to individuals in these contexts.

Just as there are facts about prison injustice that make both/and action valuable, and facts about colonial injustice that make doubling back action valuable, there can be facts about contexts of post-industrial poverty that make efforts to build without blueprints valuable. For one thing, it is a fact about contexts of post-industrial poverty that working for justice requires, in part, challenging existing systems of social organization that still support some people. In many such cases, we do not have practice living apart from such systems of social organization—there are not yet practiced alternatives available in our contexts.

The need to challenge systems of social organization is one that may be partially met through decisive action. Individuals can vote for state representatives that seem aware of the need for supporting individuals apart from their status as productive workers. We can fight for a living wage for low-income workers, and for a health care system that guarantees affordable care for everybody, regardless of income. But, in some urgent cases, and in cases where governments and economic systems have a track record of failing to meet the needs of the most impoverished, challenging such systems also requires coming up with innovative ways to meet communities' needs *now*. In such contexts, irresolute action to "build without blueprints" can be very effective.

Even without clear guides, agents may create structures for providing for themselves through the strengthening of relationships and consensus among those who most need new systems for food production, education, security, health care, and so on. While there may be some possibilities for decisively, confidently challenging systems some of us lean on, the more we lean on them, the more frightening it is likely to be to challenge them. Even in places where the systems still seem intact for some people (e.g., where some have health insurance, or where some neighborhoods have high-quality schools), the same systems are already failing some people who fall through the cracks (e.g., people who are not seen as "productive"). Meeting everyone's needs requires challenging the adequacy of these systems and, at least in some cases, building new ones. How to develop ways of life that do not depend on what we have until now depended on may be not fully clear.

5.5 CONCLUSION

As we have seen, in contexts of injustice with particular features, both/and, doubling back, and building without blueprints actions can be valuable. To be clear, note the main difference between the resolute and irresolute actions I am describing here. As I have suggested, actions can be irresolute for different reasons. In some cases actions are irresolute because they are simultaneously trying to bring about different or conflicting goals. In others, actions are irresolute when they involve an ongoing set of practices that do not work toward a goal. In still others, actions are irresolute because individuals are building new institutions without knowing how to doing so. We can *decide* to maintain actions that are irresolute, but there will still be the constant questioning, tentativeness, and openness to correction. In short, the real difference between resolute and irresolute action in these cases is the possibility or impossibility of performing them with *sureness of self*.

The kinds of action that people perform irresolutely are only one part of the collection of kinds of action against injustice. Many kinds of injustice can be addressed resolutely. As we have seen, even the complex contexts of injustice I have described have features that can be addressed decisively; my view does not entail that irresolute actions are the *only* important and useful actions within these complex contexts of injustice. Irresolute actions may not even be *required* by such contexts; I have not argued that irresolute actions are necessary. Rather, I have claimed only that one effective way to address features of complex injustices like conflicting calls to action, unmeetable responsibilities, and the need to challenge systems individual lean on is by "both/and," "doubling back," and "building without blueprints" responses to injustice, all of which are irresolute actions. My goal has been to defend the straightforward claim that irresolute actions are in some cases useful within contexts of injustice. Stepping back from this discussion, we can recall how dominant the philosophical assumption is that what it means to take a *real* stand against injustice is in every case to decide on a course of action and perform it confidently in the face of resistance. The philosophical legacy of resolvism limits understandings of actions against injustice, just as it limits philosophical understandings of moral action more generally.

Disorientations may or may not generate the three kinds of irresolute actions I have discussed (both/and, doubling back, and building without blueprints). My goal has not been to argue that they do. Whether or not disorientations generate capacities for these particular irresolute actions, if I am right that there are facts about contexts of justice where irresolute actions are helpful, then two points are important. First, individuals who believe that resolute action is required will be less likely to perform these particular kinds of useful actions. They might instead perform more resolute actions, like protesting a clinic closure or organizing a book drive. In some cases, doing so will be helpful, but in the cases I have described, it will not accomplish everything. Second, some kinds of experiences might make an agent more able to function irresolutely in contexts of injustice. Part of what has been established in chapters 3 and 4 is that disorientations can be one such kind of experience. In addition to the specific arguments I have provided for the particular capacities of disorientations to generate awareness (chapter 3) and tenderizing effects (chapter 4), in cases where disorientations generate *capacities to function without resoluteness,* such disorientations might help individuals act well in contexts of injustice where irresoluteness can be useful. We have seen that disorientations have had their beneficial effects partly by allowing agents to act even without feeling certain about what they know, or without feeling fully prepared for what will come. One need not be disoriented to be able to function without resoluteness, but in some cases, it helps.

Just as in the cases of awareness and tenderizing effects, not everyone who is disoriented will become more able to function in contexts where irresoluteness is required. In cases of disorientation where individuals gain capacities to cope with severe experiences of not-knowing-how-to-go-on, as individuals who live with disorientations often do, such abilities may themselves have political use. Given that there are contexts of injustice where irresolute action is in fact valuable, and given that people who have experienced disorientations are in some cases more able to function without resoluteness (in addition to being agents shaped by other beneficial effects), this offers a further dimension of the value of disorientations in moral life.

I have elsewhere argued for a distinct claim: that *acting responsibly against injustice can be disorienting* (Harbin 2014b). That point builds on traditions in feminist ethics and political theory from the 1980s to the 2000s that have accounted for how confronting intersecting systems of oppression can be deeply challenging and uncomfortable.[30] Some of my claims in this chapter about the particular characteristics of complex contexts of injustice also help make sense of why agents might be disoriented when trying to address such contexts. These and other complexities of contexts of injustice can be disorienting to face and respond to. The claim I have argued for here fleshes out this picture: there are *facts about some contexts of injustice* that make it such that some of the actions effective in working within such contexts will be irresolute ones.

This point holds whether agents are disoriented by such contexts or not, and whether agents gain capacities for acting irresolutely from experiences of disorientation, or in other ways.

Note finally that, political promise notwithstanding, I have not argued here for a responsibility to cultivate irresoluteness in action against injustice. Rather, I have tried to do justice to the ways that some actions that serve important purposes in some complex cases of injustice can be ones it is not possible to enact resolutely. My goal has been to defend the existence and importance of irresolute actions against injustice, rather than to make the case for the necessity of practicing or cultivating them.

[6]

DISORIENTATION AND HABITABILITY

We learn to live with the strangest things.
—Havi Carel (2008, 125)

Acceptance, non-aggrandized daily "living with" unsupported by fantasies of overcoming or restitution, may in its quiet way be as profoundly admirable as integrity in those situations which permit no reconstructive address. I would call this, simply, grace.
—Margaret Urban Walker (2003, 27)

As we have seen, unsettling as they can be, disorientations are all too common parts of life. Disruptive, difficult, and upsetting life events can be disorienting, but so can expected or exciting events. Romance, work, or aging can all be deeply disorienting even if they are completely expected. Becoming a parent—a relatively common and, for some, voluntary experience—can be anything but predictable and smooth.[1] Amidst experiences of intense fatigue, sadness, and feeling upended, it can seem for new parents like there are basically two options: take the chaos in stride or be diagnosed with a mental illness.[2] Openly recognizing how commonly people are disoriented by experiences like new parenthood is part of what can help shift the question from "Should we or should we not diagnose?" to "What can make this experience more bearable?"

I have argued for a new understanding of the position of some experiences of disorientation in individuals' moral lives. Disorientations are a spectrum of widely varying experiences that in all cases disrupt everyday ways of acting and being. As we have seen, the effects of disorientations are very different in different cases. In all cases, we have seen that particular kinds of disorientations can generate particular effects, though they do not always.

This chapter addresses the implications of my view for how we should respond to disorientations. To answer these questions, we need to first be clear about two facts about the position of individuals when disoriented: (1) disorientations are experienced and expressed by individuals in the midst of relations with others; and (2) others' responses to one's disorientations can make a difference to the effects of disorientations on one's life.

My claim that disorientations in some cases have morally beneficial effects has prescriptive implications. The extent to which disorientations can benefit agency depends in part on the ways disoriented people are responded to in communities. As such, we may have a moral responsibility to respond to the presence of disorientations in our own and others' lives in ways that facilitate their beneficial effects and a further responsibility to create social conditions that support rather than alienate or harm individuals who are disoriented.

6.1 DISMISSING DISORIENTATIONS

Disorientations can dislocate and incapacitate across various degrees of privilege, and various contexts of privilege and marginalization can support us in different ways while disoriented.

The relation of privilege to experiences of disorientation is complex. Members of privileged groups can have access to material supports less available to others, such as financial resources, professional security, access to counseling, and the general luck of being seen as someone "in a rough patch" rather than being immediately judged as unreliable, immature, or a failure. At the same time, with various kinds of privilege also can come, for example, expectations that one will be too self-controlled to be deeply disoriented or that one will be able to recover independently. Positions of privilege that provide material comforts, time, and space to experience being disoriented are not necessarily conditions hospitable to disorientations. As bell hooks (1984) attests, marginalization happens at the group level, and marginalized communities are often deeply supportive of their members. Marginalized communities may also be aware of the disorientations their members are likely to experience. At the same time, as has been clear in many of my examples, the more marginalized one is, the less leeway one can receive in contexts of medicine, education, and employment. A marginalized person's disorientation can be more likely to be seen as their own fault, and less likely to be seen as suggesting a need for social support. The specifics of how privilege shapes our experiences of disorientation are murky, like the specifics of exactly which social conditions could guarantee that disorientations have good rather than bad outcomes. But it is clear that social frameworks have the power to partly shape not only what experiences we have, but also how such experiences affect us, how we perceive them, and what we do in response.

Though disorientations have varied widely across the different contexts described throughout the book, a point that has been in the background of every case is the importance of those who are around individuals who are disoriented, who listen to and support them—that is, the *interpreters*. In some first-person accounts, interpreters are central figures. They are the family members, friends, coworkers, and medical professionals who are around the person in, for example, grief, consciousness-raising groups, or trauma. In larger studies, the role of the interpreters is sometimes less clear (though there, too, the importance of support systems is often investigated, and the researchers themselves become one kind of interpreter).

Feminist philosophers of emotion have established that what feelings an individual can have depend to some extent on what feelings they are enabled to express to others.[3] Feelings are politically salient personal experiences allowed for or prevented by those who interpret a person's expression of those feelings. As such, emotions are not equally available to or expressible by everyone.[4] It is more possible for some people to be angry and express anger than others, depending in part on their position in social groups or society writ large, and depending on the presence or absence of sympathetic interpreters.[5] As such, an individual's experience and expression of disorientation depends to some extent on people allowing her to express disorientations, and interpreting her expressions accurately as expressive of disorientation. Without an interpreter of my expression of disorientation, I may be more likely to doubt, question, or dismiss my own experience. I may not then *have* the experience of disorientation in the same way.

In some cases, disoriented individuals may be responded to by sympathetic interpreters. That is, they may find themselves able to express experiences of disorientation to others who are able to help facilitate, validate, and perhaps clarify, this expression. In other cases, disoriented individuals may be *dismissed* in the sense Sue Campbell has described:

> What we feel can be ... distorted or constricted in interpretive communities that are unsympathetic ... being dismissed [is] when what we do or say, as assessed by what we would have

described as our intentions in the situation, is either not taken seriously or not regarded at all in the context in which it is meant to have its effect.[6] (Campbell 1997, 165-166)

For instance, if someone advises a recently grieving spouse to see a doctor, having barely listened to his description of sleeplessness, anxiety, and listlessness, they may fail to allow him to express the disorientation of loss.[7] He may be seen as "just depressed." If a college student returns home the summer after freshman year questioning his religious commitments, and his family refuses to talk about his experience, they may fail to allow him to express disorientation and he may question what he actually feels. He may be seen as "just having a teenaged crisis." If a woman tells her husband how out of place she feels in her life after participating in a consciousness-raising group, trying to express that she feels she does not know how to go on, and he responds by calling the experience nonsense and encouraging her to remember how much happier they had been before she started attending such groups, she may feel deeply critical of herself and try to shake off the feeling. She may be dismissed as "silly" or "self-obsessed." If someone tells a new parent that their experience is completely normal, to be expected, or exactly what they themselves once experienced, the effect may be comforting for some ("I am not alone"), but may also aim to orient the experiencer within the disorientation ("I am overtired, this will pass, I shouldn't dwell on this"), preventing the individual from expressing (and actually experiencing) how strange life feels. They may be dismissed as "just inexperienced." Particular dismissals can be more motivated than others by a reluctance to grant authority to marginalized individuals to understand their own experiences (e.g., women, elders, or individuals with disabilities). But in all cases, the dismissal of *expressions* of disorientation can mean that such individuals are not able to *experience* disorientations in the sense that could be beneficial. If others do not understand me as disoriented, I may not understand my own experience as disorientation.

While they typically do not express having received sympathetic uptake from everyone in their lives, nor perhaps at all points in their experiences, the cases of disorientations I have discussed are ones where individuals have not been wholly dismissed in their expressions of being disoriented. Many of the individuals I have discussed received uptake and went on to express their experiences in more public ways—in writing, teaching, or performing. Their public expressions may have helped assure others who have been disoriented that they would not be alone in that experience. While being able to access others' expressions through their writing or teaching is not a substitute for being able to express one's own experiences and receive uptake by sympathetic interpreters, it is another important way of being and feeling supported.[8]

The first point I want to note in considering the responsibilities that could exist for responding to individuals who are disoriented is that being able to have and express experiences of disorientation is crucially important to the positive effects of disorientations I have tracked throughout the book. Without being able to express experiences of disorientation, individuals may not experience motivation beyond moral resolve introduced in chapter 2, the awareness described in chapter 3, or the tenderizing effects of chapter 4. In other words, the possibility that disorientations will benefit individuals as I have described depends in part on each individual's ability to have and express such experiences. And that depends on the existence of at least some sympathetic interpreters.

Further complicating the interpersonal responsibilities that may exist, people also often experience disorientations *around other people who are also disoriented* (by the same or different events). Joan Didion is disoriented in grieving her husband in the company of her friends, who are also disoriented. Feminist teachers and students in feminist classrooms may be disoriented by the same pedagogical moment. Havi Carel is disoriented by the same illness that disorients her partner. Individuals will experience disorientations differently in these cases, but multiple people may be disoriented together. In some cases, the individuals who have responsibilities to be sympathetic interpreters will be disoriented themselves.

On this point, it is important to recognize how multiple individuals can be disoriented by one event in very different ways, depending on who they are and their social identities. Returning to chapter 3's discussion of white ambush in George Yancy's *Black Bodies, White Gazes*, I think Yancy is right to assume that, in Du Bois's case of double consciousness in the schoolyard, the "tall white newcomer" acted in ways that disoriented Du Bois (refusing his visiting card), while she herself was not likely disoriented at all. In other cases, however, both individuals may be disoriented in different senses. For example, I may be disoriented by an action of mine that reveals my own racism, while that action at the same time disorients someone who is harmed by racism. Realizing this would not diminish the racism at work (the racialized person is harmed, the white person is not), but I think it should direct attention to the relational dynamics of white ambush or other disorientations. In response, I think we need to ask how the disorientations of privileged individuals in contexts of injustice can be understood alongside and in the context of the disorientations experienced by those most harmed by the injustices. When more than one individual becomes disoriented at the same time, by the same event—for example, by a hate crime in the community, or a natural disaster—the particular instances of disorientation might become more complex. How do experiences of disorientation change when multiple individuals experience them together? What implications might this have for considering repair in such cases?[9]

The role of supportive others will be very different in different cases of disorientation, but the point so far is that in all cases dismissal is possible and sympathetic interpretation required. Building on this basic sense of responsible ways of relating to those who are disoriented, I now want to turn to making two prescriptive claims: (1) members of communities can have responsibilities to create social conditions hospitable to those who are disoriented; and (2) as individuals, we can have a responsibility to respond to ourselves as disorientable. I will consider each in turn.

6.2 RESPONDING TO DISORIENTED OTHERS

If families, friend groups, political communities, schools, universities, churches, workplaces, and medical and criminal justice systems see disorientations as best avoided, disoriented individuals can face a serious lack of support and social/institutional isolation. Insistence on the social threat of disorientation and the social good of reorientation can take subtle or dramatic forms in practice. Disoriented individuals can be encouraged to distance themselves from personal relationships, can be seen as incompetent parents, asked to leave workplaces for some period of time, evaluated as academically unsuccessful, medicalized, or can face heightened surveillance by criminal justice systems. Such practices institute an imperative: reorient or face ongoing social exclusion.

Some social conditions can keep individuals in periods of disorientation not by being hospitable but by being *in*hospitable, for example, by responding to a disoriented person's behavior and needs in ways that further alienate or marginalize her. Hospitable conditions might be thought of as those that make disorientations more livable where we find ourselves, for example, through making homes, workplaces, and towns places where it is acceptable to feel and act somewhat disoriented. In cases where disorientations cause individuals to become open and susceptible to the influence of others, those who interact with us when we are disoriented can have a great deal of influence and power.

I am using the term "livable" to describe, roughly, "experiences that people can survive and not feel desperately overwhelmed by." For a period of disorientation to be livable is for it to be bearable in both the near and longer term. Because, as we have seen, different individuals have different capacities to bear experiences of different kinds, the kinds of disorientations that count as livable will differ from person to person. Any response to disorientation that drives people to forcefully reorient or to pursue violent action is clearly not livable, nor does "livable" mean just barely tolerable. I am not suggesting that there are responsibilities to create conditions that make disorientations enjoyable. Rather, I am using the term "hospitable" to describe the kinds of conditions that are accepting and supportive of people who are disoriented. As disorientations vary widely, the kinds of support individuals need when disoriented will vary from case to case. What conditions are hospitable for individuals facing serious illness may be very different from those best able to support participants in consciousness-raising groups. In general, I want to suggest hospitable conditions are those that allow people to be disoriented while having their needs met (e.g., a place to live) and while remaining connected to meaningful parts of their lives—to being able to care for loved ones, enjoy their relationships, do meaningful activities and/or work, and pursue long-term and short-term projects. Again, my intention has been to reject the received view that disorientations are inevitably bad and orientedness inevitably good, while emphasizing that disorientations are a non-homogeneous set of experiences, and without ever denying that disorientations *can be* harmful or that reorientations can be helpful.

A common way of dismissing experiences of disorientation is to encourage those who are disoriented to simply reorient. Individuals in some cases communicate (sometimes explicitly) that they would rather not discuss a person's disorientation, unless she is willing to be upbeat about it.[10] In other cases, people simply offer advice for how an individual can get over what troubles him. We might think of suggestions that cancer patients should *stay positive*. As Barbara Ehrenreich (2010) claims, responses to breast cancer too often suggest that staying positive may be sufficient to get one out of terrible circumstances, and that if one insists on remaining negative, she may be doomed to suffer. Responses to disorientations that promote positive psychology are likely to isolate individuals in their experiences, making them feel they are the only ones finding some kind of experience hard.

Through interacting with insensitive others, disoriented individuals can learn to keep their guards up. By contrast, through interacting with sensitive others while disoriented, in some cases, individuals open up. Sympathetic interpreters might ask questions that invite disoriented individuals to say more about their experience, without the demand that they put it in a positive light.[11] Sympathetic interpreters might support disoriented individuals in ways that maintain everyday routines. They might simply stay with friends who are disoriented, not leaving them too much alone.[12]

The need for hospitable responses to disorientations is clearly visible in contexts of home life, since often the people most directly involved with the disorientations of others are loved ones. The responses of family members in the broadest sense (including parents, partner(s), friends, kin, children, and extended family) to one's disorientation may be the first, most sustained, or most significant. The ways families support individuals in their disorientations—during job losses, illness and diagnosis, home foreclosures—can be the most automatic and unquestioned. Families can provide

DISORIENTATION AND HABITABILITY

individuals safe places to live, material supports, and company. At the same time, as we have seen, some kinds of disorientations are ones partly triggered or accompanied by familial conflict or absence; grief, consciousness-raising, queerness, and migration are among such examples.

Part of the way communities can be supportive of individuals who are disoriented is by generating supportive new subsets of communities, or new constellations of people. These subsets can take the form of various forms of support groups or community organizations. Taking the example of new parents as one group who may be disoriented by any number of things (related to parenting or otherwise), we can see examples of mutual support through difficult times in community groups aimed at new parents, co-operative community daycares, informal ways of sharing parenting responsibilities within and among family and friends, schools, and people who simply give parents a break from parenting or other responsibilities for shorter or longer periods of time. Such responses to the disorientations of parents are not complicated—they are simply humane responses to others in difficult times. They are responses that make it possible for disoriented individuals to remain in their lives, with additional support. Support groups also exist for people who are in grief, as in the case of one "Weekly Walkers" group in Halifax, Nova Scotia, part of a hospital-based Palliative Care Bereavement Program, providing "a safe and supportive walking group for anyone living with grief, meet every Wednesday from 11 a.m. to noon (rain or shine)." Many different support groups exist for individuals facing illness or their loved ones, as Remen (2006, 226-227) describes the Commonweal Cancer Program, a retreat center for people with cancer in Northern California that gives patients opportunities to talk about their experience of illness beyond talking about treatment plans. Church groups, addiction recovery meetings, and book clubs can serve similar purposes.

While such groups can be some of the most important supports in an individual's life while disoriented, it is important to note that they are still made up of individuals whose narratives about their own experiences may be shaped by the desire to feel (or to portray or remember themselves as feeling) oriented. As such, support groups can be dismissive of disorientations. Participation in some group may require, for instance, that new parents fit into that group's established norms (e.g., of who can be considered a mother, of what is acceptable to feed one's child, of what styles of discipline are acceptable), which means that not all new parents may have access to the support of new parenting groups, and/or they may need to be relatively oriented when it comes to certain commitments in order to be welcome. The same can be true of all support groups, including those for grief, illness, addiction, or divorce. Responses to disorientations that take distance from the person because he is perceived as too dramatic or difficult, or that position disorientations as taboo or private topics not to be discussed publically, or that question a disoriented person's reliability as a good parent, patient, co-worker, and so on, make disorientations less livable and more difficult than they already are. Such responses make it seem that people can either be good agents, or disoriented, but not both. Ehrenreich's experience of compulsory positivity in breast cancer support groups is a case of enforced norms of what it is to be a "good patient," which is to say, among other things, a case of classist and ableist norms of thinking about personal responsibility for health outcomes. If they are to truly support individuals who are disoriented, support groups must be aware of tendencies to institute requirements that individuals be or become reoriented in particular ways, and they must work against such tendencies.

Individuals may also feel more supported in disorientations when they have ongoing meaningful work to do, which opens questions about the responsibilities workplaces and other institutions may have to respond to those who are disoriented.[13] Individuals experiencing serious illness may feel more able to manage treatments if they can continue to interact with coworkers about news at work, do altered or partial tasks as they have the strength to, and look forward to returning to the familiarity and enjoyable parts of a work schedule. Ongoing possibilities for meaningful work can allow individuals to draw strength and pleasure from recognizing and exercising their capacities, even as it does not make their grief or illness less disorienting. If disorientations slow individuals down, an environment that does not force them to rush will seem to be more hospitable than one that does.[14] The call to create hospitable workplaces for individuals who are disoriented connects to claims feminists and others have made about the need to make workplaces friendly to those who have particular responsibilities and needs outside the work environment—for example, (mainly) women who have caregiving responsibilities for children and ill or older family members, or people with disabilities or chronic illness who need a work environment and schedule that allows for their needs (such as for rest or healthcare) to be met. More broadly, the call for hospitable workplaces builds on the work done by labor organizers who have ensured that workers be recognized as persons deserving of well-being quite apart from their capacities for productivity. Particularly those workplaces and coworkers that shape conditions of employment around one's needs over time (rather than just temporary family or sick leaves) support those who are disoriented while allowing them to remain in their work lives. Sometimes this is discussed in workplaces as the need to support employees in achieving "work-life balance" (though, of course, "balance" is a loaded term that can leave in place the assumption that the responsibility falls to the individual worker to perform the balancing act). The less secure one's employment is, and the more replaceable one is seen to be as a worker, the less likely supports and flexibility will be in the workplace (e.g., a tenured university professor is more likely to receive accommodation than an adjunct university instructor, who in turn may be more likely to receive accommodation than hotel cleaning staff or fast-food workers).

Supports for disoriented workers range from informal or covert efforts of coworkers to support each other (taking on more of the heavy work, covering for each other when absence is necessary) to formal stress leaves or changes in position. Subtle failures to support disoriented workers are evident when workplaces insist that workers be either completely "on" or face being fired. Workplaces are likely to be better responsive to disorientations the more they understand work to be only part of people's lives, and a more central focus at some times than others. Seeing work this way makes it more likely for individuals to remain in workplaces while disoriented during transitional periods of grief, illness, new family responsibilities, or recovery from trauma. Given that paid work is often important for our capacities to house, feed, and support ourselves, such workplaces will make disorientations more survivable. Again, different disorientations will require different responses from workplaces. Because the same aspects of life that can trigger some disorientations can make one less likely to have secure employment in the first place (e.g., racialization, queerness, migrant status), supporting all individuals who are disoriented can require more than augmenting policies for current employees, but also can require considerations of who is least likely to be hired and supported at all.

Part of what makes disorientations difficult are experiences of loss—loss of decisiveness, loss of independence, or loss of productivity. And, part of what makes such loss so difficult is that the social world is currently such that it does not make real interdependence and a life beyond productivity seem livable. Especially in conditions of austerity, individuals are often inclined to think we are responsible for our own security, to blame for acquired insecurity (e.g., of the kind when a serious illness makes it impossible to live alone, work, or self-finance), and in need of privacy above all else. Part of the big picture of what it will mean to make conditions hospitable to those who are disoriented is to recognize that individuals are not fundamentally independent, productive, financially secure workers. There are various ways to make disorientations more livable, from sympathetic listening and flexible workplaces, to a broader level of disputing the adequacy of the "American Dream."

Beyond work contexts, as I described in chapter 1, there can be a tendency in medical and psychiatric contexts to position disorientations as disorders. As such, medical contexts can be inhospitable to disorientations.[15] Such tendencies stem from the persistent sense that disorientations are dangerous and exclusively negative parts of agents' lives, experiences that only compromise and never support agency, relatively rare, and best ended or avoided. Other very serious responses to disorientations involve forced institutionalization in medical facilities, detention centers, or prisons. In such cases, individuals are often described as a threat to themselves or others. It should be considered in these cases how much the judgments about a person's threat may stem from anxieties about her as disoriented, and the harmful effects that completely removing an individual from her/his environment and communities are likely to have.

Likewise, students like those discussed in chapter 3, who experience the disorientations of feminist education, can require support. Educators can create educational contexts more hospitable to disorientations in part by becoming better able to recognize their students' capacities for experiencing disorientations. If educators and others can recognize the fragility of such moments of disorientation, they might be more likely to guard against the flippant, arrogant, and bulldozing behavior of students in such moments.

In all these contexts, the ways others respond to individuals who are disoriented can offer a "toehold," a kind of trustworthy support, often found in the secure friendship or committed presence of another or others. The main function of others as toeholds is not to interact with us in ways that reorient us, so much as to meet us in ways that make disorientations livable. They do so by relating to us in ways that do not require that we act oriented in order to interact with them, that we be on our way to reorientation, or that we understand our own disorientations. In doing so, they respond to us in ways that are generous and interpretively open to our experiences. Others can be toeholds even when disoriented themselves, as when Didion's colleagues arrive after her husband dies, and when Brison's husband cares for her after her assault. What it means to be a toehold is to stay in a relationship with a disoriented person, without the expectation that there ought to be reorientation, with a willingness to ask questions and offer help in ways that maintain the possibility of the disoriented person continuing in everyday life.

Someone might object that my claim that we should create social conditions more hospitable to disorientation is in tension with my claim that disorientations in some cases have been productive, insofar as the *strain* of being disoriented in our current context might be part of what makes disorientations productive. None of the accounts I have drawn on here identify supports that made them less disoriented, only ones that ensure they were not punished or wholly excluded from social life for being disoriented. Conditions need to be both hospitable to people who are disoriented and expectant that they will continue to be participating, responsible, relational members of a community, which is to say, not encouraged to wallow in disorientations with disregard for the needs and experiences of others. Appropriate conditions would not make disorientations any less disorienting, but would make them more livable, for however long they last.

The questions to ask when making efforts to create conditions hospitable to individuals who are disoriented should not be: How will we know in advance which disorientations will help and which will harm? And what will ensure the benefits of disorientations? Instead, central questions should be: How can we create conditions for social life that do not require individuals to be and feel oriented in order to participate? How will social conditions and ways of relating change if we come to expect that disorientations will occur and may be meaningful parts of persons' lives?

6.3 RESPONDING TO ONESELF AS DISORIENTABLE

Beyond the responsibilities we can have to support disoriented others in these ways, individuals can also have responsibilities to respond in particular ways to the possibility of becoming disoriented ourselves. We have seen that individuals relate to disorientations in part through judgments we make and cultivate about ourselves as disoriented, and the attitudes we take within experiences of disorientations and in anticipation of, or retrospection on, them.[16] To respond to ourselves as disorientable might be framed as a call to a complex combination of attitude, judgment, identification, and action. We may need to work to become able to recognize our disorientability.

Relating to oneself as disorientable within periods of disorientation is an attitude in contrast to thinking oneself immune or thinking experiences of disorientation juvenile or a luxury. The contrast case is when an individual refuses to acknowledge how disorientations might have happened in the past, might be shaping one's experience in the present, or might be affecting one's possibilities for agency in the future. We saw resistance to disorientation already in chapter 1's survey of philosophical accounts of experiences like disorientations, as in, for example, Peirce's characterization of our tendencies to "cling tenaciously" to what we believe (Peirce 1955, 10). Instead, an individual might be called to anticipate and reflect on disorientations more openly, judge himself less harshly or violently as they are happening, and to identify as disorientable. Doing so involves a degree of acceptance of disorientations as common, and of oneself as someone who can be affected by them.

Although we cannot control whether disorientations are part of our lives, the way we respond to them can alter their effects. An individual can refuse to think of himself as disorientable, perhaps thinking he does not have time to have his attention diverted, is not interested in becoming more vulnerable, or that engaging with disorientation would threaten his position or sense of self-worth. In such a refusal, the agent may accurately gauge disorientation's potential power and yet deny or block the way the effects of disorientations can benefit him. While such a response may not have the power to keep him from feeling disoriented, doing so may actually alter his experience of such disorientation. As I argued at the beginning of this chapter, interpretations of a person's experience (by himself and others) can shape what experiences the person can actually have. Refusing to acknowledge that "I am the kind of person who could experience X" does not automatically make me immune from having that experience. If I refuse to acknowledge that I could be a jealous person, I may still be jealous of my friend. But my refusal to acknowledge that I could be the kind of person who becomes jealous *can* alter the way I have, interpret, and express the experience, and in some cases it can alter the way that experience affects me. Likewise, a person's refusal to acknowledge that he might be disoriented by the diagnosis of illness can alter how he experiences, interprets, and is affected by that experience. Such refusals are not ones individuals learn on their own: dominant cultural narratives (e.g., of masculinity and invulnerability) and the reactions of others make a difference to how one is likely to see oneself.

The call to respond to ourselves as disorientable is not a call to identify as disoriented, so much as to identify as one who accepts periods of disorientation as complex and at least potentially meaningful parts of all people's lives. The call to respond to ourselves as disorientable is relevant both for when we are in periods of disorientation, and in relating to potential disorientations in the future. It is a call to recognize disorientations as ubiquitous, oneself as potentially disoriented, and (as possible) to engage in the experiences we have when we find ourselves in periods of disorientation. Responsibilities to identify as disorientable stem from a combination of responsibilities for our own moral growth (where disorientations can contribute to such growth), to relate well to others who may be disoriented alongside us, and to position disorientations as livable parts of life for everyone. I am working from an assumption that we may have responsibilities to be open to our own moral development, where and when we are able to be.

Refusing to relate to ourselves as disorientable can in some contexts mean acting irresponsibly toward others. For people facing serious illness to resist disorientations, deny that there is anything wrong, or relate to loved ones as though everything is fine would be harmful not only for themselves, but also for their loved ones. Likewise, for loved ones to fail to recognize or to actively cover over the disorienting character of the time, could also be deeply hurtful to the person who is ill. Responding to ourselves as disorientable *with others* might be necessary in order to allow them to express their own struggles in the face of fear and loss, and to make a difficult time livable for everyone involved.

Someone might suggest that cultivating capacities to respond to oneself and others as disorientable would be to cultivate a kind of virtue. For instance, the virtues of patience or honesty would help individuals both support disoriented others and live with their own disorientations in the senses I have described. I am sympathetic to this way of understanding these capacities as kinds of character traits. Note, though, an important difference between my claims about (1) what disorientations can produce and (2) what can produce our capacities to respond well to disorientations (our own or those of others). Regarding the first case, I have not described the morally beneficial effects of disorientations as virtues, and I have given reasons to think the effects of disorientation are not accurately understood as settled dispositions or character traits. Regarding the second claim, though, it is possible that individuals can cultivate capacities to support others who are disoriented, or to respond to ourselves as disorientable, by cultivating virtues. Many of the cases of disorientation I have drawn on in earlier chapters are examples of people responding to themselves as disorientable, partly by demonstrating patience when disoriented. At the same time, responding to disorientations and ourselves as disorientable seems to require a more subtle and delicate stance than many virtues. For example, the virtue of courage suggests in many philosophical accounts more resoluteness than the kinds of "living through" or acceptance that would characterize those who respond to themselves as disorientable. Perhaps the trait of responding to ourselves as disorientable is captured well by what Walker has called "grace."

Part of what it means to respond to ourselves as disorientable is to relinquish a certain kind of control. As Carel describes her experience of the disorientations of illness, "There are general issues that ill people confront. These issues can be summarized in one question: how should I face adverse circumstances over which I have no control? . . . I have no control over this illness but I have full control over my emotions and inner state" (Carel 2008, 64).[17] If individuals are able to recognize themselves as disorientable, they are also likely to want (as Carel does) to retain some degree of control. Part of my point has been to challenge understandings of "self-control" by suggesting that there is no exclusive dichotomy between positive, controlled emotions, on the one hand, and negative, uncontrolled emotions, on the other. The solution is not always to "snap out of" the latter and forcefully reorient toward the former. Perhaps more important than the fact that such reorientations are not always beneficial—a point to which I have been committed—is the fact that they are not always possible. We may need to live with disorientations more often and for longer than we would like.

Again, all this needs to be qualified by an understanding of the diversity of kinds of disorientations. How widely disorientations can vary means that the appropriate responses also vary widely. Further, the call to respond to ourselves as disorientable does not override concerns about the potential harms of disorientation; rather, it would be mitigated by the real possibilities that disorientations at some times harm more than they help. It is a conditional rather than universal call, one dependent on circumstances. An individual's ability to relate to disorientations in any way must be, of course, contingent on her particular experiences and the supports she has available. Not everyone will be able or required to relate to disorientations with grace. One's ability to relate to disorientations depends in part on one's ability to experience and express those disorientations, as well as one's ability to continue in one's life as disoriented. Of course, in unsafe environments or times of crisis individuals may need to do their best to make clear decisions to take care of their own and others' basic needs. It can be more important to survive than to identify as disorientable.

Note that I am not claiming we have responsibilities to *become* or *feel* disoriented, nor to feel any way in particular *about* disorientations, nor to recognize the benefits of disorientation while in the midst of them. My claim is just about a responsibility to position oneself in a particular way toward the disorientations that one does not choose. Being supported in living with some disorientation now might make us less resistant or more open to pursuing other disorientations for political and moral reasons in the future.[18]

6.4 BACK TO THE ROUGH WAVES

My aim in this book has been to clarify how some disorientations have had specific beneficial effects, as well as to clarify some of the most important points from a tradition that overemphasizes their danger. As I have noted throughout, social conditions shape how we experience, respond to, and benefit from disorientations. Who we are (psychological conditions) and whom we are with (social conditions) are crucial factors in our experiences of disorientation, and can make the difference between disorientations that harm and disorientations that help. I am interested in highlighting the importance of creating social conditions that make it more possible for us to live with and benefit from disorientations, though I have claimed that it is not possible to guarantee which conditions can ensure that disorientations become promising rather than debilitating. What makes one person's disorientation productive and another's destructive is complicated. Beyond the fact that their disorientations are different, their social conditions are different, complexly shaping the experience and results of their disorientations. Environments that are more hospitable to those who are disoriented may also be more livable and less oppressive in general, and more generative of responsible action toward imperfect improvements. In other words, communities where disorientations are more habitable may also be ones where relationality, humility, uncertainty, and contingency start to feel more common, expected, and un-dangerous than they otherwise would.

The risk of disorientations is that they can be powerful enough to change us without us knowing how we will be changed. Even so, that risk is reason enough neither for responsible individuals to resist experiences of disorientation for fear they will harm capacities for agency, nor for ethical theorists to neglect the potential for disorientations to spur positive moral change.

The account I have given may read, in light of some feminist philosophies, like a drastic lowering of expectations. In light of a background of thinking about transformative experiences in consciousness-raising, sustained deliberate and radical action to address injustice, and revolutionary movements to recognize and enshrine the rights of marginalized groups, my claims are about what seems a fairly narrow portion of all the kinds of improved moral and political action. I have been interested in the ways typically unchosen experiences in some cases prompt subtle shifts in how individuals relate to vulnerable others, without their having decided to do so, sometimes without their even having had clear awareness of the action needed. Narrow as this portion may be, I have become convinced that these kinds of improvements are widely experienced in day-to-day moral life, and worth careful attention.

Having acknowledged that disorientations are complex, risky, and sometimes promising experiences, a goal of this book has been to motivate future considerations of how communities and environments might support those who are disoriented. In this way, disorientations will be recognized as integral to moral life rather than antithetical to it.

NOTES

Chapter 1

1. I introduced this sense of disorientation in an article entitled "Bodily Disorientation and Moral Change" (2012).
2. Such a view is reflected in Plato's *Republic*, at 518D, where education is described as not the putting of sight into blind eyes so much as the turning of an individual's body toward the light: education as reorientation.
3. Descartes's description of the project describes what deep doubt can feel like: "This undertaking is arduous.... I fall back of my own accord into my former opinions, and fear to awake from this slumber lest the laborious wakeful hours which would follow this peaceful rest, instead of bringing me any light of day into the knowledge of truth, would not be sufficient to disperse the shadows caused by the difficulties which have just been raised" (Descartes 1971, 100–101).
4. Thomas Kuhn's *The Structure of Scientific Revolutions* (1996) may be seen as another text about the potential benefits of disorientations, though not at the level of individual agents. Kuhn understands the history of science as involving alternating "normal" periods of relatively stable accumulation of scientific understanding and "revolutionary"/"extraordinary" periods of serious challenge to the underlying assumptions of scientific disciplines, and crises of confidence in existing scientific paradigms.
5. See Silvia 2009, 2010.
6. See James, "What Is an Emotion" (1884).
7. See Dewey 1894.
8. See Henry James Sr. 1884, 65–68.

9. See Sartre 1973 and Solomon 2003, 191–192.
10. See Kierkegaard, *Fear and Trembling* (2006, 10). Likewise, Kierkegaard reads Job as having expressed disorientation and resisted a temptation to feign orientedness. As Kierkegaard writes of Job in *Repetition*: "When all existence collapsed upon you and lay like broken pottery around you, did you immediately have this superhuman self-possession, did you immediately have this interpretation of love, this cheerful boldness of trust and faith? No ... when everything went to pieces—then you became the voice of the suffering, the cry of the grief-stricken, the shriek of the terrified, and a relief to all who bore their torment in silence, a faithful witness to all the affliction and laceration there can be in a heart, an unfailing spokesman who dared to lament 'in bitterness of soul' and to strive with God" (Kierkegaard 2009, 58).
11. As Nietzsche writes in *The Birth of Tragedy*: "The struggle, the pain, the destruction of phenomena, now appear necessary to us, in view of the excess of countless forms of existence which force and push one another into life" (Nietzsche 2010, 104, §17).
12. For further phenomenological analyses of embodied experiences of disruption, see Leder 1990; Price and Shildrick 1996; and Weiss 2008.
13. See Charles Taylor's *Sources of the Self* (1989b) on identity crises in contexts of nationalism.
14. See Paul Benson's (2000) analysis of the harms of self-doubt, and Robin Dillon's (1997, 2004) considerations of compromised self-respect.
15. See Cheshire Calhoun (2008) on demoralization and loss of self.
16. See Pereboom (2014) and Balaguer (2010, especially chapter 3) who consider "torn decisions" as part of broader debates about libertarianism and determinism.
17. See Frankfurt 1987.
18. Jacques Pezeu-Massabuau's *A Philosophy of Discomfort* (2012, 58) focuses on parallel experiences of particularly spatial and physical discomforts, taking as a central example an uncomfortable early morning run. According to Pezeu-Massabuau, comfort and discomfort cannot be separated, they operate in conjunction: "The pleasure of inhabiting (and probably all well-being) seems to be founded on a specific accord between comfort and discomfort in which the latter is often masked, generally repressed and eluding consciousness. Both generate a mode of existence where they operate in conjunction and we cannot separate them" (Pezeu-Massabuau 2012, 73).
19. We can see traces of having come to terms with unpredictability in Mill's ultimate characterization of qualitative happiness as: "not a life of rapture; but moments of such, in an existence made up of few and transitory pains, many and various pleasures, with a decided predominance of the active over the passive, and having as the foundation of the whole, not to expect more from life than it is capable of bestowing. A life thus composed, to those who

have been fortunate enough to obtain it, has always appeared worthy of the name of happiness" (Mill 2011, 49).
20. I have elsewhere considered what I have called the "medicalization of struggle," where murky and difficult emotional experiences can be categorized as mental illness within diagnostic frameworks, like the DSM 5 (see Harbin, "Disorientation and the Medicalization of Struggle," 2014a). There, I consider the autobiography of Charlotte Perkins Gilman (1972) from the perspective of an analysis of disorientation and mental illness.
21. For example, the disorientations of having to navigate a health care system can accompany one's experience of pursuing treatment for an eating disorder, while not being part of the disorder itself.
22. When I say that a particular event or experience is "orienting," I mean that it can lead individuals and groups to feel, and act on the basis of feeling, oriented. When I say that an event or experience is "disorienting," I mean that it can lead individuals and groups to feel, and act on the basis of feeling, disoriented.
23. See Naomi Scheman's (2011, 159–160) discussion of standards for what can count as grief.
24. See also Naomi Scheman's introduction and Cressida Heyes's chapter in *Feminist Interpretations of Ludwig Wittgenstein*, ed. Scheman and O'Connor (2002).
25. See Fine and Gordon's "Feminist Transformations of/despite Psychology" (1992).
26. Most studies are aimed at accessing individuals' self-reports about their own experiences, some study families or couples' coping capacities at the same time, and others specifically aim to investigate phenomena like "dyadic coping" (Feldman 2006) or, for example, the importance of how a parent copes for how a child can cope with their own experience (Pelcovitz et al. 1998). Some researchers have made an effort to validate first-personal reports of effects of experiences like disorientations with second-personal reports about changes in a person's behavior following a disorienting event (Shakespeare-Finch 2012).
27. For central studies on measurements of coherence, see Antonovsky 1987, 1991, 1993; Almedom et al. 2007; and Pham et al. 2010.
28. "Autonomy-connectedness" is a term used in studies of individuals whose autonomy may be damaged (often in cases of depression or anxiety), and it means autonomy in the sense of capacity to be on one's own, as well as with others. For use of measurements of autonomy-connectedness, see Bekker 1993, 2006; and Bekker and van Assen 2006.
29. For studies that use measurements of self-efficacy, see Bandura 1977; Werner and Smith 1982; Rutter 1987; and Luthar 1991.
30. For studies designed to measure cognitive adaptation, see Taylor 1983; Taylor and Brown 1988; and Collins et al. 1990.

NOTES

31. See Janoff-Bulman (1989) for the summary of the development of this measurement. The "World Assumptions Scale" is often used to measure the effects of disorientation I survey in chapters 3 and 4.
32. See, e.g., Joseph et al. 1993.
33. See Büchi et al. 2002.
34. In practice, practitioners and researchers recognize that everything is more complex in the context of individuals' lives. One's identity and particular social circumstances make a difference to how one can cope (Lincoln et al. 2003; Chapman 2010). Still, a major goal of the research is generalizability of clinical recommendations.
35. See Connor and Davidson 2003; Pietrzak et al. 2009; and Stewart et al. 2011 on resilience.
36. See Kobasa 1979, 1982; Gentry and Kobasa 1984; Ford et al. 2000; Williams and Lawler 2001; Northouse et al. 2002; and Lang et al. 2003 on hardiness.
37. See Park et al. 1996; Armeli et al. 2001; and Weiss 2002 on stress-related growth.
38. See Folkman and Lazarus 1980; and McCrae 1984 on coping.
39. See Tedeschi and Calhoun 1996 and 2004 on post-traumatic growth.
40. Tomich and Helgeson (2004) have raised important questions from within psychology about the accuracy of the post-traumatic growth literature: study participants may exaggerate benefits because they realize that is the desired response, because they are only asked about positive effects, or to help alleviate their own distress.
41. Among the other information we get from empirical research, a meta-level of analysis can show *how such experiences have been categorized* (i.e., whether similar characteristics of disorientations among grief and political education have been able to be noticed in a given framework), and can reveal deep assumptions about likely effects of such experiences. Observing the research questions and goals of empirical projects allows for understanding and evaluating what have tended to be the most important aspects of such experiences—for example, the ways in which experiences of disorientations can compromise autonomous decision-making capacities. This gives us more information than simply data about what are or are not effects of disorientations—it tells us what we (as researchers, and in some cases as regular individuals) might be inclined to believe about such experiences, and allows for asking *why* we might be inclined to believe such things.
42. I am emphasizing the contrast between my account and *traditional* virtue ethics accounts because, as I will discuss in chapter 2, some recent feminist discussions have suggested character theories to radically revise or replace traditional virtue ethics that are more compatible with my suggestions of what disorientations' effects are.

NOTES

Chapter 2

1. In chapter 5, I discuss moral dilemmas in more depth—for now, my point is simply that moral judgments can conflict, and that while agents can choose between conflicting moral judgments, and decide to act according to one or the other, the presence of conflict can compromise their confidence in doing so.
2. Lisa Tessman (2015, 101) has written about these kinds of cases, noting how it can be possible to maintain confidence in one's action to fulfill one kind of moral requirement, while knowingly failing to fulfill another requirement that conflicts with it.
3. See also Power et al. 1989; Carpendale 2000. According to Kohlberg (1984, 202–203), in some cases conflictedness could in fact lead to moral growth, if it could necessitate agents thinking through the conflict between different approaches to a problem and resolving which would be best.
4. See Greene et al. 2001; Greene and Haidt 2002; Greene et al. 2009; and Greene 2013.
5. For summaries of different approaches to dual-systems models of moral judgment, see Greene, Sommerville, Nystrom, Darley, and Cohen 2001; Haidt 2001; Cushman, Young, and Hauser 2006; Greene 2007; Bartels 2008; Moll, De Oliveira-Souza, and Zahn 2008; Huebner, Dwyer, and Hauser 2009; Paxton and Greene 2010; Campbell and Kumar 2012; Cushman 2013; and Railton 2014.
6. See also Tversky and Kahneman 1971; Kahneman and Tversky 1984; and Kahneman 2011.
7. For instance, in her work on moral failure, Lisa Tessman has taken up dual-systems theory as clarifying what happens when one encounters a moral conflict. Tessman describes experiences of encountering situations of moral conflict such as the case of the Crying Baby dilemma used in Greene et al.'s research, where one must choose between killing one's own crying baby to save several other people who are hiding from enemy soldiers, or allowing the baby to continue crying, which will attract the soldiers who will then kill everyone (including the baby). Centrally for Tessman's purposes, in such dilemmas, the two systems of intuition and reasoning can produce incompatible moral judgments: intuition says *one must not kill one's child*, and reasoning says *the child will die either way, so it is worth killing the child to save the others in hiding* (Tessman 2015, 96). This conflictedness will not be resolved by one judgment overruling the other; acting in accordance with either judgment will mean failing to act in accordance with the other. As such, on Tessman's (2015, 97) view, the result is inevitable moral failure.
8. As Tessman clarifies, to have such a "prescriptive sentiment" "one must have the disposition not only to perform (or refrain from) an action, but also to judge it, to assess it as good or required (or forbidden, permitted, etc.)" (2015, 79).

9. See, for example, accounts of weakness of will from Hare 1952; Bratman 1979; and Jones 2003.
10. These may be failures of self-respect in Thomas Hill's (1991) or Robin Dillon's (1992, 1997) senses.
11. As Strawson describes in "Freedom and Resentment" (1962), if we have a personal relationship with someone who fails to care about or respond to our needs, we can resent them.
12. See Tedeschi and Calhoun 1996; Pargament, Smith, Koenig, and Perez 1998.
13. See Updegraff, Taylor, Kemeny, and Wyatt 2002.
14. See also Tedeschi and Calhoun 2004, 3; Triplett et al. 2012; and Calhoun and Tedeschi 2013.
15. Harbin "Prescribing Posttraumatic Growth" (2015b).
16. Researchers in clinical psychology have raised methodological worries about the post-traumatic growth research. See Tennen and Affleck 2002; Lechner 2003; and Linley and Joseph 2004.
17. Grief itself has received the most concerted treatment from philosophers who have tended to focus on characterizing what kind of a phenomenon grief is (e.g., mental state, event) and to distinguishing grief from other emotions (e.g., sadness, despair, melancholy). See Lloyd 1993; Moller 2007; Goldie 2011; and Kalman 2012.
18. The indeterminacy of grief connects to Sue Campbell's understanding of "free-style emotions": "nuanced and nameless feelings that are neither reducible to sensations nor the sorts of states that are adequately captured by the categories of the classic emotions" (Campbell 1997, 71).
19. Frantz et al. (1998) report from their study of 312 adults a year after the death of a loved one, participants report coming to feel fatalistic, that they lack control, that "life is short," "death can come at any time," and heightened awareness of the fact that while much else is uncertain, death is guaranteed.
20. See a similar description of "acute, stabbing" grief and "waves of sadness" in Jamison (2009, 159).
21. In the context of disorientation, a person committed to the idea that all moral motivation occurs through the formation of moral judgments might respond to my view in a variety of ways. They might grant that there are these different kinds of markers of moral motivation (e.g., judgments, as well as changes in action without moral judgments), and note that other theories (e.g., dual systems theories) do not aim to explain them all. This would be compatible with my view. Alternatively, they may deny that there are other distinct markers of moral motivation, and re-explain all motivational processes (including the effects of disorientation) in terms of moral judgments. Given how routinely disorientations compromise judgment, and how characteristically disorientation makes people likely to feel paralyzed, and that they do not know what to do or how to go on, re-explaining their effects as kinds of moral judgments will be difficult, if not impossible, and is more likely to result in a third

option: namely, denying that there are markers of moral motivation other than moral judgment and disregarding many of the significant effects of disorientation as cases of moral motivation. Such a denial would require articulating a non-intuitive sense of the limits of moral motivation and explaining why a change in action with morally significant effects should not count as having been morally motivated.

22. Peggy DesAutels argues further that affective dysfunction can lead to "moral oblivion," where we are "completely or mostly unaware of a moral demand being made" (2004, 73).

23. In some ways, Frankfurt's (1999, 2004, 2006) later work recognizes questions that resonate closely with mine: what can we learn about agency from investigating tumultuous moments in agents' lives when they cannot act in straightforward ways, or when they do not know how to go on? As Frankfurt summarizes his project in *The Reasons of Love*: "How should a person live? . . . The difficulties we encounter in thinking about these things may sometimes, perhaps, make us dizzy. . . . What we are hoping for is the more intimate comfort of feeling at home with ourselves" (2004, 5).

Chapter 3

1. The chapter title echoes Kant's short piece "What Is Orientation in Thinking?" (1991, 235–249). As will be clear, I maintain that disorientations are always disruptive to more than just the ways we think.
2. See Birzer 2006.
3. See Torres and Charles 2004; Lewis et al. 2013.
4. See Wilson and Mossakowski 2009.
5. See Birzer and Smith-Mahdi's (2006) qualitative study of the phenomenology of racist discrimination against black men and women in Topeka Kansas.
6. See Torres and Charles (2004) study of black university students at University of Pennsylvania. As one participant said, "I kind of find myself thinking a lot before I leave my house, like: Do I look too threatening? Like, maybe I shouldn't wear this, maybe I shouldn't wear that" (2004, 124).
7. See Torres and Charles 2004, 123. Making a similar point, Rollock et al. (2011) have described how in black Caribbean individuals' experiences of racism, individuals report gaining clarity about norms of whiteness. One participant, "Vanessa," recalls how, as a child, other school children came up to her to touch her hair and to ask if her bottom was white or black. As Rollock et al. explain, "This 'negating activity' (Fanon, 1967: 83) to which Vanessa is subjected contributes to a relational identity formation. In other words she begins to understand and examine her raced identity *in relation* to those aspects of her otherness that are picked out and met with intrigue by white peers" (Rollock et al. 2011, 1082).

NOTES

8. Patricia Hill Collins (1986) and Alison Wylie (2003), among others, have described the distinct but related benefit of an "insider-outsider standpoint."
9. As George Yancy interprets Du Bois's account, "There was a sudden annoying feeling of difference, which presumably didn't exist prior to this encounter [with the white girl]. Hence Du Bois underwent a distinctive phenomenological process of coming to appear to himself differently as one who is expelled. He moved from a sense of the familiar to the unfamiliar.... Du Bois began to experience a disjointed relationship with his body" (2008, 83, 85).
10. See also Rosemarie Garland-Thompson (2011) on the double experience of disability as fitting and misfitting.
11. I am taking for granted feminist understandings of *norms* (e.g., gender norms) as powerful but contingent standards shaping individuals' experience and action, and *normalization* as the process by which norms are experienced and enforced (Bartky 1990; Butler 1990; Bordo 1993). As Cressida Heyes notes, "Most feminists would accept the general point that gendered bodies are under constant pressure to conform to certain norms, and that Foucault's concepts of disciplinary power, docility, and normalization are productive tools for understanding how this pressure works" (2007, 36).
12. See Twine and Steinbugler (2006) and Frankenberg (1993) on the disorientations of "interracial intimacy."
13. As Yancy writes, "She was lying to herself, concealing from view the reality of her own racism in relationship to those moments on elevators or in other social spaces where she engaged in perceptual practices that criminalized or demonized the Black body" (2008, 228).
14. Discussing the white girl who refused Du Bois's visiting card, Yancy writes, her "identity is lived with epistemic certainty.... Embodying space in this raced way, she demarcated her immediate lived space as clean, untouchable, privileged.... The tall newcomer has become *absorbed* in the world of whiteness. Within the process of 'being-in' the world of whiteness.... She animates white racist scripts on cue, because they have become habituated modes of bodily enactment" (2008, 243).
15. See also Chris Cuomo's (2005) "White and Cracking Up."
16. See Williams and Williams-Morris 2000; Brown 2003, 2008; Kerig et al. 2012; and Zuberi 2013.
17. See Tatum 1997, 99.
18. Gutierrez's (1995) analysis of the efficacy of different models of Latino consciousness-raising groups in empowering individuals is interesting on this point, though not focused on what kinds of experiences are most central in such groups.
19. See Reger 2004, 212–214.
20. As Jasper describes them, "'Moral shocks,' often the first step toward recruitment into social movements, occur when an unexpected event or piece

of information raises such a sense of outrage in a person that she becomes inclined toward political action . . . the information or event helps a person think about her basic values and how the world diverges from them in some important way. . . . Whether the underlying image is a state of shock or an electrical shock, it implies a visceral, bodily feeling, on a par with vertigo or nausea. Strong emotions should flow from this" (1998, 409).
21. See Reger 2004, 212.
22. From analysis of her interviews with members of the New York City chapter of the National Organization for Women, Reger notes how "moral shocks triggering feelings of anger and alienation were caused not only by external events but also by the situations brought on by socioeconomic statuses (i.e., class, race/ethnicity, age and sexuality). . . . The women I interviewed talked about how C-R channeled their emotions and created a new perception of their experiences. . . . This new perception led women to criticize their current behavior and their understanding of interactions" (2004, 213, 215).
23. Ruíz's descriptions of experiences of gaslighting reflect the common images of disorientation as attempting to navigate deep water. As she concludes, "Cultivating a hybridly multiplicitous (rather than dual or fragmented) sense of self can also help steady the mast of our confidence when beset by gusts of setbacks . . . it can help nurture a sense of trustworthiness in our experiences of incongruence, transience, and dislocation" (2014, 203).
24. As Bartky writes, the feminist "finds herself, for awhile at least, in an ethical and existential impasse. She no longer knows what sort of person she ought to be and, therefore, she does not know what she ought to do. . . . To develop feminist consciousness is to live a part of one's life in the sort of *ambiguous ethical situation*. . . . It might be objected that the feature of feminist experience I have been describing is characteristic not of a fully emergent feminist consciousness but of periods of transition to such consciousness, that the feminist is a person who has chosen her moral paradigm and who no longer suffers the inner conflicts of those in ambiguous moral predicaments. . . . I would deny this. Even the woman who has decided to be this new person and not that old one, can be tormented by recurring doubts" (1990, 20).
25. Alexis Shotwell (2011, 85) discusses Pratt in her own account of shame, which she understands as a "paradigmatic example of discomfort" (87). Experiences of shame may occur concurrently with experiences of disorientation and may have their own disruptive effects. As Shotwell writes: "Shame can provide a gap in practice; it can stop the conceptual habits we comfortably use to navigate the world. It has a disruptive function" (2011, 90).
26. In their research on teaching about whiteness in undergraduate women's studies curriculum, Hunter and Nettles describe students' discomfort: "We attempted to teach the course from the vantage point of women of color rather than through the lens of dominant society. This displacement of whiteness from the center of

the course obviously made many students uncomfortable.... The students who felt so uncomfortable with the marginalization of whiteness spoke with us about feeling scrutinized and invalidated in class" (1999, 388).

27. See Lewis's (1990) study of resistance, frustration, and anger in feminist classrooms.
28. See Stake and Hoffman 2000; Titus 2000; and Mayberry and Rose 1999.
29. As Lewis states: "Men in the feminist classroom often state that the course readings and class discussions feel threatening and that they experience various degrees of discomfort. I would like to understand more about these feelings of threat and discomfort—where do they come from, what do they fear?" (1990, 484).
30. Boler claims that "the aim of discomfort is for each person, myself included, to explore beliefs and value; to examine when visual 'habits' and emotional selectivity have become rigid and immune to flexibility; and to identify when and how our habits harm ourselves and others" (1999, 180, 185–186; see also Freire 1973).
31. The kind of education that often takes place in critical classrooms is not simply the asking and answering of a hard question, but the generation of a "real and living doubt." To return to C. S. Peirce's account of knowledge: "Some philosophers have imagined that to start an inquiry it was only necessary to utter a question whether orally or by setting it down on paper, and have even recommended us to begin our studies with questioning everything! But the mere putting of a proposition into the interrogative form does not stimulate the mind to any struggle after belief. There must be a real and living doubt, and without this all discussion is idle" (1955, 11).
32. As Ahmed (2012) makes clear, the disorientations of universities in general and feminist classrooms in particular are not just part of students' lives—they also characterize many experiences of feminist teachers and university workers.
33. Undergraduate and graduate students can also be disoriented when trying to determine whether or how university education can support them in an uncertain economy. I have seen students in the United States and Canada bring felt uncertainty about job prospects to their degrees in Philosophy or Women and Gender Studies. They can be deeply disoriented by questions of how to identify themselves as workers. Relatedly, I have seen students disoriented by conflicts between new political knowledge and previous commitments to working in military, police, or correctional settings. As one college student described to me his uncertainty about how to negotiate questions of what to do after graduation, "Basically, I'm in what I believe is a state of lost."
34. In the case O'Reilly is describing, participants were asked to meditate and eventually develop an image of what sort of animal best expressed their

NOTES

sexual selfhood, and then to form small groups and discuss their animal identifications. Many of the women's animals were small and domesticated—cats and birds—and many of the men's were wilder and more powerful. The "click of recognition" followed one woman's description of herself as a fangless, chameleonic snake whose only protection was to change color and blend in with the environment. It was the others' recognition of how that woman had "become a housewife."

35. Susan Babbitt references a passage from Kathleen Okruhlik's analysis of these experiences: "[Okhrulik] says we experience the power and beauty of unity all the time: 'Many of those "clicks" in the early issues of *Ms.* were the sounds made by unifying conceptions falling into place. Sometimes a single concept like the "eroticisation of subordination" makes many disconnected experiences fall into place and become understandable'" (2001, 91; citing a presentation of Okruhlik's paper "Feminism and Realism").

36. As José Medina notes: "Experiencing the inability to speak on certain issues, such as one's sexuality, as well as the inability of one's interlocutors to listen to these issues, *can* make one better attuned to hermeneutical gaps, that is, more sensitive to epistemic exclusions, on the lookout for what is left out. But there is *no guarantee* that this sensitivity will always flourish or that it will go far when carried over to the experiences of others in other domains. The experience of being excluded and silenced is the fertile soil for the development of a special *sensitivity to insensitivity*" (2013, 204).

37. Of course, at the same time as one feels powerless because of new awareness, as disoriented, she can be further *rendered* powerless and untrustworthy by others who think decisiveness is the mark of intelligence, ability, and strength, or even that it is a basic requirement of a job or role in society. This distinct kind of powerlessness can be very harmful—I address it further in chapter 6.

Chapter 4

1. As I discuss in what follows, there is a substantial literature in clinical psychology and medicine on how disorienting illness can be. Alongside trauma and grief, the disorientations of illness have received the most sustained treatment in clinical research. Particular studies have documented the general disorientations of cancer (Germino et al. 1998; Pelcovitz et al. 1998; Cotton et al. 1999; Sollner et al. 1999; Holland and Lewis 2000; Cordova et al. 2001; Kiss and Meryn 2001; Tomich and Helgeson 2002, 2004; Ka'opua et al. 2007; Pinquart et al. 2007; Couper et al. 2009; Clarke et al. 2011; Kimmel and Levy 2013; Perez et al. 2014), HIV (Cadell 2007; Hackl et al. 1997; Poindexter 1997; Farber et al. 2000; Vosvick et al. 2003), neurological

and cardiological treatment (Fabbri et al. 2001; Hopp et al. 2010), amputation (Livneh et al. 2000; Cavanagh et al. 2006), genetic testing (Horowitz et al. 2001), ALS (Young and McNicoll 1998), bone marrow transplant (Rini et al. 2004), arthritis (Danoff-Burg and Revenson 2005), hepatitis C (Kraus et al. 2000), and a number of other chronic diseases (Sidell 1997; Hamilton-West and Quine 2009; Stewart et al. 2014).

2. As Susan Sontag has famously written: "Everyone who is born holds dual citizenship, in the kingdom of the well and in the kingdom of the sick. Although we all prefer to use only the good passport, sooner or later each of us is obliged, at least for a spell, to identify ourselves as citizens of that other place" (1989, 3).

3. Disorientations in the face of death are not only the most widely considered by philosophers, but also perhaps also those we most often recognize as morally significant. Death is perhaps the most widely experienced and best considered (though usually with other terminology) kind of disorientation in the western philosophical tradition, which is part of the reason I focus on other kinds here.

4. One example drawn from Wittman et al.'s qualitative study of women with lupus echoes many of the other accounts: "For Mrs. D, the most difficult aspect of SLE was the destruction of her life's plan.... Many wishes, such as having a family and a child, were disrupted, and she is afraid of losing her job because of weakness in her hands.... She also sees her dependency on others as a mainstay of her life. Some friends still remain, but nevertheless she feels somewhat isolated" (2009, 368).

5. Arthur W. Frank (2000) describes autobiographies of illness as partially aiming to re-establish narrative continuity after destabilizing experiences of illness.

6. Disorientations may be triggered by not just illness, but by the knowledge that one would not be prepared to address illness should it arise. Journalist and writer Corbyn Hightower (2011) describes her experience of losing health insurance after losing her job: "Health insurance for all of us was one of the last things we let go of when our financial crisis crested.... There is never a time that you forget that your children are uninsured. You feel like running behind them in a half-crouch, arms extended, ready to catch the sudden stumble. I wasn't prepared for how demoralizing it would feel, knowing that no one would be there to help if a member of my family was hurt or sick.... When you don't have medical insurance, you never really feel like everything is going to be all right."

7. See Danoff and Revenson's (2005, 96) study of individuals with rheumatoid arthritis.

8. Hamilton-West and Quine (2009) report these findings in a study of patients with Ankylosing Spondylitis, a kind of debilitating arthritis.

9. See Clarke et al.'s (2011) study of esophageal cancer survivors.

10. See Ka'opua et al.'s (2007) study of partners of men with prostate cancer, who became responsive to the suffering of others in cancer treatment.

11. As a practicing physician before his diagnosis, Servan-Schreiber recalled that treating patients as objects of medical attention (more than subjects with experience and insight), treating other physicians as experts to be trusted (and being treated like a medical expert himself), and feeling confident and self-assured in diagnosing and treating patients seemed normal to him. Medical establishments had been structured environments where he felt at ease, knew what to expect, and enjoyed habits of relating to others that were consistent, predictable, and self-confirming.
12. See Farber et al.'s (2000) study of adults with HIV, Hopp et al.'s (2010) study of individuals with heart failure; Sidell's (1997) study of adults with chronic illness; Pelcovitz et al.'s (1998) study of adolescents with cancer; and Stewart et al.'s (2014) study of adults with end stage liver disease.
13. See Sidell et al. 1997.
14. Tomich and Helgeson (2002, 155–156) reported this finding from their study of 164 women five years after receiving a diagnosis of breast cancer.
15. Young and McNicoll (1998) reported this finding from their study of adults with ALS (Lou Gehrig's disease). As one study participant with ALS says: "I was fooled before.... You know, you're young, you think you're going to live forever, and you think you run the show and then stuff happens, and it is totally out of your hands.... The lesson for me in this illness has been sort of the letting go, the losing control, physical control, being able to ask for help, being able to surrender" (1998, 39).
16. See Rini et al.'s (2004) study of patients receiving bone marrow transplants; and Ell's (1996) study of family members of individuals facing a variety of serious illnesses.
17. Carel (2008, 10) uses phenomenology to try to provide an account of health and illness more adequate to her experience than most of the medicalizing accounts she encountered. Her book, she says, is an attempt to make illness less secretive and less lonely. On the phenomenology of illness, see also Toombs 1992.
18. As Carel describes: "In the months that followed [diagnosis] I went through a bewildering array of emotions. At first I was shocked, then depressed, sometimes relieved that I still had decent lung function, then disillusioned as my condition deteriorated.... A new life descended on me and I gradually acclimatized to it" (2008, 5–6).
19. See Caruth 1996, 62. Studies of traumatic experiences confirm the ways they are very likely to be disorienting: the traumatic experiences of traffic accidents (Cagnetta and Cicognani 1999; Harms and Talbot 2007); being exposed to violence in war zones (Landau and Litwin 2000; Waysman et al. 2001; Dekel et al. 2009; Levine et al. 2009; Pham et al. 2010; Shrira et al. 2010; Lommen et al. 2014); and experiencing interpersonal violence of various kinds (Connor et al. 2003) have all been shown to disrupt individuals' capacities for knowing how to go on.

20. As Laura Brown explains: "'Real' trauma is often only that form of trauma in which the dominant group can participate as a victim rather than as the perpetrator or etiologist of the trauma. The private, secret, insidious traumas to which a feminist analysis draws attention are more often than not those events in which the dominant culture and its forms are expressed and perpetuated" (1995, 102).
21. See Janoff-Bulman (1989, 1992) and Janoff-Bulman and Frieze (1983) on the ways traumas can change "world assumptions."
22. See Dekel et al.'s (2009) study of war trauma survivors in Israel.
23. See Pham et al.'s (2010) study of trauma related to national violence in Congo.
24. See Cagnetta and Cicognani (1999, 556–557) on traumas of surviving serious traffic accidents.
25. As Brison and Carel describe in cases of trauma and illness, disorientations often make more visible the ways my well-being relies crucially on the work of others (see Tronto's analysis of how the ease of privileged bodies relies on the care of others rendered invisible; 1994, 101–124), and this can support morally better, potentially reciprocal, interaction with them.
26. See Couper et al.'s (2009) study of prostate cancer patients.
27. There are starting points in empirical research for thinking about how gender (Kiss and Meryn 2001), relationship status (Sollner et al. 1999), socioeconomic status (Hackl et al. 1997), age (Kraus et al. 2000), personality type (Perez et al. 2014), or the severity or duration of a given disorientation (Cordova et al. 2001) may make a difference to how disorientations affect individuals facing (or caring for others who are facing) illness.
28. See Rich (1993) and Ahmed (2006) on compulsory heterosexuality.
29. See Kitzinger and Wilkinson 1995 and Walsh, n.d.
30. See Borders et al. 2014.
31. See Ward and Winstanley (2005) on the identity negotiations of coming out in workplaces.
32. See Johnston and Jenkins 2003.
33. See Garnets et al. 1993.
34. See Jordan and Deluty's (1998) study of lesbian women who were out to greater or lesser degrees, and who suffered more the less openly queer they were able to be.
35. See Froyum (2007) on gender and sexuality in low-income black teens; and Almaguer (1993) on Chicano men and queerness.
36. See Sears (1991) on educators and queer students; and Berube's (2000) *Coming Out under Fire: The History of Gay Men and Women in World War Two*.
37. In *No Future: Queer Theory and the Death Drive*, Edelman (2004) has argued for the need for queers to embrace the lack of a future in the limited sense of reproduction.
38. Vaughan and Waehler's "Coming Out Growth Scale" has since been used to investigate not only how queers understand their own experiences of growth

related to the disorientations of queer life, but also to measure how specific aspects of their experiences (e.g., whether or for how long they have been openly queer, how difficult their coming out processes were, etc.) make it more or less likely that they will "grow" in specific domains (e.g., Cox et al. 2011). This research is helpful for beginning to understand the effects of the disorientations of queer life, but I think it is still limited by understanding "growth" in ways closely informed by the post-traumatic growth literature discussed in chapter 2.

39. Vaughan and Waehler 2010, 105. On the basis of a 2009 study of 418 queer adults, Vaughan and Waehler developed a system for measuring and further studying how the stress of queer life can promote growth in both individual and collective domains.
40. See Lewis et al.'s (2006) survey of "stigma consciousness" and the use of Pinel's (2009) Stigma Consciousness Scale.
41. See Friedman and Leaper's (2010) study of predictors of collective action among queer college women.
42. Gould describes June 1986 as one moment of moral shock. In *Bowers v. Hardwick*, the US Supreme Court decided to uphold the constitutionality of a Georgia anti-sodomy law. This decision, combined with the US government's failure to address the AIDS crisis, and in the face of suggestions that HIV-positive individuals should even be quarantined, transformed queers' ambivalence into collective direct action. As Gould writes: "Among many lesbians and gay men, there was a growing sense that their everyday routines, and for an increasing number, their very lives, were imperiled.... More and more lesbians and gay men had to acknowledge that the AIDS crisis was affecting 'me'" (2001, 153).
43. I read Stuart Hall's (1990) concept of "cultural hybridity" as one explanation for the disorientation of migration.
44. See Andreea Deciu Ritivoi's (2002) *Yesterday's Self: Nostalgia and the Immigrant Identity*.
45. Sara Ahmed reads Yasmin Hai's (2008) *The Making of Mr. Hai's Daughter: Becoming British*, as a migrant memoir: "full of ambivalence, described in terms of being happy and sad in becoming English.... Yasmin describes so well how it feels to be alienated through how you are affected by the world. Here, to be an affect alien is to experience alien affects—to be out of line with the public mood, not to feel the way others feel in response to an event" (2010, 155, 157).
46. See Bernal's (2001) research with Chicana university students.
47. See Barajas (2009) on the ways extended families shift across migration periods; and Kanaiaupuni (2000) on the role of nonmigrant women in supporting migrant families.
48. See Duke et al. (2010) on day laborers; and Finch et al. (2004) on farmworkers' health.

49. See, for example, Harsha Walia's (2013, 97–156) discussion of the work of organizers in No One Is Illegal who have fought for an end to refugee deportations, justice for migrant workers, education for migrant kids, defense of First Nations lands, against sexual violence, and against law enforcement violence.
50. This is building on what Lugones (2003, 123–146) has called "curdled logic": a conscious practice of asserting and raising awareness about multiplicious identities.
51. The ways disorientations can be too much to bear are evidenced by the high rates of mental illness, self-harm, and suicides among queers.
52. See Elliot and Gillie 1998; Araújo and Borrel 2006.
53. See Smart and Smart's (1995) study of acculturative stress for Hispanic immigrants in the United States.
54. See Miranda and Matheny 2000.
55. Marsiglia et al. 2011.
56. As Sue Campbell has argued: "That we can have expectations seems fundamental to our knowing how to go on. We could not plan what to do, even in small ways, without beliefs and attitudes about the future about what effects our actions might have, and also about what we might undergo.... Expectation gives a powerful ordering to experience by selecting what is and is not attended to and by structuring the relation of these perceptions to each other" (1999, 222–223).
57. As Susan Babbitt writes exactly on this point: "One might have thought that the disorientation consists in loss of expectations of control based upon past experience. In fact, what is disorienting is the failure to find relevantly valuable the loss of that sort of control. That is, what is disorienting is failure of the relationship between expectations of control and actual, interesting, stability of self" (2001, 69).
58. Carel works to involve patient narratives and phenomenology in medical school curricula, to make physicians more aware of how patients' experience their own vulnerabilities. She becomes involved in patient advocacy groups, patient activism (especially in campaigns for organ donation), and patient-driven research. Brison (2002, 16) lobbies to make her university campus safer for women and commits to addressing such harms in her philosophical teaching and research. Browning (1993) and other queers work for democratic shifts in definitions of civil union, marriage, parents, and family (152–159); resist arbitrary and medicalizing regulations about what kinds of sex will be recognized as "safe" (84–85); campaign for funding research into, and against delays in providing, AIDS fighting drugs (208); and make media, art, and films that better represent a broader realm of queer experience (210). Lugones creates academic programs, workshops, mentoring groups, curricula, and bodies of theory that have made it possible for many Latino/a scholars to find support and develop their own careers and activism.

NOTES

Chapter 5

1. For instance, The Unitarian Universalist Association chose the book for their 2012-13 common read, to be used in book clubs across UU congregations: http://www.uua.org/documents/lfd/commonread/crow_discussion.pdf.
2. For example, The Prisoners' Literature Project run in San Francisco encourages such prison book drive donations: http://www.prisonersliteratureproject.com/donate.
3. The Human Rights Campaign offers a voters' guide to the candidates HRC endorses: http://www.hrc.org/resources/entry/2014-endorsements.
4. There are many citizens in Halifax, Nova Scotia, Canada writing letters to try to stop the sale and development of a building that could otherwise house an indigenous health clinic: http://halifax.mediacoop.ca/story/residents-dream-future-st-pat's-alexandra-developm/31635.
5. See, for example: http://www.peopleswaterboard.org/p/donate-to-peoples-water-board-coalition.html. In Detroit, one of the major industrial cities already hard hit over decades leading up to 2008, 40% of people have never been part of the formal economy (i.e., never had a paid job in an official capacity), and the city has one of the highest rates of unemployment in the country. Less than half of Detroit's residents over the age of 16 are reported to be working (US Bureau of Labor Statistics). This, and the long history of racism and attacks on democracy in the city, means, tangibly, that people do not have access to affordable food, children often do not have access to public schools, and there is a barely functioning public transit system. Most recently, following the appointment of an unelected Emergency Manager, international attention has been drawn to the city as in the midst of rapid gentrification in some neighborhoods, at the same time water is being shut off in households where individuals cannot afford to pay rising bills, leading to serious health and safety concerns, forced eviction, and children being taken from families because of unsafe living conditions.
6. See, for example, the projects of Families against Mandatory Minimums: http://famm.org.
7. For example, one might donate to the Matthew Shepard Foundation: http://www.matthewshepard.org/our-work.
8. For example, Canadian journalist Shelagh Rogers attended hearings of the TRC and reported on them: http://www.ictinc.ca/blog/shelagh-rogers-journey-head-heart-honorary-witness-trc.
9. For example, these and other projects are the work of Keep Growing Detroit: http://detroitagriculture.net/.
10. Such a petition is part of the current Fight for 15 movement, originally based in Chicago seeking a $15/hour living wage for fast-food workers: see http://fightfor15.org/en/homepage/.

NOTES

11. As Boggs writes, "I came to Detroit in the early 1950s because as a Marxist I wanted to be part of a revolution in which the workers in the auto factories would take the struggles of the 1930s to a higher level by struggling for workers' control of production in the plant. . . . I realized that my ideas had come mostly out of books and that my expectations had little or no relationship to the reality that was rapidly changing all around me" (2012, 106).
12. In *On Being Included*, Ahmed (2012) describes this conflictedness as a reality for some "diversity workers" in universities: realizing that they have been employed and commissioned to collect data and write reports to satisfy the requirement that the university diversify, without the institution having any interest in changing its structural conditions.
13. See Conrad 2014 and Spade 2011.
14. See Calhoun 2003, chapter 5.
15. One example of this is work done by REACH Coalition (*Reciprocal Education and Community Healing on Tennessee's Death Row*) in Nashville: http://reach-coalition.wordpress.com/about/.
16. One international organization working toward this goal is Inside-Out, with programs working to create links between universities and prisons: http://www.insideoutcenter.org/programs.html.
17. See Ridgeway 2012 and Harbin's (2015a) "Prisons and Palliative Politics."
18. For example, the Critical Resistance Abolitionist Toolkit lays out strategies for working toward fewer people in prisons and, eventually, no more prisons: http://criticalresistance.org/resources/the-abolitionist-toolkit/.
19. See Haslanger 2008; Saul 2012, 2013; and Olberding et al. 2014.
20. See Alfred 2005 and McLeod 2007.
21. See Harsha Walia's (2012) recommendations for settlers involved in decolonizing institutions.
22. Simpson writes, "In my own life, I have been taught by a handful of Elders that embody Nishnaabeg [indigenous] thought in a way that I worry we are losing . . . they rejected rigidity and fundamentalism as colonial thinking . . . they didn't feel the need to employ exclusionary practices, authoritarian power and hierarchy. . . . They 'resisted' colonialism by living within Nishnaabeg contexts" (2011, 19).
23. Dr. Paulette Regan, Director of Research for the Truth and Reconciliation Commission of Canada, describes the following response to an anti-colonialist education program as follows: "For some, the very notion of 'unsettling' or decolonizing struggle seems frightening and counterintuitive. . . . Talking about the burden of history makes us feel frustrated and overwhelmed. We don't know how to put the past behind us . . . we get stuck in destructive monologues . . . we talk past each other" (2010, 20).
24. See, for example, Indigenous scholar Andrea Bear Nichols's call for indigenous language immersion in schools: http://nbmediacoop.org/2013/11/18/action-needed-to-stop-the-destruction-of-indigenous-languages/.

NOTES

25. A campaign to confront the high rates of missing and murdered Aboriginal women has been growing in Canada. Amnesty International has drawn attention to the fact that 1,017 indigenous women in Canada were found murdered between 1980 and 2012—making them three times more likely than non-Aboriginal women in Canada to suffer violent crime: http://www.amnesty.ca/our-work/issues/indigenous-peoples/no-more-stolen-sisters.
26. In 2012, the water crisis in Attawapiskat became internationally recognized, prompting Chief Theresa Spence to begin a six-week hunger strike to draw attention to the emergency in many First Nations communities: http://www.huffingtonpost.ca/2011/11/30/clean-water-native-reserves-attawapiskat_n_1120102.html.
27. Such a refusal to acknowledge the authority of the federal government and police was evident, for example, in the Oka uprising in 1990 on Mohawk territory, and many settler Canadians criticized indigenous communities for failing to respect state demands. See Conradi 2009.
28. This was the phrase used in Prime Minister Harper's June 11, 2008, apology on behalf of all Canadians for the Indian Residential Schools.
29. See, for example, work to reimagine education (http://boggsschool.org), work (http://reimaginingwork.org), community safety (http://michigan-peacenetwork.org/organizations/Detroit-Peace-Zones-for-Life), housing (http://detroitevictiondefense.org), and food security (http://detroitblackfoodsecurity.org). See an interview with Julia Putnam, who has expressed irresolute action in her work opening a new school in Detroit, where public education has been severely cut: http://vimeo.com/100701840.
30. See especially Young 2005, 2007, 2011; Walker 2003, 2006; and Sherwin 2011.

Chapter 6

1. See Spielman and Taubman Ben-Ari 2009. As a friend once described, "so far my experience of having a newborn is like a combination of the part in *Groundhog Day* when Bill Murray's character just gives in to it, and Steve Martin's 'Are You Awake?' scene from *The Jerk*."
2. These seem to be the basic options for all new parents, regardless of the age of their child, or of how that child came to be part of their family, though the diagnostic criteria most readily applied focus only on birthing parents of newborns. As Jodi Peltason (2013) describes: "The problem with that question [of whether to diagnose a new parent with post-partum depression] as our primary approach to the struggles of new motherhood is that it suggests that the postpartum experience itself is just fine, unless of course you have a legitimate clinical illness that distorts your perception of it. And the postpartum experience is not just fine. It is immensely, bizarrely complicated. It

is, at various times and for various people, grueling and joyful and frightening and beautiful and disorienting and moving and horrible. There's a lot going on there that will never make its way into the DSM V."

3. I am thinking here especially of the work of Naomi Scheman (1980, 1996), Elizabeth Spelman (1989), and Sue Campbell (1997). I take up all of their views at greater length in "Mentorship in Method: Philosophy and Experienced Agency" (Harbin 2014c). Particularly in cases of what Campbell calls "idiosyncratic emotions," the presence of interpreters, to whom individuals can express feelings, make a difference to the kinds and qualities of feelings individuals can have. Scheman (1980) challenges understandings of emotions as mental or physical states of individuals. She argues that social structures have the power to either allow individuals to have and recognize feelings, or keep them from having and recognizing their feelings.

4. Spelman (1989) disputes the assumption that emotions are equally available to and expressible by everyone. While more privileged individuals may question why those directly harmed by racism are not angrier, Spelman highlights how oppressive norms can limit individuals' opportunities to express anger.

5. Campbell (1997) offers an in-depth account of the importance of interpreters who allow individuals to *express*, and thereby to *experience* emotions.

6. In Campbell's example, Audre Lorde and other disadvantaged individuals may have their expressions of anger dismissed by privileged interpreters calling them "just bitter" (1997, 167).

7. There are a number of examples of what I read as dismissive responses even in the clinical literature on grief, trauma, and illness. Griffith and Gaby (2005) recommend therapeutic practices that counter demoralization and encourage ill patients to become more resilient and find strength in their experiences. Halstead and Fernsler (1994) recommend encouraging cancer patients to remain optimistic and confront their illness. Pietrzak and Cook (2013) recommend encouraging veterans to "handle" unpleasant feelings, bounce back, and maintain control over their lives. Wellisch and Lindberg (2001) note that in their clinic, they "encourage feelings of mastery" (335).

8. In this spirit, Stewart et al.'s (2014) study aimed to determine what would be the most important interventions to support quality of life in liver transplant patients, and found that supportive listeners were one of the most important factors.

9. I have focused throughout the book on disorientations as individual experiences, but in fact disorientations sometimes affect a broad cross-section of communities, so that many people experience disorientations triggered by the same event, at the same time. Whole groups of people can be disoriented by physical, emotional, or cognitive shifts (e.g., a major earthquake, the looping footage of planes crashing on September 11, 2001, or the introduction of a theory of evolution). The suggestion of *collective disorientation* raises a

number of questions. What kind of experience would collective disorientation be? How could the disorientations of communities be morally and politically promising in ways distinct from individual disorientations? Work could be done to establish the promise of collective experiences of disorientation in contexts of crisis, and establish a framework for evaluating the benefits of disorientations for helping groups and communities become more responsible, but that would go beyond the scope of what I have hoped to establish here.

10. See Carel 2008, 55.
11. Carel describes how her friend Catriona "has been persistent in her desire to know, to understand what [Carel is] going through" (2008, 60), and how a neighbor Sarah "walks [her] dog every morning when [Carel's] breathing is at its worst."
12. Deraniyagala (2013, 43–44) notes the importance of the people who refused to leave her alone while she faced the loss of her family in Sri Lanka.
13. Blalock et al. (2002) and Bowling (1995) focus on the importance of ongoing (in some cases adjusted) work possibilities for people with long-term illnesses.
14. This echoes Susan Wendell's claim about the disabling effects of the pace of life making impairments harder to live with (Wendell 1996).
15. I discuss the medicalization of disorientation at greater length in "Disorientation and the Medicalization of Struggle" (Harbin 2014a).
16. I follow Walker's focus on assessing the "habitability of a particular form of moral-social life" (2007b, 248)—asking what makes experiences influential and beneficial often involves asking in part what makes them livable.
17. Carel practices what she calls a kind of "emotional discipline": "I needed to say no to negative feelings. . . . I needed to stop looking at other people's lives and making up stories about their happiness. . . . I needed to recite, even by rote, all the good things in my life and to cultivate that oddly optimistic feeling I had deep down inside, that everything was going to be OK" (2008, 33).
18. Butler frames the kind of response I have in mind as desirable as a *non-violent response*: "What might it mean to undergo violation, to insist upon *not* resolving grief and staunching vulnerability too quickly through a turn to violence, and to practice, as an experiment in living otherwise, nonviolence in an emphatically nonreciprocal response?" (2005, 100).

REFERENCES

Ahmed, Sara. 2004. *The Cultural Politics of Emotion*. New York: Routledge.
Ahmed, Sara. 2006. *Queer Phenomenology: Orientations, Objects, Others*. Durham, NC: Duke University Press.
Ahmed, Sara. 2010. *The Promise of Happiness*. Durham, NC: Duke University Press.
Ahmed, Sara. 2012. *On Being Included: Racism and Diversity in Institutional Life*. Durham, NC: Duke University Press.
Alcoff, Linda Martín. 2006. *Visible Identities: Race, Gender, and the Self*. Oxford: Oxford University Press.
Alexander, Michelle. 2010. *The New Jim Crow: Mass Incarceration in the Age of Colorblindness*. New York: New Press.
Alfred, Taiaiake. 2005. *Wasáse: Indigenous Pathways of Action and Freedom*. Peterborough: Broadview Press.
Almaguer, Tomás. 1993. "Chicano Men: A Cartography of Homosexual Identity and Behavior." In *The Lesbian and Gay Studies Reader*, edited by Henry Abelove, Michèle Aina Barale, and David M. Halperin, 255–273. New York: Routledge.
Almedom, Astier M., and Douglas Glannon. 2007. "Resilience Is Not the Absences of PTSD and More than Health Is the Absence of Disease." *Journal of Loss and Trauma: International Perspectives on Stress & Coping* 12, no. 2: 127–143.
Andrews, Vernon L. 2003. "Self-Reflection and the Reflected Self: African American Double Consciousness and the Social (Psychological) Mirror." *Journal of African American Studies* 7, no. 3: 59–79.
Antonovsky, Aaron. 1987. *Unraveling the Mystery of Health: How People Manage Stress and Stay Well*. San Francisco, CA: Jossey-Bass.

REFERENCES

Antonovsky, Aaron. 1991. "The Structural Sources of Salutogenic Strengths." In *Personality and Stress: Individual Differences in the Stress Process*, edited by C. L. Cooper and R. Payne, 67–104. Chichester, UK: Wiley.

Antonovsky, Aaron. 1993. "The Structure and Properties of the Sense of Coherence Scale." *Social Science and Medicine* 36: 725–733.

Anzaldúa, Gloria. 1987. *Borderlands/La Frontera: The New Mestiza*. San Francisco, CA: Aunt Lute Books.

Araújo, Beverly, and Luisa Borrel. 2006. "Understanding the Link between Discrimination, Mental Health Outcomes, and Life Chances among Latinos." *Hispanic Journal of Behavioral Sciences* 28, no. 2: 245–266.

Armeli, Stephen, Kathleen Cimbolic Gunthert, and Lawrence H. Cohen. 2001. "Stressor Appraisals, Coping, and Post-Event Outcomes: The Dimensionality and Antecedents of Stress-Related Growth." *Journal of Social and Clinical Psychology* 20, no. 3: 366–395.

Babbitt, Susan E. 2001. *Artless Integrity: Moral Imagination, Agency, and Stories*. Lanham, MD: Rowman & Littlefield.

Bailey, Allison. 2007. "Strategic Ignorance." In *Race and Epistemologies of Ignorance*, edited by Shannon Sullivan and Nancy Tuana, 77–95. Albany: SUNY Press.

Balaguer, Mark. 2010. *Free Will as an Open Scientific Problem*. Cambridge, MA: MIT Press.

Bandura, Albert. 1977. "Self-Efficacy: Toward a Unifying Theory of Behavioral Change." *Psychological Review* 84, no. 2: 191–215.

Barajas, Manuel. 2009. *The Xaripu Community across Borders: Labor Migration, Community, and Family*. Notre Dame, IN: Notre Dame Press.

Bartels, Daniel M. 2008. "Principled Moral Sentiment and the Flexibility of Moral Judgment and Decision Making." *Cognition* 108: 381–417.

Bartky, Sandra. 1990. *Femininity and Domination: Studies in the Phenomenology of Oppression*. New York: Routledge.

Bechdel, Alison. 2007. *Fun Home: A Family Tragicomic*. New York: First Mariner Books.

Bekker, Marrie H. J., and Ursula Belt. 2006. "The Role of Autonomy-Connectedness in Depression and Anxiety." *Depression and Anxiety* 23: 274–280.

Bekker, Marrie H. J., and M. van Assen. 2006. "A Short Form of the Autonomy Scale: Properties of the Autonomy-Connectedness Scale." *Journal of Personality Assessment* 86: 51–60.

Benhabib, Seyla. 1985. "The Generalized and the Concrete Other: The Kohlberg Gilligan Controversy and Feminist Theory." *PRAXIS International* 4: 402–424.

Benson, Paul. 1994. "Free Agency and Self-Worth." *Journal of Philosophy* 91, no. 12: 650–668.

REFERENCES

Benson, Paul. 2000. "Feeling Crazy: Self-Worth and the Social Character of Responsibility." In *Relational Autonomy: Feminist Perspectives on Autonomy, Agency, and the Social Self*, edited by Catriona Mackenzie and Natalie Stoljar, 72–93. Oxford: Oxford University Press.

Bernal, Dolores Delgado. 2001. "Learning and Living Pedagogies of the Home: The Mestiza Consciousness of Chicana Students." *Qualitative Studies in Education* 14, no. 5: 623–639.

Berube, Allan. 2010. *Coming Out under Fire: The History of Gay Men and Women in World War II*. Chapel Hill: University of North Carolina Press.

Birzer, Michael, and Jackquice Smith-Mahdi. 2006. "Does Race Matter? The Phenomenology of Discrimination Experienced among African Americans." *Journal of African American Studies* 10, no. 2: 22–37.

Blalock, Andrew C., J. Stephen McDaniel, and Eugene W Farber. 2002. "Effect of Employment on Quality of Life and Psychological Functioning in Patients with HIV/AIDS." *Psychosomatics* 43, no. 5: 400–404.

Boggs, Grace Lee. 2012. *The Next American Revolution: Sustainable Activism for the Twenty-First Century*. Oakland: University of California Press.

Boler, Megan. 1999. *Feeling Power*. New York: Routledge.

Borders, Ashley, Luis A. Guillén, and Ilan H. Meyer. 2014. "Rumination, Sexual Orientation Uncertainty, and Psychological Distress in Sexual Minority University Students." *Counseling Psychologist* 42, no. 4: 497–523.

Bordo, Susan. 1993. *Unbearable Weight: Feminism, Western Culture, and the Body*. Berkeley: University of California Press.

Bowling, Ann. 1995. "What Things Are Important in People's Lives? A Survey of the Public's Judgements to Inform Scales of Health Related Quality of Life." *Social Science & Medicine* 41, no. 10: 1447–1462.

Braidotti, Rosi. 2006. "Affirmation versus Vulnerability: On Contemporary Ethical Debates." *Symposium* 10, no. 1: 235–254.

Bratman, Michael. 1979. "Practical Reasoning and Weakness of the Will." *Noûs* 13: 153–171.

Brison, Susan J. 2002. *Aftermath: Violence and the Remaking of a Self*. Princeton, NJ: Princeton University Press.

Brown, Laura S. 1995. "Not Outside the Range: One Feminist Perspective on Psychic Trauma." In *Trauma: Explorations in Memory*, edited by Cathy Caruth, 100–112. Baltimore, MD: Johns Hopkins University Press.

Brown, Tony N. 2003. "Critical Race Theory Speaks to the Sociology of Mental Health: Mental Health Problems Produced by Racial Stratification." *Journal of Health and Social Behavior* 44, no. 3: 292–301.

Brown, Tony N. 2008. "Race, Racism, and Mental Health: Elaboration of Critical Race Theory's Contribution to the Sociology of Mental Health." *Contemporary Justice Review: Issues in Criminal, Social, and Restorative Justice* 11, no. 1: 53–62.

REFERENCES

Browning, Frank. 1993. *The Culture of Desire: Paradox and Perversity in Gay Lives Today*. New York: Vintage Books.

Büchi, Stefan, et al. 2009. "Shared or Discordant Grief in Couples 2-6 Years after the Death of Their Premature Baby: Effects on Suffering and Posttraumatic Growth." *Psychosomatics* 50, no. 2: 123–130.

Butler, Judith. 1990. *Gender Trouble: Feminism and the Subversion of Identity*. New York: Routledge.

Butler, Judith. 2004. *Undoing Gender*. New York: Routledge.

Butler, Judith. 2005. *Giving an Account of Oneself*. New York: Fordham University Press.

Cadell, Susan. 2007. "The Sun Always Comes Out after It Rains: Understanding Posttraumatic Growth in HIV Caregivers." *Health & Social Work* 32, no. 3: 169–176.

Cagnetta, Eva, and Elvira Cicognani. 1999. "Surviving a Serious Traffic Accident: Adaptation Processes and Quality of Life." *Journal of Health Psychology* 4, no. 4: 551–564.

Calhoun, Cheshire. 1995. "Standing for Something." *Journal of Philosophy* 92, no. 5: 235–260.

Calhoun, Cheshire. 2003. *Feminism, the Family, and the Politics of the Closet: Lesbian and Gay Displacement*. Oxford: Oxford University Press.

Calhoun, Cheshire. 2008. "Losing One's Self." In *Practical Identity and Narrative Agency*, edited by Kim Atkins and Catriona Mackenzie, 193–211. New York: Routledge.

Calhoun, Cheshire. 2009. "What Good Is Commitment?" *Ethics* 119, no. 4: 613–641.

Calhoun, Lawrence, and Richard Tedeschi. 2012. *Posttraumatic Growth in Clinical Practice*. New York: Routledge.

Campbell, Sue. 1997. *Interpreting the Personal: Expression and the Formation of Feelings*. Ithaca, NY: Cornell University Press.

Campbell, Sue. 1999. "Dominant Identities and Settled Expectations." In *Racism and Philosophy*, edited by Susan E. Babbitt and Sue Campbell, 216–234. Ithaca, NY: Cornell University Press.

Campbell, Sue. 2003. *Relational Remembering: Rethinking the Memory Wars*. Lanham, MD: Rowman & Littlefield.

Campbell, Sue. 2014. *Our Faithfulness to the Past: The Ethics and Politics of Memory*. Oxford: Oxford University Press.

Campbell, Richmond, and Victor Kumar. 2012. "Moral Reasoning on the Ground." *Ethics* 122, no. 2: 273–312.

Card, Claudia. 1996. *The Unnatural Lottery*. Philadelphia, PA: Temple University Press.

Carel, Havi. 2008. *Illness: The Cry of the Flesh*. Durham: Acumen Publishing.

REFERENCES

Carpendale, Jeremy. 2000. "Kohlberg and Piaget on Stages and Moral Reasoning." *Developmental Review* 20, no. 2: 181–205.

Caruth, Cathy. 1996. *Unclaimed Experience: Trauma, Narrative, and History.* Baltimore, MD: Johns Hopkins University Press.

Casey, Edward S. 1987. *Remembering: A Phenomenological Study.* Bloomington: Indiana University Press.

Cavanagh, Sarah, Lisa Shin, Nasser Karamouz, and Scott Rauch. 2006. "Psychiatric and Emotional Sequelae of Surgical Amputation." *Psychosomatics* 47:459–464.

Chapman, L. Kevin, and Michael Steger. 2010. "Race and Religion: Differential Prediction of Anxiety Symptoms by Religious Coping in African American and European American Young Adults." *Depression and Anxiety* 27: 316–322.

Children of Men. 2006. Dir. Alfonso Cuarón.

Clarke, Ceara, Noleen Mccorry, and Martin Demster. 2011. "The Role of Identity in Adjustment among Survivors of Oesophageal Cancer." *Journal of Health Psychology* 16, no. 1: 99–108.

Code, Lorraine. 1991. *What Can She Know? Feminist Theory and the Construction of Knowledge.* Ithaca, NY: Cornell University Press.

Collins, Patricia Hill. 1986. "Learning from the Outsider Within: The Sociological Significance of Black Feminist Thought." *Social Problems* 33, no. 6: special section, 14–32.

Collins, R. L., S. E. Taylor, and L. A. Skokan. 1990. "A Better World or a Shattered Vision? Changes in Life Perspectives Following Victimization." *Social Cognition* 8: 263–285.

Connor, Kathryn, and Jonathan Davidson. 2003. "Development of a New Resilience Scale: The Connor-Davidson Resilience Scale (CD-RISC)." *Depression and Anxiety* 18: 76–82.

Connor, Kathryn, Jonathan Davidson, and Li-Ching Lee. 2003. "Spirituality, Resilience, and Anger in Survivors of Violent Trauma: A Community Survey." *Journal of Traumatic Stress* 16, no. 5: 487–494.

Conrad, Ryan, ed. 2014. *Against Equality: Queer Revolution, Not Mere Inclusion.* Oakland, CA: AK Press.

Conradi, Alexi. 2009. "Uprising at Oka: A Place of Non-identification." *Canadian Journal of Communication* 34: 547–566.

Cordova, Matthew J., Lauren L. C. Cunningham, Charles R. Carlson, and Michael A. Andrykowski. 2001. "Posttraumatic Growth Following Breast Cancer: A Controlled Comparison Study." *Health Psychology* 20, no. 3: 176–185.

Cotton, Sian, Ellen Levine, Cory Fitzpatrick, Kristin Dols, and Elisabeth Targ. 1999. "Exploring the Relationships among Spiritual Well-Being, Quality of Life, and Psychological Adjustment in Women with Breast Cancer." *Psycho-Oncology* 8: 429–438.

Couper, Jeremy, Sidney Bloch, Anthony Love, Gillian Duchesne, Michelle MacVean, and David Kissane. 2009. "Coping Patterns and Psychosocial Distress in Female Partners of Prostate Cancer Patients." *Psychosomatics* 50: 375–382.

Cox, Nele, Alexis Dewaee, Mieke van Houtte, and John Vincke. 2011. "Stress-Related Growth, Coming Out, and Internalized Homonegativity in Lesbian, Gay, and Bisexual Youth: An Examination of Stress-Related Growth within the Minority Stress Model." *Journal of Homosexuality* 58, no. 1: 117–137.

Cuomo, Chris. 2005. "White and Cracking Up." In *White on White/Black on Black*, edited by George Yancy, 27–34. Lanham, MD: Rowman & Littlefield.

Cushman, Fiery. 2013. "Action, Outcome, and Value: A Dual-System Framework for Morality." *Personality and Social Psychology Review* 17: 273–292.

Cushman, Fiery, L. Young, and M. D. Hauser. 2006. "The Role of Reasoning and Intuition in Moral Judgments: Testing Three Principles of Harm." *Psychological Science* 17, no. 12: 1082–1089.

Cvetkovich, Ann. 2012. *Depression: A Public Feeling*. Durham, NC: Duke University Press.

Danoff-Burg, Sharon, and Tracey Revenson. 2005. "Benefit-Finding among Patients with Rheumatoid Arthritis: Positive Effects on Interpersonal Relationships." *Journal of Behavioral Medicine* 28, no. 1: 91–103.

Davis, Angela. 2012. *The Meaning of Freedom: and Other Difficult Dialogues*. San Francisco, CA: City Lights Press.

Davis, Christopher, Cheryl Harasymchuk, and Michael J. A. Wohl. 2012. "Finding Meaning in a Traumatic Loss: A Families Approach." *Journal of Traumatic Stress* 25: 142–149.

Dekel, Rachel, and Orit Nuttman-Shwartz. 2009. "Posttraumatic Stress and Growth: The Contribution of Cognitive Appraisal and Sense of Belonging to the Country." *Health & Social Work* 34, no. 2: 87–96.

Deraniyagala, Sonali. 2013. *Wave*. New York: Knopf.

DesAutels, Peggy. 2004. "Moral Mindfulness." In *Moral Psychology: Feminist Ethics and Social Theory*, edited by Peggy DesAutels and Margaret Urban Walker, 69–81. Lanham, MD: Rowman & Littlefield.

Descartes, René. 1971. *Discourse on Method and the Meditations*. Translated by F. E. Sutcliffe. Baltimore, MD: Penguin Books.

Dewey, John. 1894. "The Theory of Emotion." *Psychological Review* 2, no. 1: 13–32.

Diagnostic and Statistical Manual of Mental Disorders 5 (*DSM* 5). 2013. Washington, DC: American Psychiatric Publishing.

Didion, Joan. 2006. *The Year of Magical Thinking*. London: Harper Perennial.

Didion, Joan. 2009. *The White Album*. New York: Farrar, Straus and Giroux.

Dillon, Robin S. 1992. "Toward a Feminist Conception of Self-Respect." *Hypatia* 7, no. 1: 52–69.

REFERENCES

Dillon, Robin S. 1997. "Self-Respect: Moral, Emotional, Political." *Ethics* 107, no. 2: 226–249.

Dillon, Robin S. 2004. "'What's a Woman Worth? What's Life Worth? Without Self-Respect!': On the Value of Evaluative Self-Respect." In *Moral Psychology: Feminist Ethics and Social Theory*, edited by Peggy DesAutels and Margaret Urban Walker, 47–66. Lanham, MD: Rowman & Littlefield.

Dillon, Robin S. 2012. "Critical Character Theory: Toward a Feminist Perspective on 'Vice' (and 'Virtue')." In *Out from the Shadows: Analytical Feminist Contributions to Traditional Philosophy*, edited by Sharon L. Crasnow and Anita M. Superson, 83–114. Oxford: Oxford University Press.

Dixon, Chris. 2014. *Another Politics: Talking across Today's Transformative Movements*. Berkeley: University of California Press.

Du Bois, W. E. B. 1996. *The Souls of Black Folk*. New York: Penguin Books.

Duke, M. R., B. Bourdeau, and J. D. Hovey. 2010. "Day Laborers and Occupational Stress: Testing the Migrant Stress Inventory with a Latino Day Laborer Population." *Cultural Diversity and Ethnic Minority Psychology* 16, no. 2: 116–122.

Edelman, Lee. 2004. *No Future: Queer Theory and the Death Drive*. Durham, NC: Duke University Press.

Ehrenreich, Barbara. 2010. *Bright-Sided: How Positive Thinking Is Undermining America*. New York: Picador.

Ell, Kathleen. 1996. "Social Networks, Social Support and Coping with Serious Illness: The Family Connection." *Social Science & Medicine* 42, no. 2: 173–183.

Elliot, Susan J., and Joan Gillie. 1998. "Moving Experiences: A Qualitative Analysis of Health and Migration." *Health & Place* 4, no. 4: 327-339.

Fabbri, Stefania, Navneet Kapur, Adrian Wells, and Francis Creed. 2001. "Emotional, Cognitive, and Behavioral Characteristics of Medical Outpatients." *Psychosomatics* 42: 74–77.

Fanon, Frantz. 1967. *Black Skin, White Masks*. New York: Grove Press.

Farber, Eugene, Jennifer Schwartz, Paul Schaper, DeElla Moonen, and Stephen McDaniel. 2000. "Resilience Factors Associated with Adaptation to HIV Disease." *Psychosomatics* 41: 140–146.

Feldman, Barry, and Anne Broussard. 2006. "Men's Adjustment to Their Partners' Breast Cancer: A Dyadic Coping Perspective." *Health & Social Work* 31, no. 2: 117–127.

Finch, Brian, Reanne Frank, and William Vega. 2004. "Acculturation and Acculturation Stress: A Social-Epidemiological Approach to Mexican Migrant Farmworkers' Health." *International Migration Review* 38, no. 1: 236–262.

Fine, Michelle, and Susan Merle Gordon. 1992. "Feminist Transformations of/despite Psychology." In *Disruptive Voices: The Possibilities of Feminist Research*, edited by Michelle Fine, 1–26. Ann Arbor: University of Michigan Press.

REFERENCES

Folkman, Susan. 1997. "Positive Psychological States and Coping with Severe Stress." *Social Science & Medicine* 45, no. 8: 1207–1221.

Ford, Julian, Christine Coutois, Kathy Steele, Onno van der Hart, and Ellert Nikenhuis. 2000. "Treatment of Complex Posttraumatic Self-Dysregulation." *Journal of Traumatic Stress* 18, no. 5: 437–447.

Frank, Arthur W. 2000. "Illness and Autobiographical Work: Dialogue as Narrative Destabilization." *Qualitative Sociology* 23, no. 1: 135–156.

Frankenburg, Ruth. 1993. *White Women, Race Matters: The Social Construction of Whiteness*. Minneapolis: University of Minnesota Press.

Frankfurt, Harry. 1987. "Identification and Wholeheartedness." In *Responsibility, Character, and the Emotions*, edited by Ferdinand Schoeman, 27–45. Cambridge: Cambridge University Press.

Frankfurt, Harry. 1999. *Necessity, Volition, and Love*. Cambridge: Cambridge University Press.

Frankfurt, Harry. 2004. *Reasons of Love*. Princeton, NJ: Princeton University Press.

Frantz, Thomas, Barbara Trolley, and Megan Farrell. 1998. "Positive Aspects of Grief." *Pastoral Psychology* 47, no. 1: 3–17.

Freire, Paolo. 1973. *Pedagogy of the Oppressed*. New York: Seabury Press.

Fricker, Miranda. 2007. *Epistemic Injustice: Power and the Ethics of Knowing*. Oxford: Oxford University Press.

Friedman, Carly, and Campbell Leaper. 2010. "Sexual-Minority College Women's Experiences with Discrimination: Relations with Identity and Collective Action." *Psychology of Women Quarterly* 34: 152–164.

Friedman, Marilyn. 2000. "Autonomy, Social Disruption, and Women." In *Relational Autonomy: Feminist Perspectives on Autonomy, Agency, and the Social Self*, edited by C. Mackenzie and N. Stoljar, 35–51. Oxford: Oxford University Press.

Froyum, Carissa. 2007. "At Least I'm Not Gay: Heterosexual Identity Making among Poor Black Teens." *Sexualities* 10, no. 5: 603–622.

Garland-Thomson, Rosemarie. 2011. "Misfits: A Feminist Materialist Disability Concept." *Hypatia* 26, no. 3: 591–609.

Garnets, L., G. M. Herek, and B. Levy. 1993. "Violence and Victimization of Lesbians and Gay Men: Mental Health Consequences." In *Psychological Perspectives on Lesbian and Gay Male Experiences*, edited by L. Garnets and D. C. Kimmel, 579–599. New York: Columbia University Press.

Gentry, W. D., and S. C. O. Kobasa. 1984. "Social and Psychological Resources Mediating Stress-Illness Relationships in Humans." In *Handbook of Behavioral Medicine*, edited by W. D. Gentry, 87–116. New York: Guilford Press.

Germino, Barbara, Merle Mishel, Michael Belyea, Lorna Harris, Andrea Ware, and James Mohler. 1998. "Uncertainty in Prostate Cancer: Ethnic and Family Patterns." *Cancer Practice* 6, no. 2: 107–113.

REFERENCES

Gilligan, Carol. 1982. *In a Different Voice: Psychological Theory and Women's Development*. Cambridge, MA: Harvard University Press.

Gilman, Charlotte Perkins. 1972. *The Living of Charlotte Perkins Gilman*. New York: Arno Press.

Goldie, Peter. 2011. "Grief: A Narrative Account." *Ratio* 24, no. 2: 119–137.

Gould, Deborah. 2001. "Rock the Boat, Don't Rock the Boat, Baby: Ambivalence and the Emergence of Militant AIDS Activism." In *Passionate Politics: Emotions and Social Movements*, edited by Jeff Goodwin, James Jasper, and Francesca Polletta, 135–157. Chicago: University of Chicago Press.

Greene, Joshua. 2008. "The Secret Joke of Kant's Soul." In *Moral Psychology*, vol. 3, *The Neuroscience of Morality*, edited by Walter Sinnott-Armstrong, 35–79. Cambridge, MA: MIT Press.

Greene, Joshua. 2013. *Moral Tribes: Emotion, Reason, and the Gap between Us and Them*. New York: Penguin.

Greene, Joshua, and Jonathan Haidt. 2002. "How (and Where) Does Moral Judgment Work?" *Trends in Cognitive Science* 6: 517–523.

Greene, Joshua, R. Brian Sommerville, Leigh Nystrom, John Darley, and Jonathan Cohen. 2001. "An fMRI Investigation of Emotional Engagement in Moral Judgment." *Science* 293: 2105–2108.

Greene, Joshua, Sylvia Morelli, Kelly Lowenberg, Leigh Nystrom, and Jonathan Cohen. 2008. "Cognitive Load Selectively Interferes with Utilitarian Moral Judgment." *Cognition* 107: 1144–1154.

Greene, Joshua, F. A. Cushman, L. E. Stewart, K. Lowenberg, L. E. Nystrom, and J. D. Cohen. 2009. "Pushing Moral Buttons: The Interaction between Personal Force and Intention in Moral Judgment." *Cognition* 111: 364–371.

Greene, Maxine. 1988. *The Dialectic of Freedom*. New York: Teachers College Press.

Greenspan, Patricia. 1980. "A Case of Mixed Feelings: Ambivalence and the Logic of Emotion." In *Explaining Emotions*, edited by Amélie Rorty, 223–250. Berkeley: University of California Press.

Griffith, James, and Lynne Gaby. 2005. "Brief Psychotherapy at the Bedside: Countering Demoralization from Medical Illness." *Psychosomatics* 46: 109–116.

Groundhog Day. 1993. Dir. Harold Ramis.

Gutierrez, Lorraine. 1995. "Understanding the Empowerment Process: Does Consciousness Make a Difference?" *Social Work Research* 19, no. 4: 229–237.

Hackl, Kristin, Anton Somlai, Jeffrey Kelly, and Seth Kalichman. 1997. "Women Living with HIV/AIDS: The Dual Challenge of Being a Patient and Caregiver." *Health & Social Work* 22, no. 1: 53–62.

Hai, Yasmin. 2008. *The Making of Mr. Hai's Daughter: Becoming British*. London: Virago Press.

Haidt, Jonathan. 2001. "The Emotional Dog and its Rational Tail." *Psychological Review* 108: 814–834.

REFERENCES

Haidt, Jonathan, Fredrik Björklund, and Scott Murphy. 2000. "Moral Dumbfounding: When Intuition Finds No Reason." Unpublished manuscript, University of Virginia.

Halifax Palliative Care Bereavement Program. http://www.cdha.nshealth.ca/media-centre/news/weekly-walkers-supportive-walking-group-anyone-living-grief.

Hall, Stuart. 1990. "Cultural Identity and Diaspora." In *Identity: Community, Culture, Difference*, edited by Jonathan Rutherford, 222–237. London: Lawrence & Wishart.

Halstead, Marilyn, and Jayne Fernsler. 1994. "Coping Strategies of Long-Term Cancer Survivors." *Cancer Nursing* 17, no. 2: 94–100.

Hamilton-West, Kate, and Lyn Quine. 2009. "Living with Ankylosing Spondylitis: The Patient's Perspective." *Journal of Health Psychology* 14: 820–830.

Harbin, Ami. 2012. "Bodily Disorientation and Moral Change." *Hypatia* 27, no. 2: 261–280.

Harbin, Ami. 2014a. "Disorientation and the Medicalization of Struggle." *International Journal of Feminist Approaches to Bioethics* 7, no. 1: 99–121.

Harbin, Ami. 2014b. "The Disorientations of Acting against Injustice." *Journal of Social Philosophy* 45, no. 2: 162–181.

Harbin, Ami. 2014c. "Mentorship in Method: Philosophy and Experienced Agency." *Hypatia: A Journal of Feminist Philosophy* 29, no. 2: 476–492.

Harbin, Ami. 2015a. "Prisons and Palliative Politics." In *Death and Other Penalties: Philosophy in a Time of Mass Incarceration*, edited by Lisa Guenther, Geoffrey Adelsberg, and Scott Zeman, 158–173. New York: Fordham University Press.

Harbin, Ami. 2015b. "Prescribing Posttraumatic Growth." *Bioethics* 29, no. 9: 671–679.

Hare, R. M. 1952. *The Language of Morals*. Oxford: Clarendon Press.

Harms, Louise, and Michelle Talbot. 2007. "The Aftermath of Road Trauma: Survivors' Perceptions of Trauma and Growth." *Health and Social Work* 32, no. 2: 129–137.

Haslanger, Sally. 2008. "Changing the Culture and Ideology of Philosophy: Not by Reason (Alone)." *Hypatia* 23, no. 2: 210–222.

Hatab, Lawrence. 2000. *Ethics and Finitude: Heidegger's Contributions to Moral Philosophy*. Lanham, MA: Rowman & Littlefield.

Heidegger, Martin. 1962. *Being and Time*. Translated by John Macquarrie and Edward Robinson. New York: Harper & Row.

Herman, Judith Lewis. 1992. *Trauma and Recovery*. New York: Basic Books.

Heyes, Cressida. 2007. *Self-Transformations: Foucault, Ethics, and Normalized Bodies*. Oxford: Oxford University Press.

Hightower, Corbyn. 2011. "Will Everything Be Alright?" http://corbynhightower.com/will-everything-be-all-right/.

REFERENCES

Hill, Thomas. 1991. *Autonomy and Self-Respect*. Cambridge: Cambridge University Press.

Holland, Jimmie, and Sheldon Lewis. 2000. *The Human Side of Cancer: Living with Hope, Coping with Uncertainty*. New York: Harper Collins.

hooks, bell. 1984. *Feminist Theory from Margin to Center*. Cambridge: South End Press.

Hopp, Faith Pratt, Nancy Thornton, and Lindsey Martin. 2010. "The Lived Experience of Heart Failure at the End of Life: A Systematic Literature Review." *Health and Social Work* 35, no. 2: 109–117.

Horowitz, Mardi, Eva Sundin, Andrea Zanko, and Roger Lauer. 2001. "Coping with Grim News from Genetic Tests." *Psychosomatics* 42: 100–105.

Huebner, Bryce, Susan Dwyer, and Marc Hauser. 2009. "The Role of Emotion in Moral Psychology." *Trends in Cognitive Science* 13, no. 1: 1–6.

Hunter, Margaret L., and Kimberly D. Nettles. 1999. "What about the White Women?: Racial Politics in a Women's Studies Classroom." *Teaching Sociology* 27, no. 4: 385–397.

Jaggar, Alison. 1997. "Love and Knowledge: Emotion in Feminist Epistemology." In *Feminist Social Thought: A Reader*, edited by Diana Tietjens Meyers, 384–404. New York: Routledge.

James, Henry, Sr. [1884] 1970. *The Literary Remains of Henry James*, ed. William James. Reprint. Upper Saddle River, NJ: Literature House.

James, William. 1884. "What Is an Emotion?" *Mind* 9: 188–205.

Jamison, Kay Redfield. 2009. *Nothing Was the Same: A Memoir*. New York: Knopf.

Janoff-Bulman, R. 1989. "Assumptive Worlds and the Stress of Traumatic Events: Applications of the Schema Construct." *Social Cognition* 7: 113–136.

Janoff-Bulman, R. 1992. *Shattered Assumptions: Towards a New Psychology of Trauma*. New York: Free Press.

Janoff-Bulman, R., and I. H. Frieze. 1983. "A Theoretical Perspective for Understanding Reactions to Victimization." *Journal of Social Issues* 39: 1–17.

Jasper, James. 1998. "The Emotions of Protest: Affective and Reactive Emotions in and around Social Movements." *Sociological Forum* 13, no. 3: 397–424.

Johnston, Lon, and David Jenkins. 2003. "Coming Out in Mid-Adulthood: Building a New Identity." *Journal of Gay & Lesbian Social Services* 16, no. 2: 19–42.

Jones, Karen. 2004. "Trust and Terror." In *Moral Psychology: Feminist Ethics and Social Theory*, edited by Peggy DesAutels and Margaret Urban Walker, 3–18. Lanham, MD: Rowman & Littlefield.

Jordan, Karen, and Robert Deluty. 1998. "Coming Out for Lesbian Women: Its Relation to Anxiety, Positive Affectivity, Self-Esteem, and Social Support." *Journal of Homosexuality* 35, no. 2: 41–63.

Kahneman, Daniel. 2003. "A Perspective on Judgment and Choice." *American Psychologist* 58, no. 9: 697–720.

REFERENCES

Kahneman, Daniel. 2011. *Thinking Fast and Slow*. New York: Farrar, Straus, and Giroux.

Kahneman, Daniel, and Amos Tversky. 1984. "Choices, Values, and Frames." *American Psychologist* 39: 341–350.

Kalman, Hildur. 2012. "Feelings of Loss and Grieving: Selves between Autonomy and Dependence." *PhaenEx* 7, no. 2: 1–27.

Kanaiaupuni, Shawn Malia. 2000. "Sustaining Families and Communities: Nonmigrant Women and Mexico-U.S. Migration Processes." Center for Demography and Ecology Working Paper, University of Wisconsin Madison.

Kant, Immanuel. 1991. *Political Writings*. Edited by Hans Reiss. Cambridge: Cambridge University Press.

Ka'opua, Lana Sue I., Carolyn C. Gotay, and Patricia S. Boehm. 2007. "Spiritually Based Resources in Adaptation to Long-Term Prostate Cancer Survival: Perspectives of Elderly Wives." *Health & Social Work* 32, no. 1: 29–39.

Kerig, Patricia, Diana Bennett, Mamie Thompson, and Stephen Becker. 2012. "'Nothing Really Matters': Emotional Numbing as a Link between Trauma Exposure and Callousness in Delinquent Youth." *Journal of Traumatic Stress* 25: 272–279.

Kierkegaard, Søren. 2006. *Fear and Trembling*. Cambridge: Cambridge University Press.

Kierkegaard, Søren. 2009. *Repetition and Philosophical Crumbs*. Oxford: Oxford University Press.

Kim, David Haekwon. 1999. "Contempt and Ordinary Inequality." In *Racism and Philosophy*, edited by Susan E. Babbitt and Sue Campbell, 108–123. Ithaca, NY: Cornell University Press.

Kimmel, Ryan, and Mitchell Levy. 2013. "Brief Psychotherapy for Demoralization in Terminal Cancer: A Case Report." *Psychosomatics* 54: 84–87.

Kiss, Alexander, and Siegfried Meryn. 2001. "Effect of Sex and Gender on Psychosocial Aspects of Prostate and Breast Cancer." *British Medical Journal* 323, no. 3: 1055–1058.

Kitzinger, Celia, and Sue Wilkinson. 1995. "Transitions from Heterosexuality to Lesbianism: The Discursive Production of Lesbian Identities." *Developmental Psychology* 31: 95–104.

Kobasa, S. C. 1979. "Stressful Life Events, Personality, and Health: An Inquiry into Hardiness." *Journal of Personality and Social Psychology* 37: 1–11.

Kobasa, S. C., S. R. Maddi, and S. Kahn. 1982. "Hardiness and Health: A Prospective Study." *Journal of Personality and Social Psychology* 42: 168–177.

Koggel, Christine. 1998. *Perspectives on Equality: Constructing a Relational Theory*. Lanham, MD: Rowman & Littlefield.

Kohlberg, Lawrence. 1971. "From Is to Ought: How to Commit the Naturalistic Fallacy and Get Away with It in the Study of Moral Development."

In *Cognitive Development and Epistemology*, edited by T. Mischel, 153–235. New York: Academic Press.

Kohlberg, Lawrence. 1981. *The Philosophy of Moral Development: Moral Stages and the Idea of Justice*. New York: Harper and Row.

Kohlberg, Lawrence. 1984. *The Psychology of Moral Development: The Nature and Validity of Moral Stages*. New York: Harper and Row.

Kraus, Michael, Arne Schafer, Herbert Csef, Michael Scheurlen, and Hermann Faller. 2000. "Emotional State, Coping Styles, and Somatic Variables in Patients with Chronic Hepatitis C." *Psychosomatics* 41: 377–384.

Kuhn, Thomas. 1996. *The Structure of Scientific Revolutions*. Chicago: University of Chicago Press.

Kurashige, Scott. 2012. "Introduction." In *The Next American Revolution: Sustainable Activism for the Twenty-First Century*, by Grace Lee Boggs, 1–27. Oakland: University of California Press.

Landau, Ruth, and Howard Litwin. 2000. "The Effects of Extreme Early Stress in Very Old Age." *Journal of Traumatic Stress* 13, no. 3: 473–487.

Lang, A., C. Goulet, and R. Amsel. 2003. "Lang and Goulet Hardiness Scale: Development and Testing on Bereaved Parents Following the Death of Their Fetus/Infant." *Death Studies* 27, no. 10: 851–880.

Lechner, S. C., et al. 2003. "Do Sociodemographic and Disease-Related Variables Influence Benefit-Finding in Cancer Patients?" *Psycho-Oncology* 12: 491–499.

Leder, Drew. 1990. *The Absent Body*. Chicago: University of Chicago Press.

Lehman, Darrin, Camille Wortman, Susan Bluck, and David Mandel. 1993. "Positive and Negative Life Changes Following Bereavement and Their Relations to Adjustment." *Journal of Social and Clinical Psychology* 12, no. 1: 90–112.

Levine, Stephen, Avital Laufer, Einat Stein, Yaira Hamama-Raz, and Zahava Solomon. 2009. "Examining the Relationship between Resilience and Posttraumatic Growth." *Journal of Traumatic Stress* 22, no. 4: 282–286.

Lewis, C. S. 1961. *A Grief Observed*. London: Faber and Faber.

Lewis, Jioni A., Ruby Mendenhall, Stacy A. Harwood, and Margaret Browne Huntt. 2013. "Coping with Gendered Racial Microaggressions among Black Women College Students." *Journal of African American Studies* 17: 51–73.

Lewis, Magda. 1990. "Interrupting Patriarchy: Politics, Resistance, and Transformation in the Feminist Classroom." *Harvard Educational Review* 60, no. 4: 467–488.

Lewis, Robin, Valerian Derlega, Eva Clarke, and Jenny Kuang. 2006. "Stigma Consciousness, Social Constraints, and Lesbian Well-Being." *Journal of Counseling Psychology* 53, no. 1: 48–56.

Lincoln, Karen, Linda Chatter, and Robert Joseph Taylor. 2003. "Psychological Distress among Black and White Americans: Differential Effects of Social Support, Negative Interaction and Personal Control." *Journal of Health and Social Behavior* 44, no. 3: 390–407.

REFERENCES

Linley, Alex, and Stephen Joseph. 2004. "Positive Change Following Trauma and Adversity: A Review." *Journal of Traumatic Stress* 17, no. 1: 11–21.

Livneh, Hanoch, Richard Antonak, and John Gerhardt. 2000. "Multidimensional Investigation of the Structure of Coping among People with Amputations." *Psychosomatics* 41: 235–244.

Lloyd, Genevieve. 1993. *Being in Time: Selves and Narrators in Philosophy and Literature*. New York: Routledge.

Lommen, Miriam, Iris Engelhard, Rens van de Schoot, and Marcel A ven den Hout. 2014. "Anger: Cause or Consequence of Posttraumatic Stress? A Prospective Study of Dutch Soldiers." *Journal of Traumatic Stress* 27: 200–207.

Lorde, Audre. 1997. *The Cancer Journals*. San Francisco, CA: Aunt Lute Books.

Lugones, María. 1987. "Playfulness, World-Travelling, and Loving Perception." *Hypatia* 2, no. 2: 3–19.

Lugones, María. 2003. *Pilgrimages/Peregrinajes: Theorizing Coalition against Multiple Oppressions*. Lanham, MD: Rowman & Littlefield.

Luthar, S. 1991. "Vulnerability and Resilience: A Study of High Risk Adolescence." *Child Development* 62, no. 3: 600–616.

Mayberry, Maralee, and Ellen Cronan Rose, eds. 1999. *Meeting the Challenge: Innovative Feminist Pedagogies in Action*. New York: Routledge.

McCrae, Robert. 1984. "Situational Determinants of Coping Responses: Loss, Threat, and Challenge." *Journal of Personality and Social Psychology* 46, no. 4: 919–928.

Mackenzie, Catriona, and Natalie Stoljar. 2000. *Relational Autonomy: Feminist Perspectives on Autonomy, Agency, and the Social Self*. New York: Oxford University Press.

McLeod, Neal. 2007. *Cree Narrative Memory: From Treaties to Contemporary Times*. Saskatoon: Purich Publishing.

Mancini, Anthony, Gabriele Prati, and Sarah Black. 2011. "Self-Worth Mediates the Effects of Violent Loss on PTSD Symptoms." *Journal of Traumatic Stress* 24, no. 1: 116–120.

Mansson, Sven-Axel. 1992. "Dead-End or Turning Point: On Homosexuality and Coping with HIV." *Journal of Psychology & Human Sexuality* 5, nos. 1–2: 157–176.

Marsiglia, Flavio, Stephen Kulis, Hilda Garcia Perez, and Monica Bermudez-Parsai. 2011. "Hopelessness, Family Stress, and Depression among Mexican-Heritage Mothers in the Southwest." *Health & Social Work* 36, no. 1: 7–18.

Medina, José. 2002. *The Unity of Wittgenstein's Philosophy: Necessity, Intelligibility, and Normativity*. Albany: SUNY Press.

Medina, José. 2013. *The Epistemology of Resistance: Gender and Racial Oppression, Epistemic Injustice, and Resistant Imaginations*. Oxford: Oxford University Press.

Meyers, Diana Tietjens. 1997. "Emotion and Heterodox Moral Perception: An Essay in Moral Social Psychology." In *Feminists Rethink the Self*, edited by Diana Tietjens Meyers, 197–218. Boulder, CO: Westview Press.

REFERENCES

Meyers, Diana Tietjens. 2004. *Being Yourself: Essays on Identity, Action, and Social Life*. Lanham, MD: Rowman & Littlefield.

Mill, John Stuart. 2009. *The Autobiography of John Stuart Mill*. Huntington, MA: Seven Treasures Publications.

Mill, John Stuart. 2011. *Utilitarianism*. Peterborough: Broadview Press.

Mills, Charles. 2007. "White Ignorance." In *Race and Epistemologies of Ignorance*, edited by Shannon Sullivan and Nancy Tuana, 13–38. Albany: SUNY Press.

Minkler, Meredith. 1979. "Role Shock: A Tool for Conceptualizing Stresses Accompanying Disruptive Role Transitions." *Human Relations* 32, no. 2: 125–140.

Miranda, Alexis, and Kenneth Matheny. 2000. "Socio-Psychological Predictors of Acculturative Stress among Latino Adults." *Journal of Mental Health Counseling* 22, no. 4: 306–318.

Moll, J., R. De Oliveira-Souza, and R. Zahn. 2008. "The Neural Basis of Moral Cognition: Sentiments, Concepts, and Values." *Annals of the New York Academy of Sciences* 1124: 161–180.

Moller, Dan. 2007. "Love and Death." *Journal of Philosophy* 104: 301–316.

Murphy, John Michael, and Carol Gilligan. 1980. "Moral Development in Late Adolescence and Adulthood: A Critique and Reconstruction of Kohlberg's Theory." *Human Development* 23: 77–104.

Nagel, Thomas. 1979. *Mortal Questions*. New York: Cambridge University Press.

Nietzsche, Friedrich. 2010. *The Birth of Tragedy* and *The Case of Wagner*. Translated by Walter Kaufman. New York: Knopf Doubleday.

Northouse, Laurel, Darlene Mood, Trace Kershaw, Ann Schafenacker, Suzanne Mellon, Julie Walker, Elizabeth Galvin, and Veronica Decker. 2002. "Quality of Life of Women with Recurrent Breast Cancer and Their Family Members." *Journal of Clinical Oncology* 20, no. 19: 4050–4064.

Olberding, Amy, Sherri Irvin, and Stephen Ellis. 2014. "Best Practices for Fostering Diversity in Tenure-Track Searches." *APA Newsletter on Feminism and Philosophy* 13, no. 2: 27–36.

O'Reilly, Jane. 1971. "The Housewife's Moment of Truth." *New York Magazine*. December 20.

Pargament, K., B. Smith, B. W. Koenig, and L. Perez. 1998. "Patterns of Positive and Negative Religious Coping with Major Life Stressors." *Journal of Scientific Study of Religion* 37: 711–725.

Park, Crystal, Lawrence Cohen, and Renee Murch. 1996. "Assessment and Prediction of Stress-Related Growth." *Journal of Personality* 64, no. 1: 71–105.

Paxton, J. M., and Joshua Greene, J.D. 2010. "Moral Reasoning: Hints and Allegations." *Topics in Cognitive Science* 2, no. 3: 511–527.

Peirce, Charles S. 1955. *Philosophical Writings of Peirce*. New York: Dover.

Pelcovitz, David, Barbara Goldenberg Libov, Francine Mandel, Sandra Kaplan, Mark Weinblatt, and Aliza Septimus. 1998. "Posttraumatic Stress Disorder and Family Functioning in Adolescent Cancer." *Journal of Traumatic Stress* 11, no. 2: 205–221.

Peltason, Jodi. 2013. "Before I Forget: What Nobody Remembers about New Motherhood." http://www.theatlantic.com/sexes/archive/2013/04/before-i-forget-what-nobody-remembers-aboutnew-motherhood/274981/.

Pereboom, Derk. 2014. *Free Will, Agency, and Meaning in Life.* Oxford: Oxford University Press.

Perez, Sandra, María José Galdón, Yolanda Andreu, Elena Ibáñez, Estrella Durá, Andrea Conchado, and Etzel Cardeña. 2014. "Posttraumatic Stress Symptoms in Breast Cancer Patients: Temporal Evolution, Predictors, and Mediation." *Journal of Traumatic Stress* 27: 224–231.

Pezeu-Massabuau, Jacques. 2012. *A Philosophy of Discomfort.* London: Reaktion Books.

Pham, Phuong, Patrick Vinck, Didine Kaba Kinkodi, and Harvey Weinstein. 2010. "Sense of Coherence and Its Association with Exposure to Traumatic Events, Posttraumatic Stress Disorder, and Depression in Eastern Democratic Republic of Congo." *Journal of Traumatic Stress* 23, no. 3: 313–321.

Piaget, Jean. 1932. *The Moral Judgment of the Child.* London: Kegan Paul, Trench, Trubner and Co.

Pietrzak, Robert, and Joan M. Cook. 2013. "Psychological Resilience in Older U.S. Veterans: Results from the National Health and Resilience in Veterans Study." *Depression and Anxiety* 30: 432–443.

Pietrzak, Robert, Douglas C. Johnson, Marc B. Goldstein, James C. Malley, and Steven M. Southwick. 2009. "Psychological Resilience and Postdeployment Social Support Protect against Traumatic Stress and Depressive Symptoms in Soldiers Returning from Operations Enduring Freedom and Iraqi Freedom." *Depression and Anxiety* 26: 745–751.

Pinel, E. C. 1999. "Stigma Consciousness: The Psychological Legacy of Social Stereotypes." *Journal of Personality and Social Psychology* 76: 114–128.

Pinquart, Martin, Cornelia Fröhlich, and Rainer K. Silbereisen. 2007. "Cancer Patients' Perceptions of Positive and Negative Illness-Related Changes." *Journal of Health Psychology* 12: 907–921.

Pippin, Robert. 2000. *Henry James and Modern Moral Life.* Cambridge: Cambridge University Press.

Plato. 1956. *Great Dialogues of Plato.* Chicago: New American Library.

Plato. 1981. *Five Dialogues.* Cambridge: Hackett.

Poindexter, Cynthia Cannon. 1997. "In the Aftermath: Serial Crisis Intervention for People with HIV." *Health & Social Work* 22, no. 2: 125–132.

Power, Clark, Ann Higgins, and Lawrence Kohlberg. 1989. *Lawrence Kohlberg's Approach to Moral Education.* New York: Columbia University Press.

Pratt, Minnie Bruce. 1984. "Identity: Skin, Blood, Heart." In *Yours in Struggle: Three Feminist Perspective on Anti-Semitism and Racism,* by Elly Bulkin, Minnie Bruce Pratt, and Barbara Smith, 11–63. Brooklyn, NY: Long Haul Press.

REFERENCES

Railton, Peter. 2014. "The Affective Dog and Its Rational Tale: Intuition and Attunement." *Ethics* 124, no. 4: 813–859.

Regan, Paulette. 2010. *Unsettling the Settler Within: Indian Residential Schools, Truth Telling, and Reconciliation in Canada.* Vancouver: UBC Press.

Reger, Jo. 2004. "Organizational 'Emotion Work' through Consciousness-Raising: An Analysis of a Feminist Organization." *Qualitative Sociology* 27, no. 2: 205–222.

Remen, Rachel Naomi. 2006. *Kitchen Table Wisdom: Stories that Heal.* New York: Riverhead Books.

Rich, Adrienne. 1993. "Compulsory Heterosexuality and Lesbian Existence." In *The Lesbian and Gay Studies Reader,* edited by Henry Abelove, Michèle Aina Barale, and David M. Halperin, 227–254. New York: Routledge.

Ridgeway, James. 2012. "The Other Death Sentence." *Mother Jones,* September. http://www.motherjones.com/politics/2012/09/massachusetts-elderly-prisoners-costcompassionate- release.

Rini, Christine, Sharon Manne, Katherine N. DuHamel, Jane Austin, Jamie Ostroff, Farid Boulad, Susan K. Parsons, Richard Martini, Sharon Williams, Laura Mee, Sandra Sexson, and William H. Redd. 2004. "Changes in Mothers' Basic Beliefs Following a Child's Bone Marrow Transplantation: The Role of Prior Trauma and Negative Life Events." *Journal of Traumatic Stress* 17, no. 4: 325–333.

Ritivoi, Andreea Deciu. 2002. *Yesterday's Self: Nostalgia and the Immigrant Identity.* Oxford: Rowman & Littlefield.

Rollock, Nicola, David Gillborn, Carol Vincent, and Stephen Ball. 2011. "The Public Identities of the Black Middle Classes: Managing Race in Public Spaces." *Sociology* 45: 1078–1093.

Ruíz, Elena Flores. 2014. "Musing: Spectral Phenomenologies: Dwelling Poetically in Professional Philosophy." *Hypatia* 29, no. 1: 196–204.

Rutter, Michael. 1987. "Psychosocial Resilience and Protective Mechanisms." *American Journal of Orthopsychiatry* 57, no. 3: 316–331.

Sartre, Jean-Paul. 1973. *Existentialism & Humanism.* London: Methuen.

Saul, Jennifer. 2012. "Ranking Exercises in Philosophy and Implicit Bias." *Journal of Social Philosophy* 43, no. 3: 256–273.

Saul, Jennifer. 2013. "Implicit Bias, Stereotype Threat and Women in Philosophy." In *Women in Philosophy: What Needs to Change?,* edited by Fiona Jenkins and Katrina Hutchison, 39–60. Oxford: Oxford University Press.

Scheman, Naomi. 1980. "Anger and the Politics of Naming." In *Women and Language in Literature and Society,* edited by Sally McConnell-Ginet, Ruth Borker, and Nelly Furman, 174–187. New York: Praeger Publishers.

Scheman, Naomi. 1996. "Feeling Our Way toward Moral Objectivity." *Minds and Morals: Essays on Cognitive Science and Ethics,* edited by Larry May, Marilyn Friedman, and Andy Clark, 221–236. Cambridge, MA: MIT Press.

Scheman, Naomi. 2011. *Shifting Ground: Knowledge and Reality, Transgression and Trustworthiness.* Oxford: Oxford University Press.

REFERENCES

Scheman, Naomi, and Peg O'Connor, eds. 2002. *Feminist Interpretations of Ludwig Wittgenstein*. University Park: Penn State University Press.

Scherkoske, Greg. 2010. "Integrity and Moral Danger." *Canadian Journal of Philosophy* 40: 335–358.

Scherkoske, Greg. 2012. *Leading a Convincing Life: Integrity and the Virtues of Reason*. New York: Cambridge University Press.

Schwartzberg, Steven. 1993. "Struggling for Meaning: How HIV-Positive Gay Men Make Sense of AIDS." *Professional Psychology: Research and Practice* 24, no. 4: 483–490.

Sears, J. T. 1991. "Educators, Homosexuality and Homosexual Students: Are Personal Feelings Related to Professional Beliefs?" *Journal of Homosexuality* 22: 29–48.

Servan-Schreiber, David. 2008. *Anti-Cancer: A New Way of Life*. New York: Harper Collins.

Shakespeare-Finch, Jane, and Allysa Barrington. 2012. "Behavioural Changes Add Validity to the Construct of Posttraumatic Growth." *Journal of Traumatic Stress* 25: 433–439.

Sherwin, Susan. 1998. "A Relational Approach to Autonomy in Health Care." In *The Politics of Women's Health: Exploring Agency and Autonomy*, edited by Susan Sherwin, 19–47. Philadelphia: Temple University Press.

Sherwin, Susan. 2011. "Relational Autonomy and Global Threats." In *Being Relational: Reflections on Relational Theory and Health Law and Policy*, edited by Jocelyn Downie and Jennifer Llewellyn, 13–34. Vancouver, BC: UBC Press.

Shotwell, Alexis. 2011. *Knowing Otherwise: Race, Gender, and Implicit Understanding*. University Park: Penn State University Press.

Shrira, Amit, Yuval Palgi, Menachem Ben-Ezra, and Dov Shmotkin. 2010. "Do Holocaust Survivors Show Increased Vulnerability or Resilience to Post-Holocaust Cumulative Adversity?" *Journal of Traumatic Stress* 23, no. 3: 367–375.

Sidell, Nancy. 1997. "Adult Adjustment to Chronic Illness: A Review of the Literature." *Health & Social Work* 22, no. 1: 5–11.

Sifneos, P. E. 1973. "The Prevalence of 'Alexiythymic' Characteristics in Psychosomatic Patients." *Psychotherapy and Psychosomatics* 22, nos. 2–6: 255–262.

Silvia, Paul J. 2009. "Looking Past Pleasure: Anger, Confusion, Disgust, Pride, Surprise, and Other Unusual Aesthetic Emotions." *Psychology of Aesthetics, Creativity, and the Arts* 3, no. 1: 48–51.

Silvia, Paul J. 2010. "Confusion and Interest: The Role of Knowledge Emotions in Aesthetic Experience." *Psychology of Aesthetics, Creativity, and the Arts* 4, no. 2: 75–80.

Simpson, Leanne. 2011. *Dancing on Our Turtle's Back: Stories of Nishnaabeg Re-creation, Resurgence, and a New Emergence*. Winnipeg: Arbeiter Ring Publishing.

REFERENCES

Smart, Julie, and David Smart. 1995. "Acculturative Stress: The Experience of the Hispanic Immigrant." *Counseling Psychologist* 23, no. 1: 25-42.

Sollner, Wolfgang, Martina Zingg-Schir, Gerhard Rumpold, and Matthias Augustin. 1999. "Interactive Patterns of Social Support and Individual Coping Strategies in Melanoma Patients and Their Correlations with Adjustment to Illness." *Psychosomatics* 40: 239-250.

Solomon, Robert, ed. 2003. *What is an Emotion? Classic and Contemporary Readings*. Oxford: Oxford University Press.

Sontag, Susan. 1989. *Illness as Metaphor and AIDS and its Metaphors*. New York: Picador.

Spade, Dean. 2011. *Normal Life: Administrative Violence, Critical Trans Politics, and the Limits of Law*. Cambridge, MA: South End Press.

Spelman, Elizabeth V. 1989. "Anger and Insubordination." *Women, Knowledge, and Reality: Explorations in Feminist Philosophy*, edited by Ann Garry and Marilyn Pearsall, 263-274. Boston: Unwin Hyman.

Spelman, Elizabeth V. 2002. *Repair: The Impulse to Restore in a Fragile World*. Boston: Beacon Press.

Spielman, Varda, and Orit Taubman-Ben-Ari. 2009. "Parental Self-Efficacy and Stress-Related Growth in the Transition to Parenthood: A Comparison between Parents of Pre- and Full-Term Babies." *Health & Social Work* 34, no. 3: 201-212.

Stake, Jayne, and Frances L. Hoffman. 2000. "Putting Feminist Pedagogy to the Test: The Experience of Women's Studies from Student and Teacher Perspectives." *Psychology of Women Quarterly* 24, no. 1: 30-38.

Stewart, Donna, and Tracy Yuen. 2011. "A Systematic Review of Resilience in the Physically Ill." *Psychosomatics* 52: 199-209.

Stewart, Karen, Robert Hart, Douglas Gibson, and Robert Fisher. 2014. "Illness Apprehension, Depression, Anxiety, and Quality of Life in Liver Transplant Candidates: Implications for Psychosocial Interventions." *Psychosomatics* 55: 650-658.

Strawson, P. F. 1962. "Freedom and Resentment." *Proceedings of the British Academy* 48: 1-25.

Sullivan, Shannon, and Nancy Tuana, eds. 2007. *Race and Epistemologies of Ignorance*. Albany: SUNY Press.

Talbot, K. 2002. *What Forever Means after the Death of a Child: Transcending the Trauma, Living with the Loss*. New York: Brunner-Routledge.

Tatum, Beverly Daniel. 1997. *Why Are All the Black Kids Sitting Together in the Cafeteria? And Other Conversations about Race*. New York: Basic Books.

Taylor, Charles. 1989a. "Embodied Agency." In *Merleau-Ponty: Critical Essays*, edited by Henry Pietersma, 1-21. Washington, DC: University Press of America.

Taylor, Charles. 1989b. *Sources of Self: The Making of the Modern Identity*. Cambridge: Cambridge University Press.

REFERENCES

Taylor, Shelley. 1983. "Adjustment to Threatening Life Events: A Theory of Cognitive Adaptation." *American Psychologist* 38: 1161–1173.

Taylor, Shelley, and Jonathon Brown. 1988. "Illusion and Well-Being: A Social Psychological Perspective on Mental Health." *Psychological Bulletin* 103, no. 2: 193–210.

Tedeschi, Richard, and Lawrence Calhoun. 1996. "The Posttraumatic Growth Inventory: Measuring the Positive Legacy of Trauma." *Journal of Traumatic Stress* 9: 455–472.

Tedeschi, Richard, and Lawrence Calhoun. 2004. "Posttraumatic Growth: Conceptual Foundations and Empirical Evidence." *Psychological Inquiry* 15, no. 1: 1–18.

Tennen, Howard, and Glenn Affleck. 2002. "The Challenge of Capturing Daily Processes at the Interface of Social and Clinical Psychology." *Journal of Social and Clinical Psychology* 21, no. 6: 610–627.

Titus, Jordan. 2000. "Engaging Student Resistance to Feminism: 'How Is This Stuff Going to Make Us Better Teachers?'" *Gender and Education* 12, no. 1: 21–37.

Tomich, Patricia, and Vicki Helgeson. 2002. "Five Years Later: A Cross-Sectional Comparison of Breast Cancer Survivors with Healthy Women." *Psycho-Oncology* 11: 154–169.

Tomich, Patricia, and Vicki Helgeson. 2004. "Is Finding Something Good in the Bad Always Good? Benefit Finding among Women with Breast Cancer." *Health Psychology* 23: 16–23.

Torres, Kimberly, and Camille Charles. 2004. "Metastereotypes and the Black-White Divide: A Qualitative View of Race on an Elite College Campus." *Du Bois Review* 1, no. 1: 115–149.

Triplett, K. N., R. G. Tedeschi, A. Cann, L. G. Calhoun, and C. L. Reeve. 2012. "Posttraumatic Growth, Meaning in Life, and Life Satisfaction in Response to Trauma." *Psychological Trauma: Theory, Research, Practice, and Policy* 4: 400–410.

Tronto, Joan C. 1994. *Moral Boundaries: A Political Argument for an Ethic of Care.* New York: Routledge.

Tversky, Amos, and Kahneman, Daniel. 1971. "Belief in the Law of Small Numbers." *Psychological Bulletin* 76: 105–110.

Twine, France Winddance, and Amy Steinbugler. 2006. "The Gap between *Whites* and *Whiteness*: Interracial Intimacy and Racial Literacy." *Du Bois Review* 3, no. 2: 341–363.

Updegraff, J. A., et al. 2002. "Positive and Negative Effects of HIV-Infection in Women with Low Socioeconomic Resources." *Personality and Social Psychology Bulletin* 28: 382–394.

Vaughan, Michelle, and Charles Waehler. 2010. "Coming Out Growth: Conceptualizing and Measuring Stress-Related Growth Associated with

REFERENCES

Coming Out to Others as a Sexual Minority." *Journal of Adult Development* 17: 94–109.

Vosvich, Mark, Cheryl Koopman, Cheryl Gore-Felton, Carl Thoresen, John Krumboltz, and David Spiegel. 2003. "Relationship of Functional Quality of Life to Strategies for Coping with the Stress of Living with HIV/AIDS." *Psychosomatics* 44: 51–58.

Waldrop, Deborah. 2007. "Caregiver Grief in Terminal Illness and Bereavement: A Mixed-Methods Study." *Health & Social Work* 32, no. 3: 197–206.

Walia, Harsha. 2012. "Decolonizing Together." In *Organize! Building from the Local for Global Justice*, edited by Aziz Choudry, Jill Hanley and Eric Shragge, 240–253. Oakland, CA: Independent Publishers Group.

Walia, Harsha. 2013. *Undoing Border Imperialism*. Oakland, CA: AK Press.

Walker, Margaret Urban. 2003. *Moral Contexts*. Lanham, MD: Rowman & Littlefield.

Walker, Margaret Urban. 2006. *Moral Repair: Reconstructing Moral Relations after Wrongdoing*. Cambridge: Cambridge University Press.

Walker, Margaret Urban. 2007a. "Moral Psychology." In *The Blackwell Guide to Feminist Philosophy*, edited by Eva Feder Kittay and Linda Martín Alcoff, 102–115. Oxford: Blackwell.

Walker, Margaret Urban. 2007b. *Moral Understandings: A Feminist Study in Ethics*. 2nd ed. Oxford: Oxford University Press.

Walls, Jeannette. 2009. *The Glass Castle: A Memoir*. New York: Simon & Schuster.

Walsh, Clare F. 2007. "Narratives of Lesbian Transformation: Coming Out Stories of Women Who Transition from Heterosexual Marriage to Lesbian Identity." Master's thesis, University of South Florida.

Ward, James, and Diana Winstanley. 2005. "Coming Out at Work: Performativity and the Recognition and Renegotiation of Identity." *Sociological Review* 53, no. 3: 447–475.

Waysman, Mark, Joseph Schwarzwald, and Sahava Solomon. 2001. "Hardiness: An Examination of Its Relationship with Positive and Negative Long Term Changes Following Trauma." *Journal of Traumatic Stress* 14, no. 3: 531–548.

Weiss, Gail. 2008. *Refiguring the Ordinary*. Bloomington: Indiana University Press.

Weiss, T. 2002. "Posttraumatic Growth in Women with Breast Cancer and Their Husbands: An Intersubjective Validation Study." *Journal of Psychosocial Oncology* 20, no. 2: 65–80.

Wellisch, David, and Nangel Lindberg. 2001. "A Psychological Profile of Depressed and Nondepressed Women at High Risk for Breast Cancer." *Psychosomatics* 42: 330–336.

Wendell, Susan. 1996. *The Rejected Body*. New York: Routledge.

Werner, E. E., and R. E. Smith. 1982. *Vulnerable but Invincible: A Study of Resilient Children*. New York: McGraw-Hill.

REFERENCES

Williams, Bernard. 1982. *Moral Luck*. Cambridge: Cambridge University Press.
Williams, D., and K. A. Lawler. 2001. "Stress and Illness in Low-Income Women: The Roles of Hardiness, John Henryism, and Race." *Women and Health* 32, no. 4: 61–75.
Williams, David R., and Ruth Williams-Morris. 2000. "Racism and Mental Health: The African American Experience." *Ethnicity & Health* 5, nos. 3–4: 243–268.
Wilson, George, and Krysia Mossakowski. 2009. "Fear of Job Loss: Racial/Ethnic Differences in Privileged Occupations." *Du Bois Review* 6, no. 2: 357–374.
Wittgenstein, Ludwig. 2001. *Philosophical Investigations*. Translated by G. E. M. Anscombe. Oxford: Blackwell Publishing.
Wittman, Lutz, Tom Sensky, Luzia Meder, Beat Michel, Thomas Stoll, and Stephan Büchi. 2009. "Suffering and Posttraumatic Growth in Women with Systemic Lupus Erythematosus (SLE): A Qualitative/Quantitative Case Study." *Psychosomatics* 50: 362–374.
Wylie, Alison. 2003. "Why Standpoint Matters." In *Science and Other Cultures: Issues in Philosophies of Science and Technology*, edited by Robert Figueroa and Sandra Harding, 26–48. New York: Routledge.
Yancy, George. 2008. *Black Bodies, White Gazes: The Continuing Significance of Race*. Lanham, MD: Rowman & Littlefield.
Young, Iris Marion. 2005. *On Female Body Experience: "Throwing like a Girl" and Other Essays*. Oxford: Oxford University Press.
Young, Iris Marion. 2007. *Global Challenges: War, Self Determination, and Responsibility for Justice*. Cambridge: Polity Press.
Young, Iris Marion. 2011. *Responsibility for Justice*. Oxford: Oxford University Press.
Young, Jenny, and Paule McNicholl. 1998. "Against All Odds: Positive Life Experiences of People with Advanced Amyotrophic Lateral Sclerosis." *Health & Social Work* 23, no. 1: 35–43.

INDEX

ACT UP, 113
ability to live unprepared, 105–106, 108–110
acting despite oneself, 122
adaptation, 50
   cognitive, 27, 179n30
adjustment disorders, 12
Adorno, Theodor, xi
adversarial growth, 28
affect, 98
Ahmed, Sara
   and diversity work, 186n32, 194n12
   and migrant experiences, 117, 191n45
   and orientation, 9, 97
   and queer disorientations, xiii, 11, 24, 84–85
Alcoff, Linda Martín, 74, 92
Alexander, Michelle, 127
alexithymia, 12
ambivalence, 49
Andrews, Vernon, 71
anti-colonialism, 139–144. *See also* decolonization; settlers
anxiety, 6, 12, 102
Anzaldua, Gloria, 117–118
attunement, 31
autonomy, 29, 59
autonomy-connectedness, 27, 179n28
awareness, xviii

and non-resolvism, 63, 88–95
of oppressive norms and their contingency, 67, 69–70, 73, 76, 88
of political complexity, 67, 77, 80, 83, 86, 87–88

Babbitt, Susan, 187n35, 192n57
Bailey, Alison, 92
Bartky, Sandra, 10, 81–82, 184n11, 185n24
Bechdel, Alison, 54–55
benefit-finding, 50
Benson, Paul, 80, 178n14
Boggs, Grace Lee, 130, 194n11
Boler, Megan, 85–86, 186n30
Bordo, Susan, 184n11
both/and action, 130, 135–138
   and conflicting goals, 131–138
   and heterosexism, 131–134, 138
   and mass incarceration, 134–135, 138
   and sexism, 131
Braidotti, Rosi, 125
Brison, Susan, xii, 11, 24, 108–110, 168
Brown, Laura, 190n20
Browning, Frank, 113–114
building without blueprints, 144, 148–149
   and post-industrial poverty, 145–149
   and sexism, 144–145
Butler, Judith, xi, xiii, 24, 123, 184n11, 197n18

INDEX

Calhoun, Cheshire, 49, 61, 133, 138, 178n15
Campbell, Sue
   on emotional expression, 156–158, 182n18, 196n3, 196n5
   on expectation, 120, 192n56
   on memory, 59
   on resistant identification, 94
Camus, Albert, xiii
cancer, 102–104, 162–164, 187n1, 189n14
Card, Claudia, 61, 132–133
Carel, Havi
   on disorientation of illness, 122, 153, 159, 172–173, 197n17
   on experience of diagnosis, 105–106, 189n18
   and use of phenomenology, 189n17
Caruth, Cathy, 24, 189n19
Casey, Edward, 9
churches, xix, 110, 144, 160, 163
citizenship, 67, 115–116, 118, 123, 132
click experiences, 89–90, 92, 187n35
climate, 114
clinical psychology
   methodology of, 179n26, 180n40, 180n41, 182n16
   and research on grief, 53–56
   and research on illness, 102–103, 105, 187n1
   and research on trauma, 107–110
   as source of information on disorientations, 4, 12, 23, 24–25
   as source of information on effects of disorientations, 26, 27
Code, Lorraine, 59
coherence, 27, 108, 179n27
collective disorientation, 158–159, 196n9
Collins, Patricia Hill, 184n8
colonialism, 139–144
comfort, 9, 115, 157, 178n18
Coming-Out Growth Scale, 190n38
commitment, 61
communities of origin, 93, 94
community organizations, 146, 193n5, 195n29
compulsory heterosexuality, 111, 190n28

confidence, 39–41,
conflictedness, 38, 49, 72, 131, 138, 181n1, 181n7
confusion, xv, 5, 69, 80
consciousness-raising, xviii, 10, 11, 77, 78
   as disorienting, 66, 79–81, 82–83, 157
   and feminist movements, 77, 78–79, 82–83, 185n22
contingency, 116, 174
control, 95, 105, 121, 172, 173
conversion, xiii, 157
coping, 28, 108
criminal justice systems, 160. *See also* police; prisons
crisis of faith, xiii, xiv, 56
Critical Resistance, 194n18
Cuomo, Chris, 184n15
curdled logic, 192n50
Cvetkovich, Ann, 11, 24

Davis, Angela, 135
death, xiii, 6, 14, 53–57, 103, 106, 114, 188n3. *See also* grief
decision making, 37, 44, 126
decisiveness, xvii, 30, 126, 130, 148
decolonization, 140–144
depression, 11, 12
Deraniyagala, Sonali, 1, 197n12
DesAutels, Peggy, 183n22
Descartes, René, 4, 65, 177n3
desire, 49, 110
Detroit, 128, 130, 146, 193n5, 195n29
Dewey, John, 5
Diagnostic and Statistical Manual of Mental Disorders, 5, 12. *See also* mental illness
Didion, Joan, 54, 56, 63, 97, 158
Dillon, Robin, 61–63, 178n14, 182n10
disability, 33, 184n10, 197n14
discomfort, 69–70, 74, 79, 85, 178n18
dismissal, 154, 156–158, 196n7. *See also* emotional interpretation
disorientability, 169–174
disorientation
   and anti-resolutionary effects, 59
   deliberate pursuit of, 3, 173–174
   duration of, 18

INDEX

and family resemblance, 13–22, 24
hospitable responses to, 160–169
and irresolute actions against injustice, 150–152
minor instances of, xv, 2
and negative effects, xix, 29, 118, 123–124, 168–169, 174
and non-resolutionary effects, 59, 126
self-perception of, 20, 170, 173–174
variation in kinds of, 2–3, 13–14, 173
Dixon, Chris, 147
dogmatism, 125
double consciousness, 68, 75
as disorienting, 69, 70–71, 159
empirical studies of, 69, 183n5, 183n6, 183n7
and W. E. B. Du Bois, 11, 67, 71, 184n9
double ontological shock, 10, 81–82
doubling back actions, 138–139, 142–144
and implicit bias, 139
and North American colonialism, 139–142
doubt, 4, 10, 177n3
Du Bois, W. E. B., 6, 24
account of double consciousness, 11, 67, 71, 159, 184n9
and *Souls of Black Folk*, 32, 71
dual-systems models of moral judgment, 44–48

ease, 72, 79, 98, 115–117, 121
Edelman, Lee, 190n37
Education
in critical classrooms, xviii, 67, 77, 83, 167
as disorienting, 66, 84–87, 158–159
and resistance to learning about oppression, 88, 185n26, 186n27
Ehrenreich, Barbara, 162, 164
elevator, 75
emotion
and expression, 156, 157
philosophy of, 4, 156–158
role in moral judgment, xvii, 44–48
emotional interpretation
and disorientation, 155–160

and sympathetic interpreters, 155
empathy, 103
epistemic humility, 91–93
epistemology, 4. *See also* feminist epistemology; social epistemology
existentialism, 6
expectation, 99–100, 119–122
exploitation, 127
expression, 155–160. *See also* emotion; emotional interpretation; uptake

fallibility, 93
Families Against Mandatory Minimums, 193n6
family, 160, 162–163
family resemblance, 13–22
fast-food workers, 127, 129, 136
fear, 39
feeling white, 74. *See also* white privilege
feminist epistemology, 23, 67, 76, 77
feminist methodology, xv–xvi, 22–34
Fight for 15, 129, 193n10
first-person accounts, xv, 4, 23, 26, 155
from philosophers, 10, 11
food, 118, 128
food security, 145–149
foreclosures, 145, 147
forlornness, 7
Frank, Arthur, 188n5
Frankfurt, Harry, 49, 63, 183n23
free-style emotions, 182n18
Fricker, Miranda, 92
Friedman, Marilyn, 59

Garland-Thompson, Rosemarie, 184n10
gaslighting, 80
gender, xvi, 33, 86, 123, 133, 184n11, 190n27
generalizability, xvi, 27
Gilligan, Carol, 23, 43
Gilman, Charlotte Perkins, 179n20
Gould, Deborah, 113–114, 191n42
government, 148
grace, 153, 172
Greene, Joshua, 44–48
Greene, Maxine, 65

INDEX

grief
  and caregiving, 53–54
  as disorienting, 53–57, 157
  effects of, 54–57
  and family resemblance, 15–19
  first-person accounts of, 11, 54–57
  philosophical accounts of, 182n17
  and support groups, 163

habit, xviii, 34, 119–122
habitability, 161. *See also* hospitability; livability
Haidt, Jonathan, 44–48
Hall, Stuart, 191n43
happiness, 3, 10
hardiness, 28, 50
Haslanger, Sally, 194n19
Hatab, Lawrence, 7
health, 100, 145–149
health care systems, 101, 118, 147, 179n21
  and insurance, 145, 148, 188n6
health disparity, 111
Heidegger, Martin, xiii, 6
Herman, Judith, 24, 107
heteronormativity, 112. *See also* norms
Heyes, Cressida, 179n24, 184n11
Hill, Thomas, 182n10
HIV, 113–114, 133, 191n42
hooks, bell, 155
hope, 99
hospitality, 160–169, 174
Human Rights Campaign, 128, 193n3
humility, 91–93

ignorance, 34, 67, 92, 112
ill-fit, 110
illness, 40, 98, 101, 187n1. *See also* health; health care systems
  as disorienting, 100–101, 172–173
  effects of, 101–106
  first-person accounts of, 11, 103–106
immunity, 123, 169
implicit bias, 34, 92, 139
in-this-togetherness, 112–114
incarceration, 127, 134. *See also* prisons; prison industrial complex

independence, 101, 167
Indian Boarding School System, 128, 144. *See also* Truth and Reconciliation Commission
individualism, 60, 119
injustice, xviii–xix, 32–33, 60, 82, 86–88, 90, 122, 127–130
insecurity, 108. *See also* vulnerability
insider-outsider standpoint, 184n8
integrity, 49
interdependence, 100, 121
interruption, 99–100
intuitions, 45–48
invulnerability, 105, 121, 170. *See also* immunity; independence; individualism
irresolute action, xviii, 126–127, 130, 149–152
  and both/and actions, 137–138
  and building without blueprints, 147–149
  and doubling back actions, 142–144
isolation, 109

Jaggar, Alison, 90
James, Henry (Jr.), 6
James, Henry (Sr.), 6
James, William, 6
Jasper, James, 184n20
Job (Biblical), 178n10

Kahnemann, Daniel, 45
Kant, Immanuel, 47, 183n1
Kierkegaard, Søren, 8, 178n10
Koggel, Christine, 59
Kohlberg, Lawrence, 23, 43
Kuhn, Thomas, 177n4
Kurashige, Scott, 125

Lewis, C. S., 11, 36
livability, xix, 161, 164, 166, 168, 171. *See also* habitability; hospitality
Lorde, Audre, 103–104, 196n6
Lugones, María, 115–116, 192n50

Mackenzie, Catriona, 59
marginalization, 22, 32, 154–155
marriage, 131–134

INDEX

masculinity, 170
Matthew Shepard Foundation, 193n7
meaning-making, 50
medicine, 23. *See also* health; health care systems; illness
Medina, José, 16–17, 92, 187n36
mental illness, 2, 12, 76, 118, 153
mestiza consciousness, 117
Meyers, Diana Tietjens, 59
migration, 98
   as disorienting, 114–116
   and documentation, 114–115
   effects of, 116–118
military combat, 106
Mill, John Stuart, 10–11, 178n19
Mills, Charles, 92
moral development, 43–44
moral dilemmas, 136–137, 181n2, 181n7
moral dumbfounding, 46
moral judgments, 30, 38, 44–48, 181n5
   conflicting, 38–39
   and emotion, 44–48
   and intuition, 45–48
   and reasoning, 38, 44–48
moral luck, 61
moral motivation, xvi, 29, 37
   without moral resolve, 42, 58–59, 88–95
moral resolve, xvii, 34, 37, 38, 41
   acting without, 41, 42, 58–59, 64, 119, 121–122
   awareness without, 88–95
   dual meaning of, 41
   and moral development, 43–44
   and moral failure, 49–50
   and moral growth, 50–53
   and moral judgment, 38, 40, 42, 47–48, 182n21
   and resolutionary power of experience, 41, 58
moral shock, 79, 113, 184n20, 185n22
mortality, 101. *See also* death

Nagel, Thomas, 61
National Organization for Women, 185n22
Nietzsche, Friedrich, xiii, 178n11
No One Is Illegal, 192n49

norms, 184n11
   of citizenship, 115–118, 123
   of gender, 123
   of health, 112, 123, 164
   of invulnerability, 123
   living against the grain of, 116–118
   and racism, 70
   of straightness, 112–113
   and tenderizing effects, 119–120, 121, 123
Nussbaum, Martha, 11

O'Reilly, Jane, 89, 186n34
ocean
   as metaphor for disorientations, 2–3, 5, 54, 65, 125, 185n23
   and natural disasters, 1, 97
orientedness, 5, 9, 22, 81, 161
outlaw emotions, 90–91

pain, 125
paradigm shift, xiii
parenting, 153, 157, 163, 195n1, 195n2
pedagogy of discomfort, 85–86, 186n30
Peirce, Charles Sanders, 5, 169–170, 186n31
perception, 40
personal identity, 9–10
phenomenology, 4, 8, 178n12
philosophy of race, 68
Piaget, Jean, 43
Pippin, Robert, 6
Plato, 4, 177n2
police, 115, 128–129, 136–137
positive psychology, 162
post-industrial cities, 145–147
post-partum conditions, 153. *See also* parenting
post-traumatic growth, 28, 50–53
   five domains of, 51
post-traumatic stress disorder, 12, 107
powerlessness, 95, 187n37
Pratt, Minnie Bruce, 11, 24, 82–83, 94, 185n25
prefigurative politics, 147
prisons, 111, 128–129, 134–135, 167
prison industrial complex, 134
privilege, 33, 154–155. *See also* white privilege

INDEX

productivity, 115, 117, 148–149, 165–166
psychiatry, 167. *See also* clinical psychology
psychic disunity, 62

queer ambivalence, 113
queerness, xiii, 84–85, 98
  and coming out, 110–113
  as disorienting, 110–111, 112
  effects of, 111–114
  first-person accounts of, 11, 113–114

racialization, 70, 76, 92, 93
racism, 23, 66, 68, 76
  and anti-racism, 74
  and double consciousness, 67, 68, 159
  and white privilege, 66, 159
REACH Coalition, 194n15
reactive attitudes, 49
Regan, Paulette, 144, 194n23
Reger, Jo, 184n19, 185n22
relational autonomy, 59, 63
relationality, 59–60, 113–114, 120, 174
  and responses to disorientations, 154
Remen, Rachel Naomi, 56–57
reorientation, 8, 162. *See also* orientedness
reproductive justice, 127
resilience, 28, 50–51
resistant identification, 93–95
resolute action, 137, 149–150
resoluteness, 151
resolutionary power of experience, 41, 59, 63, 66. *See also* moral motivation
resolvism, 43, 58–60, 63. *See also* moral resolve
role shock, 115
Ruíz, Elena Flores, 80–81, 185n23

safety, 100. *See also* security
same-sex marriage, 128–129, 131–134
Sartre, Jean-Paul, 7, 178n9
Saul, Jennifer, 194n19
Scheman, Naomi, 19, 179n23, 179n24, 196n3
Scherkoske, Greg, 49
schools, 127, 145–149
security, 146–147, 166
self-determination, 146

self-efficacy, 27, 179n29
self-knowledge, 170
self-mastery, 50
self-respect, 49, 182n10
sensing vulnerability, 102–104
sensitivity to insensitivity, 92, 187n36
Servan-Schreiber, David, 104, 189n11
settlers, 140–142
sexism, 33, 77, 83, 90, 92, 104, 135
Sherwin, Susan, 59, 195n30
Shotwell, Alexis, 185n25
Simpson, Leanne, 140, 194n22
social epistemology, 67, 76
Socrates, 4
Solomon, Robert, 178n9
Sontag, Susan, 188n2
soundwave, 85, 86, 92, 95
Spelman, Elizabeth, xi, 196n3, 196n4
stereotype, 115–116
stigma consciousness, 191n40
Stoljar, Natalie, 59
stop and frisk, 128. *See also* police
Strawson, Peter, 182n11
stress-related growth, 28, 180n37
Sullivan, Shannon, 92
support groups, 163–164
sureness of self, 149. *See also* resolute action; resoluteness
sympathy, 103

Tatum, Beverly Daniel, 74, 184n17
tenderizing effects, xviii, 99, 119–123
Tessman, Lisa, 61–62, 137, 181n2, 181n7, 181n8
testimony. *See* first-person accounts
toehold, 167, 168
Toombs, Kay, 189n17
torn decisions, 10, 178n16
trauma, xii, 11, 98
  as disorienting, 106–107
  effects of, 107–110
Tronto, Joan, 190n25
Truth and Reconciliation Commission (Indian Residential Schools), 128, 139, 193n8
Tuana, Nancy, 92
Tversky, Amos, 45

INDEX

uncertainty, 110, 174
unconscious action, 34
unpredictability, 63, 106, 121
uptake, 156–160. *See also* emotional interpretation

vastation, 6
vertigo, 82
violence, 106–107, 145–149, 197n18
   gendered, 66, 127
   state, 114
virtues
   as burdened, 61–62
   as character traits, 48, 61, 122
   in critical character theory, 61–62
   in responding to disorientations, 171–172
   in traditional virtue ethics, 30–31, 61, 91, 180n42
voting, 148
vulnerability, 62, 87, 102–106, 121, 123

Walia, Harsha, 192n49, 194n21
Walker, Margaret Urban, 23, 60–61, 153, 172, 195n30, 197n16
Walls, Jeannette, 56
war on drugs, 128
water, 118, 128, 145–149, 195n26
weakness of will, 182n9
Wendell, Susan, 197n14
white ambush, 73, 75–77, 159, 184n13
white privilege, 66, 73–75, 82–83, 159, 184n14
wholeheartedness, 30, 49
Williams, Bernard, 61
Wittgenstein, Ludwig, 16, 19
work, 101, 111, 145–149, 164–165
   and contingent labor, 191n48
workplaces, 111, 160, 164–167
World Assumptions Scale, 180n1
Wylie, Alison, 184n8

Yancy, George, 24, 75, 159, 184n9
Young, Iris Marion, 195n30

www.ingramcontent.com/pod-product-compliance
Ingram Content Group UK Ltd.
Pitfield, Milton Keynes, MK11 3LW, UK
UKHW021330310725
7175UKWH00033B/326